READING ECCLESIASTES

Reading Ecclesiastes explores the literary style and themes of the Book of Ecclesiastes, investigating its overall theological messages and the cultural perspectives which readers bring to bear on their act of reading. Examining the meaning found in Ecclesiastes through the use of two important contemporary reading methods – narrative criticism and cultural exegesis – Mary E. Mills breaks new ground. Highlighting the range of theological meaning attached to the book of Ecclesiastes as a result of treating the text as a form of narrative and a story told in the first person, this innovative book will appeal to all those interested in narrative criticism, literary studies and interpretation and Wisdom tradition and the ancient world more widely, as well as biblical scholars.

HEYTHROP STUDIES
IN CONTEMPORARY PHILOSOPHY, RELIGION & THEOLOGY

Series Editor
Laurence Paul Hemming, Heythrop College, University of London, UK

Series Editorial Advisory Board
John McDade SJ; Peter Vardy; Michael Barnes SJ; James Hanvey SJ;
Philip Endean SJ; Anne Murphy SHCJ

Drawing on renewed willingness amongst theologians and philosophers to enter into critical dialogues with contemporary issues, this series is characterised by Heythrop's reputation for openness and accessibility in academic engagement. Presenting volumes from a wide international, ecumenical, and disciplinary range of authors, the series explores areas of current theological, philosophical, historical, and political interest. The series incorporates a range of titles: accessible texts, cutting-edge research monographs, and edited collections of essays. Appealing to a wide academic and intellectual community interested in philosophical, religious and theological issues, research and debate, the books in this series will also appeal to a theological readership which includes enquiring lay-people, Clergy, members of religious communities, training priests, and anyone engaging broadly in the Catholic tradition and with its many dialogue partners.

Published titles
Biblical Morality – Mary E. Mills
Religion Within the Limits of Language Alone – Felicity McCutcheon
Challenging Women's Orthodoxies in the Context of Faith – Edited by
Susan Frank Parsons
Radical Orthodoxy? – A Catholic Enquiry – Edited by
Laurence Paul Hemming

Forthcoming titles include:
Essays Catholic and Critical – Edited by
Philip G. Zeigler and Mark Husbands
A Moral Ontology for a Theistic Ethic – Frank G. Kirkpatrick
God as Trinity – James Hanvey

Reading Ecclesiastes

A literary and cultural exegesis

MARY E. MILLS

ASHGATE

Published by
Ashgate Publishing Limited
Gower House
Croft Road
Aldershot
Hants GU11 3HR
England

Ashgate Publishing Company
Suite 420
101 Cherry Street
Burlington, VT 05401-4405
USA

Ashgate website: http://www.ashgate.com

British Library Cataloguing in Publication Data
Mills, Mary E.
    Reading Ecclesiastes : a literary and cultural exegesis. -
(Heythrop studies in contemporary philosophy, religion &
theology)
    1. Bible. O.T. Ecclesiastes - Criticism, interpretation,
etc.
    I. Title II. Heythrop College
    223.8'06

Library of Congress Cataloging-in-Publication Data
Mills, Mary E.
    Reading Ecclesiastes : a literary and cultural exegesis / Mary E. Mills.
        p. cm. -- (Heythrop studies in contemporary philosophy, religion & theology)
    Includes bibliographical references and index.
    ISBN 0-7546-1667-3 (alk. paper)
    1. Bible. O.T. Ecclesiastes--Socio-rhetorical criticism. I. Title. II. Heythrop studies in
contemporary philosophy, religion & theology.

    BS1475.52 .M56 2002
    223'.806--dc21

                                                                            2002021436

ISBN 0 7546 1667 3

Typeset in Times by N²productions
Printed and bound in Great Britain by MPG Books Ltd, Bodmin, Cornwall.

Contents

Preface

This commentary on the book of Ecclesiastes is written from the perspective of narrative criticism and cultural exegesis. It approaches Ecclesiastes as an autobiographical work. The first two chapters and the last two chapters form a narrative frame for this exploration. They contextualize the commentary within debates concerning methods of reading biblical texts (outer border) and the particular nature of literary and cultural criticism (inner border). Inside this frame the commentary on Ecclesiastes operates itself as a piece of narration, which 'pictures' the meanings of the text and so offers the reader an instance of the exercise of biblical imagination described in the framing chapters.

Many of the secondary reading tools involved in this exercise are drawn from the fields of literary criticism and cultural studies. Only some of these have a specifically biblical focus and, then, not necessarily a focus on Ecclesiastes as such. This is a deliberate choice. The purpose of this particular set of readings of Ecclesiastes is to draw upon new and different tools for reading. In this mode, commentaries by biblical scholars become themselves cultural artefacts which are suitable for examination as examples of the afterlife of a text in differing social worlds.

PREAMBLE

Chapter 1

The Exercise of Biblical Imagination

This book deals with a reading of Ecclesiastes from the perspectives of literary and cultural criticism. It moves away from the historical-critical method of exegesis, which has been so dominant in modern biblical criticism. Whereas the historical method seeks the one true meaning of the original writer or context, literary criticism engages with the final text as it has been handed down to the present day and cultural exegesis deals with the social settings which influence the formation of ideas through literature. While the historical method of biblical criticism has long had its clear boundaries of operation in the tools of source, form and redaction criticism, newer methodologies have frameworks, that are not as yet so clearly defined.[1]

A reader may ask of these approaches to biblical literature, 'What exactly is the intention here?' This enquiry is necessary because the modern reader of the Christian Bible, living in Western Europe, faces a range of possible meanings to life, combined with the cultural impact of subjectivism and globalization. There is no longer an agreed consensus that a single overarching meaning can be obtained from texts or that a single message can be found to answer all questions about life's meanings. This perceived lack of a stable centre for social and personal existence casts a gloomy shadow on biblical interpretation and especially on the view that biblical texts may help readers to form valid moral vision. The term 'moral vision' is to be understood as a set of values which help to shape readers' actions, with positive consequences for the individual and for society.

Interpreting Biblical Texts

Yet postmodern society offers freedoms of action and belief for the sections of society that might be marginalized under older cultural forms.[2] All is not lost. There are opportunities here to explore fresh lines of textual interpretation. 'Biblical imagination' is a term that can be coined as a way of speaking about alternative methods of reading the Christian Bible. Walter Brueggemann, for example, sets out a basic model for using imagery as a reading tool in *Texts under Negotiation*. He takes as his base 'the human capacity to picture, portray, receive and practice the world in ways other than it appears to be at first glance when seen through a dominant, habitual ... lens'. In this approach, it can be argued that all human thought involves imaginative construal. 'The world we take as "given" is a long established act of imagination.'[3] All thoughts about the contemporary world are only partial accounts of reality. Humans read the meaning of an event 'as' and the force of this is that different, and even opposing, images of reality may emerge, each formulated in an 'as' clause.[4]

When this view is applied to textual criticism, Brueggemann argues that this imaginative 'asness' can have a critical, subversive function.[5] The meanings of texts thus become relative and subject to change. 'All claims to reality, including those by theologians, are fully under negotiation ... Reality ... is no longer a fixed arrangement ... but it is an ongoing, creative, constitutive task in which imagination ... has a critical role to play.'[6] The function of biblical interpretation is to engage in that creative task, among the pluriformity of social groups, and in the setting of a global community created by the market forces of capitalist economies. Brueggemann's ideas are one example of the search for new exegetical and theological tools under the heading of 'imagination'. His work recognizes the need to move on from the perspectives of post-Enlightenment biblical exegesis, where the challenge was to prove that biblical literature could be taken seriously in a time period when the empirical pursuit of reason provided the frame for intellectual activity. The insights of 'modern' biblical criticism are not to be slighted. But the European culture that undergirded these insights has passed away; a different cultural context requires other exegetical approaches.

Biblical Imagination

The 'biblical imagination' approach to reading biblical texts, like previous methodologies, is founded on a scholarly examination of texts, with special regard for the original language versions of these texts. In addition, this method includes the recognition that these works are meant for reading, and that readers make a contribution to textual meanings. The symbiosis of readers and ancient inherited texts influences cultures, and can itself be studied with regard to the religious dimension of life in society. Where Christianity has been the dominant religion, as in Western Europe, a variety of cultural links exists between religious language and the wider traditions and customs of the social world. Since Europeans have taken their religious traditions into parts of Africa and Asia there also the biblical books have interacted with cultural systems, though with different results from those in Europe. Now, within Europe, Christianity is living alongside other world religions and this, too, produces new social readings of the meaning of texts.

If half of the term 'biblical imagination' concerns the biblical texts and their impact on readers, the other half focuses on the concept of imagination as a creative tool for biblical exegesis. Pursuit of meaning in biblical works is not simply a matter of logical construction of interpretations derived from explorations of what can be gleaned from the original sources of the literature.

Rather, it involves a reaching out beyond the construction of meaning in short prose comments to engage with the poetic and metaphorical nature of biblical language. This creative use of imagination on the part of the interpreter is a method which has recently come more into prominence. Doubting that the historical method can ever achieve its aim of finding a single truth, and doubting that such an enterprise is itself a sensible goal, biblical exegetes, such as Timothy Luke Johnson, have sought out the human imagination as a key to finding meaning in biblical material.[7]

'If Scripture is ever again to be a living source for theology, those who practice theology must become less pre-occupied with the world that produced Scripture and learn again how to live in the world Scripture produces. This will be a matter of imagination, and perhaps of leaping.'[8] Christian Scriptures produce a 'Christian world' with its own parameters. Johnson argues that this world is like a city, 'a living city that one might inhabit'.[9] Citizens of this world, that is readers of biblical texts, both bring that city to life with their reception of biblical material via the imagination, and are creatively led to act in different ways because of the appropriation of that 'city' to the communities of their earthly existence.

Biblical Interpretation and Use of Language

The edifices of the biblical city consist of a rich environment of metaphor and imagery, the materials of which biblical texts are constructed. It is in the nature of this type of language to be thick-stranded and to offer plurality of meanings. Thus the reader's imagination can play over the buildings of the biblical city, viewing them now in one light and now in another. This inherent plurality of biblical language can reasonably dialogue with the open-ended nature of postmodern culture. The spin off for biblical interpretation is that positive value can be attached to 'open-ended' language as the bearer of true moral vision. For the delineation of biblical material as expressed in figurative language can give rise to the query, 'so, can metaphor, symbol and myth be vehicles of truth-giving insight into the foundational realities of the universe?' 'Can they become paths to the divine?'[10] Paul Avis emphasizes the positive nature of creative human imagination: 'As Coleridge (among others) suggested, human imaginative creativity is an echo, a spark, of the divine creativity that is poured out in the plenitude of creation.'[11] In this manner human imagination lies parallel to transcendence and opens many paths to that Other.

The task, then, is to explore, to take on, images found within biblical books and to investigate these through the use of 'biblical imagination'. This task is both a rational exercise and one which engages the field of human lived experience. It can be argued that certain key symbols recur within biblical books and that these symbols produce a coherent ground for investigation of textual meaning. Within texts, 'God/deity', 'human person', 'social setting' and 'heavenly/cosmic world' are concepts constantly explored through character, plot, and time and space settings. Yet the nature of the deity as a character varies from text to text and the major human characters in narratives have their individualities. Time and place are not always the same. To meet this variety of material 'biblical imagination' itself involves both stability and instability. But this does not undermine the value of the tool. Avis claims that 'symbols are not arbitrary ... but powerful, cognitive and to be handled with care', and argues that 'metaphors are the vehicles of fresh insight and thus constitutive of our apprehension of truth'.[12] This approach does not mean that there is a one-to-one likeness between the metaphor and the reality it connotes, but it does mean that windows of imagination open up vistas on that which is beyond immediate daily experience.

Metaphors build up a longer piece of literature, a poem or a narrative, for instance. This longer literary piece shares the nature of the language of which it is formed. If metaphors can act as symbols of authentic meaning so can these longer pieces. 'Narrative is a creative, idealised and stereotyped relation of the paths and journeys on which individuals and communities find themselves.'[13] It can be noted that the Old Testament, in particular, contains a great many narratives in which individual characters and whole communities find themselves on journeys through time and space. These narratives and their component images – their constructions of 'God', 'human person', 'human community' and 'heavens and earth' – offer a means for the reader to stand outside everyday experience and view it from a fresh angle. This action of taking a new stance leads on to the broader critique of an existence now seen from a different perspective. These narratives and their images do not form a systematic understanding of the divine transcendent or of the human state, but they are the raw material for human thought concerning these matters. Avis concludes that, 'what the Bible gives us is not doctrinal propositions, but "an imaginative vision of God" and God's dealings with human beings'.[14]

Textual Meaning and Cultural Context

It is within societies and their cultures that readers of the Christian Bible take up the method of reading with imagination. Any particular example of 'biblical imagination' is the product of the engagement of individual readers with specific cultural contexts with a given text. William Blake, in nineteenth-century Britain, is one example which can be cited. Blake's engravings for the story of Job are derived from the biblical story but have been shaped by his own personal creativity in theological thought. It is noticeable, for instance, that God and Job are constantly portrayed as alike in features. Solomon remarks that,

Blake repeatedly equates God with the human imagination; and it is action instigated by the creative imagination that brings us this *meaning*. I would say that this has the quality of divinity – not of divinity as a matter of externalised religious belief, but as the very substance and driving force of life.[15]

For Blake, Job's story describes a human being's progress to true religion and away from formalized and destructive institutions, from the control of social institutions to an inner freedom of fresh vision. This interpretation fits with Blake's own social context in the Britain faced with American Independence and Revolutionary France. For Blake saw signs of hope in the collapse of the past order and the possibility of new growth not only in material conditions but also in moral vision as a source of human action. The example of Blake provides a picture of 'biblical imagination', an indication of the role of biblical books in creating and contextualizing meanings, both religious and spiritual. There is a symbiosis here between the reader and the text. The biblical book sparks the creative imagination of the reader to apply what is read to the particular context of his/her day.

Blake himself formed messages for his own revolutionary time from his biblical resources, entitling some of his writings 'Prophecies' for America, for Europe. The most well known image among these prophecies is probably that of London as a 'New Jerusalem', a city fit for free human beings to dwell in, aligned with the divine cosmic energy. In the last scenes of his Job engravings, Blake shows Job standing upright and free before a cosmic deity which is no longer a copy of Job himself. Arms outstretched, like a crucifixion, Job radiates knowledge born of painful suffering. Finally he heads his renewed household, leading their song, as they live, interiorly in touch with the divine, in a cosmos of great promise. Comparisons between Plates 1 and 21 show the boundaries of Blake's religious thought: the subjection of human beings to false religious systems balanced with their religious freedom once their inner religious vision is corrected and freed.

Moving within the wisdom books of the Old Testament it is possible to consider how 'biblical imagination' might be applied to Ecclesiastes. At first sight this might appear to be a difficult task since this biblical text, unlike that of Job, contains few images connected with divine appearances or cosmic visions. Yet, this work also makes use of metaphor for the communication of its messages. The first chapter introduces what will be a dominant symbol for moral vision, the concept of advantage or commercial gain (*yitrôn*). It is in the everyday language of work and its advantageous consequences that human affairs are evaluated. It is from within the human perspective of life under the sun that the overarching role of the deity as creator and judge can be situated. Chapter 3 raises the possibility that ordinary time has an extension in eternity, but this is unproven since there is no evidence that human beings have ever experienced life as eternal. Although God is consistently equated with the cosmic order, dealing out each person's portion of good and bad fortune, the gap between humanity and divinity is unmistakable and the relationship between universal order and human activity is problematic, linguistically contained within the view that all is *hebel*.

Although the 'I' who narrates the text puts great value on being wise, not even wisdom can survive death, since both wise and foolish come together to the grave. The elder figure who speaks to the young in the final chapters urges an enjoyment of life while it is on offer, but there remains a brooding image of a deity who is judge and to whom the human spirit returns. Since, in chapter 12: 7–8, reference to this figure is immediately followed by the comment on the ambiguity or meaninglessness of life, it seems likely that humans are thought of as subject to a cosmic order, which does not include the image of 'happy ever after'. However, in terms of 'biblical imagination', chapter 12 provides a major setting for the use of creative interpretation. The symbols of the storm and the house offer the reader a wide vista on the significance of human enjoyment of life.

Selfhood and Religious Meaning

These brief reviews of Job and Ecclesiastes illuminate the idea of 'biblical imagination' as an exegetical tool. Such an exegetical method involves a search for the 'asness' of the text. In Ecclesiastes the imaginative model used is that of the personal voice of a self. Autobiography here is a tool of biblical imagination through which the concept of selfhood is explored. The model involves, within the book of Ecclesiastes, a self who is both same and other. That is, Qohelet is the voice that both speaks of the grave as the true destiny of human effort and yet also urges the reader to eat, drink and enjoy material pleasures. These two evaluatory strands of thought create both a single voice and a combination of two voices. The model includes as well the versions of selfhood created by the written comments of the 'many voices' of readers of this book. Within this model 'Qohelet' is both a single figure whose identity is determined by the content of an original text, and a self whose identity is composed of all the readers of Qohelet's words, who empathize with this character in such a way as to add new layers of meaning to a 'Qoheletic self'.

Selfhood is thus a concept explored by personal voices and a source of religious meaning. In the investigation of personal meaning the horizontal viewpoint of human beings who gaze across their existence, seeking the path from there to the world which is beyond the sun, has the major part to play. Here biblical imagination involves an evaluation of the world as that which is 'as' the individual human being finds it to be. The deity exists within this framework, both as the expression of world order and as the being through whom human beings are created, given a portion of good and bad fortune, a number of days to live, and are judged according to their actions within their allotted span.

This tool provides one example of the interface between a given text and a reader who appropriates that text by use of the human imagination. The core concepts and images in the text form the means by which this appropriation takes place. As indicated above, it is possible to move from this particular example of interaction between reader and text to consider how such an approach to reading biblical books might work with regard to Ecclesiastes. This exploration of meaning opens up two further areas for examination, the nature of the text as literature and the cultural role of the text. The next chapter will begin a consideration of these two aspects in relation to the book of Ecclesiastes.

Notes

1   There are classifications of literary criticism, for instance, but these tools have not yet been fully integrated with biblical studies, especially with regard to the Old Testament. D. Gunn and D. Fewell (1993) have provided the basis for further work in their treatment of narrative art in the Bible. Much work has been carried out with regard to the Gospel books in the New Testament. See here the foundational study by A. Culpepper, *The Anatomy of the Fourth Gospel* (Minneapolis, Fortress), published in 1983.

2   It is important to note here, especially, the link between feminist biblical studies and the postmodern cultural milieu. The freedom to move away from master narratives can be aligned with the search for women in biblical texts; characters whose actions, in a story, are often subordinated to the interests of the dominant male concerns of the narrator.

3   W. Brueggemann, *Texts under Negotiation: The Bible and Postmodern Imagination* (Minneapolis, Fortress/Augsburg, 1993), p. 13.

4   Ibid., p. 14.

5   Ibid., p. 15.

6   Ibid., p. 17.

7   Timothy Luke Johnson's essay is part of a volume of essays that explore the possible implications for theology of using an imaginative method of reading biblical texts.

8   T. Johnson, 'Imagining the World Scripture imagines', in G. Jones and J. Buckley (eds) *Theology and Scriptural Imagination* (Oxford, Blackwell, 1998), p. 3.

9   Ibid., p. 5.

10   P. Avis, *God and the Creative Imagination: Metaphor, Symbol and Myth in Religion and Theology* (London, Routledge, 1999), p. vii.

11   Ibid., p. ix.

12   Ibid., p. 11.

13   Ibid., p. 53.

14   Ibid., p. 65.

15   A. Solomon, *Blake's Job: A Message for our Time* (London, Palambron, 1993), pp. 52–3.

Chapter 2

The Person and the World

That the biblical books were written for a particular social world and its time is, of course, a truism. But it reminds the reader that texts do not exist in a vacuum or as examples only of literary style but rather that they come into being within the worldview of a particular historical period and are meant to communicate with readers belonging to that period. This means that texts are, at core, social realities. Once a particular text is copied and exists in manuscript form, obviously it is no longer fixed to its social origins, but that does not lessen its social identity. For it now becomes available to another set of readers who will approach the text from within the social and cultural context of their own time.

Looked at in this manner, therefore, biblical texts are essentially cultural entities, which operate within broader cultural paradigms, which arise among human beings living in social communities. Biblical texts can themselves contribute to these cultural paradigms and will certainly be understood by readers wearing the spectacles of a given social environment. It is, then, entirely appropriate to consider Old Testament texts in the light of cultural studies.

Cultural Studies

The term 'culture' is itself a broad term, capable of many variant interpretations. In this context of 'cultural studies' the focus is on the serious investigation of social values from an academic perspective. Here it is important to note the shifts in scholarly approach in the twentieth century. Whereas culture was originally thought of as an aesthetic matter relating to the dissemination of social values through art, music and literature, it has now come to include the 'whole of life'.[1] The aesthetic model of culture largely restricted the subject to a 'high' form, that of the educated elite groups in a given society. The inclusive model of culture brings in the life experience of a 'low' or 'popular' culture, that of the mass of ordinary citizens. Thus cultural studies comes to overlap in some ways with the approach of social anthropology.[2]

The Christian Bible as a social artefact can be situated within this frame. Cheryl Exum and Stephen Moore refer to the Bible's status as a cultural icon in Western Europe.[3] This status is created by a diffusion of biblical concepts and language, through media and through daily speech forms. This is to be expected since Christianity has been the dominant official religion in Western Europe since late antiquity and has thus contributed covertly, as well as directly, to social images of self-identity. The interrelationship between Bible and contemporary society is thus a complex one. According to Exum and Moore, it is not just a matter of 'the Bible influencing culture or culture re-appropriating the Bible, but of a process of unceasing mutual redefinition in which cultural appropriations constantly recover the Bible, which in turn constantly impels new appropriations'.[4]

The Bible and the Modern World

The study by David Clines, which operates under this title, is one example of a biblical scholar making an investigation of the role of the Bible in the context of cultural studies: in this case, the cultural impact of the Christian Bible in contemporary English society.[5] Clines begins by noting a paradox – for the academic world, Bible means a Hebrew or Greek book, whereas for W. H. Smith, booksellers, the Bible is an English book. Academics view the Bible as an ancient book, a product of the past, an inheritance which 'cannot be understood ... except through reference to the historical circumstances of its composition'.[6] By contrast the English Bible now functions as a cultural artefact of modern British society.

This poses for the reader a new set of perspectives. Viewing the Bible as an ancient reality means treating it as a fixed object, which can be understood on its own terms. But spotlighting the English Bible as a living cultural artefact entails evaluating the function of such an item in the contemporary world, in relation to its input to cultural values. What is to be asked is a matter of critique, such as 'What does coming into contact with a Bible do to you?' 'Whether it is moral to restrict one's scholarly concern to mere understanding.'[7] The Christian Bible is to be assessed, rather, for its actual impact on a living historical society, which uses it.

One of the issues raised by Clines' work is the way in which phrases or images from the Christian Bible serve as cultural symbols. Tina Pippin in *Apocalyptic Bodies* addresses this popular reuse of biblical material via a consideration of the role of the 'Jezebel' figure.[8] She traces the manner in which a biblical character, already nuanced in the text as a 'bad woman whose dead body is eaten by dogs',[9] becomes a cultural stereotype for any woman who is sexually aware and is using her sexuality as a social tool in making relationships.[10] 'Jezebel is a fantasy space. She is, in effect, a personality, a lifestyle, an ethical way of being female in the world.'[11] Although the dominant social stereotype of Jezebel is negative – a whore or a vamp – the boldness and wildness of the biblical character in her own story makes Jezebel also a positive symbol for women seeking an independent identity. 'Even though in popular Western culture to be called a Jezebel is not a compliment, there is a strange connection/disconnection to Jezebel. Women read themselves as Jezebel as having the "Jezebel spirit".'[12] In this example one biblical character turns from containment within the text to a further and separate existence as a metaphor for women's behaviour in contemporary social worlds.

Cultural Symbols

In the instance discussed above biblical materials provided an icon for cultural evaluation. This can be put into a wider frame of social identity construction. Taking the view that cultural study involves an examination of the 'whole of life' it is possible to seek evaluative cultural symbols in the everyday affairs of a group. Roland Barthes' work has given a basis for this process of discovering social/cultural symbols.[13] In his book *Mythologies* Barthes explores French cultural symbolism via the media images which lead a society to its self-definition. In his article 'Wine and Milk' he points out the manner in which French society has taken possession of wine as an icon for self-identity. 'Wine is felt by the French nation to be a possession which is its very own ... It is a totem-drink, corresponding to the milk of the Dutch or the tea ceremonially taken by the British Royal Family.'[14] The corollary of this approach to wine is that one can only be truly French if one conforms to this cultural image, which Barthes calls a social myth. 'A Frenchman who kept that myth at arm's length would expose himself to minor but definite problems of integration, the first of which, precisely, would be that of having to explain his attitude.'[15] Here wine becomes a 'moral substance', something which exemplifies the positive ethos of French sociability.

The role of the cultural symbol is thus integrative of the individual to the whole. The identity of the whole group is established by the mirror of life provided by the icon, whose values are transmitted by media and by social critics; in turn the group owns that image and offers it to potential members as a guide to belonging. Yet Barthes is operating with 'tongue in cheek' in his articles on French social myths. He does not see these icons as innocent and pure transmitters of positive values.[16] Wine, for instance, is a product of French capitalist society, grown at the expense of minority economic interests such as those of Algerian labourers. In Part Two of his book Barthes develops further his critique of the 'aggressive nature' of social mythology. He argues that social symbols attack individuals and require conformity.[17] Culture itself can be viewed not as a neutral good but as another face of ideology in which vested social interests pressurise society as a whole for acceptance. The 'mythologist' needs to stand back and to examine social icons of the daily world with care, and with attention to their function in endorsing a particular mode of class structure.[18]

Social Icons in Ecclesiastes

'Cultural symbolism' refers to the setting up of social images drawn from the 'whole of life' and to the critique of how such social images operate as a source of social identity. Barthes' study examines French society through a number of cultural icons. The focus is on the role of language as a tool of social communication. In Barthes' view, popular journals, which combine texts and picture, especially fulfil the social function of language.

It can be argued that the same consideration can be given to the cultural content of ancient works. It is likely that ancient texts also offer their readers a means of socio-religious identity. It is possible to move from modern cultural studies to the written text of biblical works and to show that there are comparable cultural moves taking place within biblical material. The language and core concepts of an ancient text will derive from and be related to the social interests of the community for which the text was produced. With regard to the book of Ecclesiastes it can be argued that the messages of this work are conveyed through a series of images which are drawn from a 'whole of life' perspective in which religious ideas are transmitted and evaluated in the language of everyday activity.

It has been shown that there are few direct references to the deity in Ecclesiastes and that there is no use of the metaphors of revelation and transcendence, such as throne theophany, which are largely present in other parts of the Old Testament.[19] Ecclesiastes sets out the issues about life and meaning in terms of human experience under the sun. As Elizabeth Huwiler has recently argued, Ecclesiastes uses language derived from money and commerce to express religious concepts: 'This is not to say that Qohelet's only concern is financial ... It is, however, significant that Qohelet describes both tangible and intangible outcomes in the language of finance and commerce more frequently than, for example, in the parlance of agriculture or the royal court.'[20]

The text's programmatic question itself turns on a commercial idiom, that of profit and loss. 'Of what advantage is it for a human being to live?' Is it profit or loss for a person? Life here contains the idea of labour or toil. It is something that has to be worked at rather than passively received. When a person has made an effort to engage with life experience, is that profitable or not? The answer given is that there is no clear profit to be made. The use of the term *hebel* may point to the total lack of profit (that is, loss) or it may indicate that the nature of any possible profit is ambiguous or uncertain. That question and answer found at the start of chapter 1 of the book is repeated across the rest of the text and covers a range of varying life events. Thus is it profitable to make money and collect wealth, is it profitable to have a family and many sons, is it profitable to be educated and to have 'wisdom'?

This use of cultural icons from ordinary experience to critique life as a metaphysical whole is found regularly in the middle sections of the book. In chapter 4: 1–5, 20, for example, the segments are 'connected by the theme of the human individual, both in isolation and in relationships within social, familial, and religious systems'.[21] And these, in turn, are evaluated under the headings of a concern with labour and material prosperity. Thus the writer points out, in Ecclesiastes 4: 4, that what motivates human enterprise and material endeavour is a spirit of competition with other humans. This is defined as envy and subjected to ideological suspicion. In Ecclesiastes 4: 8 the writer observes those who have no one to share wealth with, in terms of family members, but who ceaselessly toil to gain more possessions without asking what the point of all this struggle is. In these instances the text is exploring the long-term meaning and goal of human life not through supernatural ideas nor through theological language but through an adding up of life as a form of commercial transaction. The use of commercial imagery fills the space belonging to religious terminology and so its ultimate signification is in conveying a religious critique of daily life.

In combining social and religious issues Qohelet implicitly queries the cultural icons of commerce and money making, in his time. The narrator creates caricatures of the daily reality in order to highlight the problem. In chapter 6, for example, he speaks of a man with a hundred sons and a long life. But this man does not have the means to enjoy the years and his sons do not bother to provide him with a decent burial.[22] Thus the profit of family and age are negated by lack of benefit attached to these social goods. The writer of Ecclesiastes, like Barthes, not only employs cultural images drawn from life experience in the broadest sense to map existing social value systems, but also stands back from these cultural myths and offers a critical perspective on the cultural network as a self-promoting reality. Whereas Barthes utilizes images drawn from popular journals, Ecclesiastes uses cultural icons derived from the world of business and commerce. In both writers the goal appears to be a deeper understanding of what it means to belong to a certain society, with its traditional explanations of meaning.

From Culture to Ideology

'Culture' is taken, here, to be a neutral term, defining overarching social reality, but it can easily become the vehicle by which one social group extends its control over other groups – usually in the form of a dominant group over minorities. It can be said that 'culture' is taken over by 'ideology', making of 'ideology' a matter for careful scrutiny. This scrutiny is one in which a negative attitude, suspicious of cultural issues in a text on the grounds that there are 'distortions' of reality present, dominates the enquiry into social realities. J. Dyck, for instance, in discussing the framework of the term 'ideology' deals with the role of ideology in legitimating political power. Ideological arguments operate both to authenticate a political system and to limit the freedom of the citizens living within this system.[23]

These two concepts, culture and ideology, can be applied to biblical criticism. Ecclesiastes' use of money images can be seen as a neutral cultural imagery, but, equally, it can be viewed suspiciously as the manner in which one particular group seeks to dominate social consciousness and so hold power. In Ecclesiastes' case this would be the educated elite, which has access to power and wealth in its community. This is not a bourgeoisie in modern terms, but it is certainly not the peasantry, even though a labourer's life is idealized in the text (Eccles. 5: 12).[24] Reading Ecclesiastes from the perspective of an ideology of power would be to view the writer as spokesperson for dominant class interests in post-exilic Judaism. In this setting the book would be seen as dealing with the nature of existence, a common human debate, but doing so only within the cultural interests of the elite governing class. Only someone with surplus wealth, for example, would be concerned with the risks of venture capital (cf. Eccles. 5: 13). The world-weary tone of the work, adduced by Fox, would stem from an upper-class malaise, a suspicion that the advantage of wealth and status confers no absolute profit in terms of life as a whole.[25]

So far the focus has been on the writer of the text and his/her cultural ideology. But while texts offer the reader a view from the writer's ideological position the reader also comes from a social context and has his/her own cultural and ideological agendas.[26] 'The reader is not an innocent bystander but an active participant with particular interests, whether or not these are articulated in terms of a specific agenda.'[27] When a reader from a different time period reacts to an ancient text the act of reading will engage the reader as a person whose social concerns affect what is understood about the text.

Reader and Text

The phrase 'cultural studies' comes, then, to cover both a text (and its writer) and a reader. The question can be asked 'What does a text do to you if you read it?' But equally important is the query 'What does a reader do to a text in the act of reading?' In the modern world much reading is a private matter in which, through the possession of literacy skills, one individual engages with a text in a direct and personal manner. It is reasonable to describe the reader as a 'self', a unit of being which is aware of its own individuality, with its boundaries and value systems. When the reader-as-self interacts with the text, the act of engagement mirrors his selfhood, as the reader finds a textual message about what it means to be an individual. Investigating this process allows the student to move from cultural to literary criticism as a tool for biblical exegesis.

In Qohelet there is a clear point of contact with the self-conscious reader in the 'I' who narrates the work. It is through the eyes of a 'self' that evaluative messages about life experience are expressed. Moreover this is not a 'disembodied' narrator whose voice is never identified within the text. Rather the speaker is one who has taken on a personalized critique of life in relation to received religious traditions and who deliberately records his findings. The scene is set in Ecclesiastes 1 where the source of the information to come is located as Qohelet (Ecclesiastes), a preacher, and a self in Solomonic guise.[28] Verses 12–17 focus the reader on the narrative persona – I applied MY mind … I have seen everything … I said to Myself … I applied MY mind. A case can be made for describing the 'I' who speaks as a character within the book, which in turn can be labelled as an autobiography. As Eric Christiansen argues 'Ecclesiastes gives us a radically individualised statement … his use of the "I" is uniquely narrative bound.'[29] This individuality is rooted in the autobiographical nature of the text. 'The autobiographical form lends stable integrity to a narrative, for autobiography is concerned with the self of the narrator, and the narrative "I" is the great adhesive quality of such a narrative.'[30] Life may be transient and knowledge partial, as a general principle, but, for the personal voice of Ecclesiastes, life and wisdom are pinned down to specific, if many-layered, ideas.[31] The frame for Qohelet, then, is clearly provided in the text and a character emerges: 'frames with symmetry provide the reader with a sense of origin and ending … This is precisely what Qohelet's frame narrator does. By giving us an origin … and a context … the frame narrator wins our trust and summons our attention.'[32]

The Emerging Character

The next question to be asked is 'What character emerges?' It has already been demonstrated that Qohelet emerges in the text as royal and as a sage. In the material narrated by Qohelet the royal attribution is clearest in chapter 2 and fades away after that. But the conceptual framework revealed by the narrative voice informs the reader concerning other aspects of characterization. The social rank indicated is that of the elite stratum which has access to wealth and education. This is evidenced by the way in which the 'I' who speaks assumes that wealth as a possible good is an important issue and that wisdom is a key possession to have. The references to 'making money' (as in Eccles. 4: 7) imply a commercial background whether through trade or agriculture. The narrator is male and an older man, evidenced by references to having seen, that is experienced, much of life. He is probably a family man, judging by his references to the married life in chapter 9: 9. However, his attitude to women is ambiguous as seen by the difficult passage in chapter 7: 26ff.

Moving from material context to philosophical reflection, Qohelet is concerned with both 'body' and 'inner self'. He focuses on the value of intelligence and reasoning at the same time as upholding the value of physical pleasure – houses, vineyards, gardens, pools, slaves – in chapter 2. There is, indeed, frequently a tension between these two aspects of life, with each held as equally weighty, but not adding up to a single total. 'Body' and 'inner self' are constitutive elements of Qohelet's character, but the reader cannot

determine their exact relationship. For body shapes the human being within
time and space, and, by going into the grave, ends the self. Yet the inner self is
still capable of being set apart from body and wisdom is worthy of pursuit
even in the face of death and forgetfulness.

In a parallel manner, Qoheleth is both 'religious' and 'secular'. God is seen
as the ultimate creator, giver of gifts and judge, but there is little stress on
cult and priestly matters or on the nature of divinity. Even the worship
references in chapter 5 are viewed from the perspective of the folly of human
activity with regard to vows rather than from a directly other world approach.
Chapter 3's examination of time can be taken as a case study here. The first
basis for discussing time is the human one of times and seasons for human
events to occur, but this opens out into a consideration of the concept of *'ôlām*
(eternity). Yet this, too, is conducted from a human viewpoint and the topic
falls back within the limits of human mortality. Key to this investigation is the
concept of the *lēb* (heart), which represents the inner dimension on which
the idiosyncratic self establishes its deeper foundations. The *lēb* is the seat
of reason and of self-conscious activity; as such it is the initiator and the
evaluator of the actions in which the self engages.

The Heart and the Self

Eric Christiansen develops the theme of the *lēb* in a manner central to the
idea of Selfhood in Ecclesiastes. He situates the term in the wider biblical
context. 'The word is used more than any other in the biblical literature to
make reference to the metaphysical "insides" of a person. It conveys a wide
range of emotional, intellectual and physical experiences'.[33] These cover the
intellectual aspect of life – to speak in one's heart refers to an inner thought
process.[34] In Ecclesiastes the heart is already mentioned in chapter 1 in
connection with Qohelet's first introduction of himself as an 'I' (Eccles.
1: 13). 'Because Qohelet invokes his Lēb as a *separate* entity, he invites the
reader to explore and observe his inner person as he does … The Lēb enjoys
this privileged place as Qohelet's intellectual centre, and it is from here that all
of his observations will flow.'[35] It is through this entity that Qohelet processes
his life experiences and what emerges is evaluative criticism of the world
order.

Qohelet's heart/self can lament moral evil in the world and comment
critically on the behaviour of the wicked and of rulers and judges he has
encountered – as in chapters 3: 16, 4: 1–3, 5: 8. More personally, the 'moral
self' seeks an ethos or moral vision for living. The settling on death rather
than life, as in chapter 7, fits into this moral heart/self. Yet the heart, too, can
be pleasured by good physical and material experiences. Peace at the centre of
a family who sit around a table equipped with the fullness of food and wine
is something that carries its own moral vision. In chapter 8: 15, for instance,
he commends enjoyment as the reality of goodness under the sun, eating,

drinking and enjoying himself. Out of these observations Qohelet creates his own idiosyncratic self. 'By thinking ... by centring the place of experience and by feeling the weight of absurdity so deeply he acknowledges that the self is not simply a mental peg on which to hang his ideas and observations. The self is the centre.'[36] In this treatment by Christiansen, the character Qohelet is profiled as a thinking self who is at the centre of human action. This thinking self produces images not only of personal experience but also of the cosmos within which all acts take place. The character, the *lēb*, and the name Qohelet thus cohere in a single mode.

The Self and the World

It is from the centring of his own self-knowledge that Qohelet reaches out to an understanding of the world at large. According to Brown, 'Qohelet's grand experiment reveals an important part of his self-characterisation, namely his unchallenged, authoritative position of power and understanding.'[37] Qohelet's self is distanced from active participation in the world. 'Qohelet's perspective is that of a stranger to the world.'[38] In this detachment he can view the world as a place of absurdity, a view which 'reflects an understanding of the world that is in tension with the framework of human expectations and hopes.'[39] The challenge here is not only to the world but also to the individual's relationship with it. 'Thus the Absurd is a collision between his expectations and the world, but also [stems] from a collision with himself.'[40]

By such a self-awareness of self and world Qohelet can examine also the notion of human self-identity and evaluate many human self-definitions as absurd also. Even the pursuit of intellectual truth comes into this category. Yet that does not empty life of all meaning or destroy a valid concept of the self. Qohelet's moral vision of the self is one that reconstructs character. And this is achieved by the force of the 'inner self' coming to viable conclusions about life and meaning. 'Qohelet by sheer intellectual force steps back and observes life and the cosmos in their meaningless, self-contained whole and returns in resignation.'[41] This resigned state of acceptance finds answers in the simple and passing pleasures of daily life.

Time and Narrative Voice

Qohelet's self-presentation as an 'I' who engages in thought stands at the end of a long process of living and so holds together the lifetime's development of character in a single line with one central question being repeatedly asked. But within this profile there exist separate stages in the line of search. The early chapters tell of the original initiative of seeking answers and then of the first stages in that exploration, as the younger man builds his palaces and utilizes his wealth and good fortune. As the narrative progresses there are numerous observations made, based on 'seeing the world for what it is'. Each instance of observation has its rationale and content, but is joined to others by the narrative comment 'then I saw' and it was *hebel*. Each observation is ultimately subsumed into the overarching ambiguity of life experience.

Thus meaning is associated with the relationship between time and the narrative voice. Gerard Genette sets down the view that 'the chief temporal determination of the narrating instance is ... its position relative to the story'.[42] In Ecclesiastes this position is at the end of life. In addition Genette refers to the convergence in an autobiographical narrative between the time of its first narration and the final time of the 'I', as a type of temporal isotopy. 'In first person narrative ... this isotopy is evident from the beginning, where the narrator is presented right away as a character in the story, and where the final convergence is the rule.'[43] Thus Qohelet, the older sage, waits at the end of the story for his younger self to develop and achieve that breadth of experience which will produce the final moral vision of the narration.

Between each moment of the narration and the different stages of the story the interval is variable.[44] Thus the experiences of a lifetime are, in Ecclesiastes, shortened to twelve chapters. This use of narrative time illustrates the progression of the sage's education-through-life and its links with inherited wisdom, expressed especially in proverbial form. The moral aspects of Qohelet as a 'self' are hereby reinforced. The narrative voice can be defined by the part the narrator takes in the story he tells: the relationship he maintains with it.[45] This is both an emotional contact and a moral and intellectual one. In Ecclesiastes, the narrator's part fits Genette's ideas of the role of the narrator to the extent that the 'I' who speaks offers a commentary on events which delineate both pessimistic and positive possibilities concerning human life. The viewpoint on human existence thus gained by the 'I' of Qohelet is then available to shape the 'I' of the reader.

Notes

1   C. Exum and S. Moore (eds) *Biblical Studies: Cultural Studies* (Sheffield, Sheffield Academic Press, 1998), p. 20.
2   Ibid., p. 21.
3   Ibid., p. 35.
4   Ibid.
5   D. Clines, *The Bible and the Modern World* (Sheffield, Sheffield Academic Press, 1997).
6   Ibid., p. 10.
7   Ibid., p. 24.
8   T. Pippin, *Apocalyptic Bodies* (London, Routledge, 1999), ch. 3.
9   See here the text of 2 Kings 9.
10   Pippin, *Apocalyptic Bodies*, p. 32.
11   Ibid., p. 39.
12   Ibid., p. 42.
13   This comment assumes that R. Barthes is a forerunner of a new style of cultural studies

which uses popular media communication as a type of culture, and links this approach with that of structuralism. R. Barthes, *Mythologies* (New York, Hill and Wang, 1972).

14   Ibid., p. 58.

15   Ibid., p. 59.

16   Ibid., p. 61.

17   Ibid., p. 124.

18   'Mythogist' here refers to Barthes' particular meaning of one who studies these cultural symbols/social myths.

19   See here the New International Bible Commentary on Ecclesiastes, R. Murphy and E. Huwiler, *Proverbs, Ecclesiastes and the Song of Songs* (Carlisle, Paternoster, 1999), p. 173.

20   E. Huwiler on Ecclesiastes in Murphy and Huwiler, *Proverbs, Ecclesiastes and the Song of Songs*.

21   Ibid., p. 191.

22   Since this work does not know of a viable afterlife, peace, for a human being, is to be found through a good death and through proper burial rites. For more detail on this matter, see Tremper Longman III, *The Book of Ecclesiastes* (Grand Rapids, Mich., Eerdmans, 1998).

23   J. Dyck, *A Map of Ideology for Biblical Critics* in M. Daniel Carroll (ed.) *Rethinking Contexts, Rereading Texts* (Sheffield, Sheffield Academic Press, 2000), p. 123.

24   Understanding 'bourgeoisie' here as meaning the particular content given by Marxist philosophy: a meaning derived from European society.

25   M. Fox, *A Time to tear down and a Time to build up* (Grand Rapids, Mich., Eerdmans, 1999). Fox revises his earlier theory towards a more positive evaluation of meaning for life in the book of Ecclesiastes. Qohelet is not a nihilist, though, see pp. 48–9.

26   D. Clines, *Interested Parties* (Sheffield, Sheffield Academic Press, 1995), ch. 1.

27   Exum and Moore, *Biblical Studies*, p. 128.

28   There is an ambiguity in meaning here. 'Preacher' is the usual translation of 'Qohelet', though that word is ambivalent. It is a feminine noun, though the subject appears to be male, and it is unclear what role exactly is designated here. The translation as preacher follows the Greek and Latin versions.

29   E. Christiansen, *A Time to Tell* (Sheffield, Sheffield Academic Press, 1998), p. 134.

30   Ibid., p. 36.

31   Ibid.

32   Ibid., p. 121.

33   Ibid., p. 183.

34   Ibid., p. 185.

35   Ibid., p. 195.

36   Ibid., p. 213.

37   W. Brown, *Character in Crisis* (Grand Rapids, Mich., Eerdmans, 1996), p. 122.

38   Ibid., p. 129.

39   Ibid., p. 131.

40   Ibid., p. 132.

41   Ibid., p. 135.

42   G. Genette, *Narrative Discourse: An Essay in Method* (New York, Cornell University Press, 1983), p. 216.

43   Ibid., p. 221.

44   Ibid., p. 225.

45   Ibid., p. 256.

PART I
NARRATIVE CRITICISM

Chapter 3

Narrative Fiction as Social Commentary

The scene has now been set for the major part of this treatment of Ecclesiastes, in its broadest categories. The foundation for a reading methodology has been established under the heading of 'biblical imagination'. Within this setting both literary criticism and cultural exegesis have been given a preliminary exploration with regard to reading Ecclesiastes. Following the introductory section of this work, which began to consider the use of literary critical methods of reading as exegetical tools for the book of Ecclesiastes, it is now appropriate to consider these matters in greater detail. It was established above that Ecclesiastes can be examined as a narrative work, in which a narrator relates a first person account within the framing borders of editorial, third person comments made at the start of chapter 1 and at the end of chapter 12.[1] The establishment of this point allows for the work to be explored through the sub-themes of characterization, plot and time setting.

Wayne Booth and the Rhetoric of Fiction

Before any such detailed examination takes place, it is important to return to the broader aspects of narrative criticism and to consider some features of narrative fiction. One important aspect of this is the perspective that stories are works of commentary. The root of this concept is the manner in which stories are narrated. As an internal narrator tells a story, the reader is provided with extra information with regard to characters and events, which helps to shape his/her response to the narrative. But these extras are not so readily available in daily life story-events. They are, instead, a feature of narrative fiction, according to Wayne Booth. 'In life such views are not to be had. The act of providing them in fiction is itself an obtrusion by the author.'[2] By both 'showing' and 'telling' the reader how the story is evolving the narrative voice provides extra dimensions of understanding with regard to the manner in which events build up complex systems of relationships between persons. In this way narrative fiction operates as a form of social commentary.

In pursuing this concept of narrative fiction as social commentary it is important to consider the social role of fiction. The symbolic world of a literary work lies alongside the real world of a reader's experience. The relation between these two worlds is a symbiotic one. The reader brings everyday experience to the act of reading a story and applies ideas formed via that act of reading to the daily world of social interaction. Reading a story and responding to it provides a space for the interaction of these two worlds of character, plot and setting, on the one hand, and persons, events and contexts, on the other hand.

Narratives create social worlds, which are in themselves explorations of the nature of human relationships and the quality of human experience. At the same time they offer tools for evaluating life experience. It is not, however, the case that there is any exact, ideal geometrical measurement of the distance between these two worlds of text and reader. The connection between these worlds is not precisely calculated by author or reader: 'the closer we look at the concept of distance the more complicated it appears.'[3] If critics regarded all criticism as tending towards one kind of involvement only, then rules could perhaps be formulated to govern such involvement. 'But is our experience with actual works ever as simple as this approach suggests? Every literary work of any power – whether or not its author composed it with his audience in mind – is in fact an elaborate system of controls over the reader's involvement and detachment along various lines of interest.'[4]

The type of social commentary novels offer is diverse and varied, according to the way in which the telling of the story impinges upon the human interests of readers, potential and actual. For Booth, a high point here is the ability of a given narrator to combine intellectual and aesthetic interests with those of the imagination. 'If he is clear about where his focus lies, a great artist can of course do some justice to the complexities of the world and still achieve a high degree of emotional involvement.'[5] At the centre of this ability to engage the reader while exploring deeply lies the role of the narrator. Every narrator 'must either report dialogue alone or support it with "stage directions" and description of setting'.[6] But each narrator evidences a personal style in carrying through this necessary activity. Booth suggests that this individual act of narration occurs as part of a four-way relationship between author, narrator, other characters and the reader. 'Each of the four can range, in relation to each of the others, from identification to complete opposition, on any axis of value, moral, intellectual, aesthetic and even physical.'[7] It is this complex interrelational system which creates the category of fiction as social commentary.

The role of the narrative voice is thus key to the consideration of social commentary. As well as matters of distance, identification with and opposition to other characters in the novel, the narrator must be examined for reliability or otherwise. A reliable narrator provides a clear line of social commentary on persons and events. One example of this is an obtrusive narrator, who intervenes in the telling, interrupting events to guide the reader as to what to think about characters and events involved in the story.[8] But even an unobtrusive narrator is giving some slant to the story simply by the manner of showing the successive scenes to the reader. How far can these commentaries be taken at their face value by the reader? How far might a narrator 'lead a reader up the garden path' to an understanding of events which is later revealed as an illusion. Booth argues that 'if impersonal narration had been limited to ambiguous heroes who narrate or reflect their own lives, our problems would have been great enough'.[9] He continues by pointing out extra complications, as evidenced in the works of Henry James. James, in *The Turn of the Screw*, pursuing a desire for ' "gradations and suppositions of effect" that will produce "a certain fullness of truth", seeks to give us one character's "troubled vision" as "reflected in the vision, also troubled enough", of an observer'.[10]

It is possible that the narrator may not be omniscient with regard to the events and persons in a story and may thus produce a meaning for events which is itself limited or 'unreliable'. In Ecclesiastes the role of the narrator is central since the narrative voice and the main character are one and the same. It could seem, at the opening of the story, that Qohelet will be a thoroughly reliable commentator since his views have been personally synthesized and his search has constantly been for a unitive meaning to human existence. This aspect of the narrator produces a social commentary which is pessimistic in tone, because the first and very strong line of commentary in the text is that of *hebel*.[11] This term offers mystery, ambivalence and potential lack of meaning as a social commentary on life. But the reader then comes to passages where this viewpoint appears to be challenged by a second line, which encourages readers to engage more optimistically with events. Thus, in chapter 2, Qohelet describes a test of pleasure he underwent. He tried out all the physical delights and found them wanting. In verse 11, for instance, Qohelet announces 'and I myself looked at all the works which my hands had made and at all the toil at which I had laboured to carry out and behold the whole thing was *hebel* and chasing after wind and there was no *yitrôn taḥat ha ššemešš*'. Yet in chapter 2: 24 he asserts 'there is no good for man except to eat and drink and to give pleasure to his self through his toil. This also I saw that it was from the hand of Elohim'. What is more the term *ȧmal*, which he has previously used to indicate worthless labour and toil, now operates as a positive concept, something to produce contentment.

The second narrative voice undermines the first and shows it to be less than totally reliable. This mixture of two narrative moods leads to a complex depth in the social commentary. Any attempt to hold the two voices together needs great negotiation on the part of the reader. But the failure to contain the two narratorial approaches in a single view leads ultimately to a fragmentation of the story as a whole into two different, opposing social commentaries on the world 'under the sun'.[12]

While the narrative voice appears to deconstruct itself in Ecclesiastes it can also be argued that it is this voice which brings together the random collection of experiences, traditional knowledge[13] and personal evaluation which form the material content of the narrative. In this regard Qohelet may be compared with Montaigne in his *Essais*. Here is an example of studying 'commentary when it has no function other than to be itself'.[14] Booth states that Montaigne, as a character within his own story, is a consciously constructed narrator who reveals his own self-development as a foundational part of the social commentary contained within the autobiographical narrative. 'It is this created fictional character who pulls the scattered thoughts together. Far from dispersing otherwise coherent materials, as intrusive commentary does in *Charlotte Summers*, in this work it confers unity ... on what would otherwise be intolerably diffuse.'[15]

Ecclesiastes, then, can be explored as a work of narrative fiction in which the narrator offers his own kind of social commentary on the meaning of life. As Qohelet tells his story he provides the readers with perspectives on daily life – in the royal household, in families, in matters of commerce and cult. The reader's imagination is engaged as a series of 'snapshot' scenes pass before the eyes of the mind. But as the social commentary in this text gathers force and the narrator produces meaning, so the process of narration erodes its own conviction and the reader finds a choice opening up between two apparently opposing 'Qohelets',[16] each of whom offers an intellectual view on social reality. This may be seen in the area of the family, for example, where two views are evidenced. The first view points to the pains of family life while the second stresses the family as the main focus for a man's happiness. Thus in Ecclesiastes 6: 3, Qohelet states that 'If a man begets a hundred offspring and lives a great number of years and great are the days of his years but he does not take pleasure from the good things and also there is not a burial for him, I say better than he is an untimely birth.' But in Ecclesiastes 9: 9 Qohelet argues 'enjoy living with the wife whom you love all the days of your *hebel* life which he gives to you *taḥat ha ššemešš* ... for this is your lot in life'. These two views offer potentially competing evaluations of the family as a symbol of social values. They can be reconciled as parallel strands of thought, but pushing each independently to its extreme limit produces a viewpoint in which 'family' is at best an ambivalent term denoting social reality and, at worst, one that comments very negatively on social existence.

Frederic Jameson and the Political Unconscious

Whereas Booth's study tends towards the development of the concept of social commentary as a broad term to describe the role of narrative fiction, Jameson pursues a Marxist, materialist theory which posits an intimate connection between language and social activity. The work of narrative fiction arises from and realizes, the interests of the particular culture in which it originates. Jameson adds to this Marxist base an element of Greimas' thought, that of binary opposition as a structuring force in literature.[17] The structuralist theory of Lévi-Strauss produces a ground plan for the argument that there is an open-ended symbiosis between text and society.[18] In this setting 'ideology is not something which informs or invests symbolic production; rather the aesthetic act is itself ideological, and the production of aesthetic or narrative form is to be seen as an ideological act in its own right'.[19]

This viewpoint entails a close knit process of text production. 'The whole paradox of ... the sub text may be summed up in this, that the literary work or cultural object, as though for the first time, brings into being that very situation to which it is also, at one and the same time, a reaction.'[20]

Thus the connection between text and cultural phenomena is a dialogical one, which can be expressed through Bakhtinian theory.[21] This dialogical process makes it possible for the binary opposition within the text to create a socio-literary class conflict. In this perspective the battle of Good and Bad forces within a fairy tale is rooted not in a transcendent realm but in the daily clash of interests between competing social groups. It forms a particular expression of the opposition between Them and Us[22] in which peasant culture undermines the aristocratic epic genre. The consequence of such an approach to literature is that narrative criticism must always be regarded as an exploration of the historical and particular nature of culture and not abstracted to an investigation of overarching and constant literary structures. 'The forms of human consciousness and the mechanisms of human psychology are not timeless and everywhere essentially the same, but rather situation-specific and historically produced.'[23] Ideology does not represent the views of an individual writer or reader but expresses the social connections between human groups in a manner which can be described as 'anagogical', 'in which even ... individual visions of Utopian transfiguration are rewritten in terms of the collective, of the destiny of the human race'.[24] Thus the very nature of the text is that of social commentary because the text is a social artefact.

When this mode of reading text is applied to Ecclesiastes it yields new interpretations of meaning. The text is not written in an age conscious of Marxist thought, but, in this sense, belongs to a pre-scientific age, yet it can be viewed as sharing in the pattern of binary oppositions and tensions. Picking up the point made above of Qohelet as an unreliable narrator it is reasonable to view the two voices of Qohelet as a type of binary opposition through which the text explores social reality. The voice of pessimism expresses an alienation from the social world of family and status, from the tradition that society has a deeper value, expressed through the established social norms of an elite society. The voice of optimism reasserts the ongoing significance of that traditional lifestyle of the household of a rich man. The 'I' of the autobiographical format holds both modes of analysis together in a manner which reveals some fissures in putting confidence in the social world of the upper classes. In the two aspects of the autobiographical self, these fissures are examined through their realization in a literary form.

Narrative fiction, it can be said, is inherently tied into cultural reality and expresses the social forces feeding into its creation. Thus, reading from a Jamesonian approach entails understanding the two opposing faces of the 'I' who narrates as creating, exploring and analysing social perspectives which are in tension with each other. In the process of narration social reality materializes. In Booth's approach the reader deals also with the mimetic role of narrative.[25] But, here, the narrator does not construct material reality, instead he offers the reader an alternative world in which the relationships of people and events in the real world can be symbolically played out. Both interpretations of the role of narrative fiction have in common the link between the individual and the community, making the act of reading into a socially symbolic act. Ecclesiastes, of course, is not a novel but a work of fiction expressed in autobiographical form. It is appropriate, therefore, to apply the concept of narrative fiction as social commentary to the autobiographical account of a life to be found in Ecclesiastes.

A Profile of Autobiography

First it is necessary to consider the autobiographical genre as such. L. Marcus offers a basic definition of autobiography as a 'cultural and literary form which demonstrates temporal scope, interprets the past from a present standpoint, and understands life as a process which can be viewed as a coherent and patterned whole'.[26] Thus a later self reconstructs an earlier 'I' and, in doing so, produces a narrative of selfhood. J. Olney points out that whereas such a literary work could be viewed as a holistic account with a straightforward approach to self-definition, the critique of autobiography has come to shed doubt on the clarity and wholeness of the self.[27] If Gusdorf has raised 'le probleme de la connaissance de soi',[28] Foucault, Derrida and Lacan have tended to the view that the text takes on a life of its own in which the self that was not really in existence in the beginning is ultimately a matter of the text. 'Self is a fiction and so is the life.'[29] Here it is possible to make a comparison with Jameson's view that fiction creates a social world. This time it is the identity of an individual self which is the focus of the social meaning created by the text.

As the tale of the self opens up from a single layer to many layers it adds a range of ambiguities in which the narrator confronts existential uncertainty. This process appeals to readers through a telling in which the autobiographical narrative meets the needs of a fascination with the self and an anxiety about personal reality, 'an anxiety about the dimness ... of that entity that no-one has ever seen'.[30] In the unfolding of these many levels of the self, several strands can be discovered. At one level the past (history) is created through the presentation of the author's life.[31] On another level the varieties of selfhood can be investigated through its meaning in relation to just one life. Then again, the autobiography may act as a kind of apologetics for the narrated self.[32] At the opposite end to a justification of a life after the events of living lies the re-creation of actuality through fiction – not as the person was but as s/he believes or wishes the self to be. This, then is an exercise of the imagination.[33]

Summarizing these faces of the self it is possible to adopt the views of Renza. 'We might view autobiography as a unique, self-defining mode of self-referential expression, one that allows then inhibits, its ostensible project of self-representation, of converting oneself into the present promised by language.'[34] This leads into an approach to autobiography as a 'moral' form in that it has meaning beyond the trivial or commonplace. The autobiographical narrative reveals an 'I' seeking to confess his/her own struggles and weaknesses, as in St Augustine's *Confessions*, which exemplify this autobiographical mode. Overall there is a tension implicit in the autobiographical form between establishing selfhood as a viable coherent category of existence and a deconstructive mode in which the narrated self is viewed as illusionary. This model can be applied to a reading of Qohelet in which the optimistic voice fits the first definition and the pessimistic voice fits the deconstructive perspective.

Autobiography and Social Constraints

In autobiography there is a form of social commentary. The 'I' of the text is offered as a living being who speaks directly to the reader. But such a figure is often narrated within an editorial framework, which acts as a social modifier of the message of the 'I'. G. Whitlock discusses the impact of the editorial framing on women's autobiography in *An Intimate Empire*.[35] In the case of Mary Prince, for example, the slave woman's own story is told within the parameters set out by an editorial amanuensis who 'embodies at the scene of writing the epitome of English womanhood as it was understood in terms of the cult of domesticity'.[36] Whitlock notes that the ' "truthful" subject position, which Prince is required to embody, is a particular ensemble of race, gender and sexual characteristics that allows her to speak to the good people of England in the abolitionist cause in 1831'.[37] In this structure the inner self of the main text is controlled by the boundaries of meaning set by editorial contextualizing. In Ecclesiastes, too, Qohelet is constructed within editorial parameters. To this extent, the meaning of the 'I' of Qohelet is modified by the social setting provided by the editors and becomes a socially constructed reality. The first of the final editorial comments, for instance, constructs Qohelet as a great and socially beneficial ruler.

Such a social construction of the autobiographical self operates with the tools of accepted paradigms of behaviour. Whitlock demonstrates that in accounts of emigration by colonists from Britain the normal paradigms of male/female behaviour are followed in telling the story of life on the edges of civilized land. Catherine Traill's book *The Backwoods of Canada* adapts actual experience to the format of the conduct book and the memoir, 'mapping out the appropriate behaviours, morals and competencies for women of the author's rank'.[38] But autobiography may also challenge these socially constructed boundaries to self-expression. Thus, in the story of Mrs Seacole, a Creole woman, Whitlock points out how shifting patterns of social behaviour may be explored through autobiography.[39] Mrs Seacole, a social outsider, tells a tale which leads the reader to re-examine accepted social values. In a similar manner the second and third editorial framings of Qohelet provide an ambivalent profile of the wise king and teacher.

The second editorial frame in which the self of the text is evaluated changes the first viewpoint, which stated 'and as well as Qohelet being wise, in addition he taught the people knowledge'. Now the words of the textual self are socially difficult, 'the sayings of the wise are as goads and as nails firmly fixed are the masters of sayings given by one shepherd'. There is a warning attached to this autobiographical self. The reader should not press the boundaries of thought any further, as verse 13 argues. This may well be a recognition that the interior narrative pushes out the parameters of social commentary. The very image of a king as a source of social order is challenged when Qohelet argues that a poor man can be of greater social value than the rich, in Ecclesiastes 9: 13–15. 'This also have I seen, wisdom *tahat ha ššemešš* and it was great to me ... a little city ... and a great king came against it ... and was found in it a poor wise man and he rescued the city by his wisdom.' The second editorial frame, then, deals with an 'I' who is prepared to deconstruct existing social patterns and to challenge the authority of established tradition.

The Death of the Subject

The deconstructionist critique of autobiography leads to the view that the self produced by a narrative telling is one that constantly evades historical reality and is found only within the words of the text. Paul Jay notes that Nietzsche, in stating that the self's 'real' existence as a spiritual force is contradicted by its discursive origins, moved to the attitude that the self is a product of literary activity, without deeper or permanent significance.[40] Indeed there is a death of the self, since the 'I' who speaks is denied any worth as a subject. Impermanence is here the marker of illusion. But it is possible to turn this round and to argue that it is from the edge of death that the self gives a valid account of subjectivity. 'Deconstructionist themes ... with their suspicion of the categories of subjectivity and experience, seem to point back to an image of autobiography as funerary architecture.' [41]

In Ecclesiastes the funerary theme takes on special life with the use of *mot* in the text. The event of physical death reduces human beings to dust and thus the term *ȧpar* becomes the tool for defining the parameters of the valid self. It constitutes a boundary to the 'I', which cannot be transcended in any real terms. The concept of selfhood must contain the concept of death and the self must be constructed by the inevitability of the death of the self as a living subject. Thus, in chapter 7, mourning is better than mirth and a funeral gathering better than one for a birth. Death is a constant accompaniment to the 'I' who speaks, and acts as the commentary on the worth of individual existence.

Qohelet and Montaigne

These interpretations of the deconstructionist aspect of the personal voice of Qohelet, allied to the more socially constructive aspects of his voice, produce social commentary involving shifting patterns of identification and varying viewpoints on social reality. This is a form of autobiography that is rambling and diffuse, not so much a clear evaluation of the place of an 'I' as a mixed bag of personal snapshots on lived experience. As such its nearest relative may be Montaigne's *Essais*. 'Montaigne's book, a rambling collection of opinions about this and that, owes whatever dramatic coherence it has to the consistently inconsistent portrait of the author himself, in his character as a writer.'[42] It is this created, fictional 'I' who pulls the scattered thoughts together. This style, which might elsewhere appear to manipulate the reader, provides, in this work, a unified picture of events, which would otherwise be lacking.

Montaigne argues that he is making *essais*, that is trials, of life. Through this means he is conducting excursions into meaning in which each visit to the site of human experience takes a different form and produces another variant meaning. This concept of making an experiment is matched in Ecclesiastes 2, where Qohelet describes his deliberate attempts to test pleasure as a meaning for human existence. The overlapping of the two texts in this basic area of narrative purpose legitimizes the development of comparisons between the two works. In support of this endeavour it is possible to quote D. Fewell. 'No text exists in a vacuum. All texts are embedded in a larger web of related texts. We cannot ... understand any text without some appeal to other texts.'[43] T. Beal, also, argues that every text suggests an indeterminate surplus of meaningful possibilities and that interpretation is always a production of meaning from that surplus.[44] Placing Montaigne and Ecclesiastes side by side makes it possible to gain a further perspective on the experimental self as evidenced in Qohelet. This is, of course, an intertextuality that owes something to the mind of the interpreter who juxtaposes disparate texts in a creative fashion.[45]

Experimental Selves in Montaigne and Ecclesiastes

Building on these comments on the role of intertextuality, it is possible to advance to a consideration of the experimental selves created by the narrative in these two works. The lines of interpretation which open up here cover both the content of self-identity and the role of self-reflection. A key metaphor for Qohelet is that of *yitrôn*, the profit that can be made on business transactions. It is this image which Qohelet uses to evaluate life understood as effort or labour. As effort is put into a business deal in order to gain some advantage, so a human being puts effort into life itself. Through this programmatic language,[46] drawn from everyday life, Qohelet constructs a social commentary. Montaigne also draws on commercial vocabulary in his comments on life and its meaning. In Book 1/22, 'That one man's profit is another's loss', Montaigne comments on an Athenian judgement against profit as a form of oppression of others. He points out that all sorts of gains in life take place at the expense of other people and he extends this principle to the very roots of life. 'For natural scientists hold that the birth, nourishment, and growth of each thing means the change and decay of something else.'[47] Despite their differences of approach both Montaigne and Qohelet, in these examples, utilize the material reality of human experience in order to formulate philosophical answers to the question of what value to attach to life itself.

In this form of social commentary the broader issues for debate emerge naturally from, and are answered in relation to, the material events of life as experienced by a self who is able to think and reflect on meaning. More is known of Montaigne's background than that of Qohelet and it is useful to understand the ancient autobiographer through the prism of an administrative officer of a later age. Such a person is constantly engaged in observing and relating to the activities of politics and commerce, while himself standing outside affairs and occupying the role of magistrate. For the core of the narrative, in both works, turns on the individual person who can observe what happens and can then narrate his reactions to those events.

Qohelet makes frequent use of the introductory phrase 'I saw' while Montaigne also describes himself as an observer, as in Book1/28, 'As I was observing the way in which a painter in my employ goes about his work.'[48] Qohelet's 'seeings' form a collection of mental snapshots, which are his learning resources for the task of critical evaluation. Montaigne, too, engages with a series of anecdotes, which he has culled from daily life, as in Book1/21, on the power of the imagination. It is through the memory that the visual observations of these two selves turn into independent analysis. The intellect can take the memories of experience as the ground for acts of self reflection. Thus Qohelet speaks of the use of the inner self as a means of testing what has been observed, as in Ecclesiastes 3: 17 'I said to myself in my *lēb*.' Montaigne, for his part, speaks of the mind and its use for testing and knowing in Book 1/10. It should be noted here that the heart in ancient semitic usage performs the same tasks as the mind in later European usage. Both autobiographers stress the evaluative work of an inner dimension of the self, activity in which seeing becomes perceiving.

The focus on life which emerges for both experimental selves in these texts is one of caution. This can be defined as pessimism possibly, or, more positively, as moderation. Thus Qohelet defines life as *hebel* and frequently mentions the role of death as an intellectual signpost to value, while Montaigne comments on the ambiguity of beautiful thoughts, as in Book 2/17. 'I have always an idea in my mind ... but I cannot grasp and develop it.'[49] He owns his desire for moderation also in that chapter. 'Where others seek the reputation for an active and ready mind, I would be praised for my steadiness.'[50] For both of these commentators on social meaning ambiguity is a key issue. Life's meaning is not clearcut. It is possible to read Qohelet's '*hebel*' here in tones of moderation rather than pessimism, as a linguistic signpost warning that an overenthusiastic investment in maximizing social success will not produce happiness.

In this context of identifying what appropriate social action would entail, Qohelet remarks on the fact that all human acts have a proper time for their exercise. This view is present in chapter 3 where the pairs of action referred to are attached to proper times, headed by verse 1. 'For everything a season and a time for every matter *taḥat ha ššemešš.*' Montaigne's view is that all things have their season, the good as well as the rest. Like Qohelet, Montaigne picks up the significance of death as an intellectual marker, since it is an inevitable material event. 'That is why the earlier acts of our lives must be proved on the touchstone of our last breath. There comes the supreme day that is the judge of all the rest.'[51] Like Qohelet, Montaigne reflects on the inevitable judgement of a person's worth which the deity will require. Since there will be a right time for that judgement, after the cessation of personal existence, human time and the span of a life come into true focus. Time's end is the key to the meaning of individual moments of time, and all social activity from start of life to its finish will be measured in balance with that end point.

The role of the thinking self, in these reflections, is to assess carefully the messages derived from a great variety of different and even opposing human experiences. Such an endeavour tends to produce caution, since the meaning of one event may be countered by that of the next. Only by standing far back from the immediate material context can an 'I' decide on what meaning-for-me emerges overall. This approach leads both Qohelet and Montaigne to explore the significance of the act of thought itself. In Book 3/13 Montaigne discusses the need to weigh evidence from life carefully. 'Reason has so many shapes that we do not know which to take hold of; experience has no fewer.'[52] Qohelet focuses on the difficulty of arriving at an accurate mental analysis of meaning when he states in chapter 7: 23 'All these have I tested by wisdom I have said I will be wise and this was far from me.'

The bottom line to these searches for meaning, therefore, is the weight attached to evaluative wisdom. It is not the accumulation of facts drawn from observation that counts, but the use that is made of the collected experiences of a spectator by the thinking self. Montaigne remarks that 'philosophical enquiries and reflections serve only as food for our curiosity'. And he adds, 'I would rather understand myself well by self-study than by reading Cicero.'[53] The crux of wisdom here is personal intellectual action rather than a passive encounter with the minds of others. This view seems to be very much the kind of opinion held by Qohelet, who holds on to the validity of self-reflection even when this can be shown to be a flawed exercise. He argues that the wise man has a better path through life, for his eyes are open to examining life's affairs (Ecclesiastes 2: 13–14). Yet that watchful quality cannot keep death at bay. For both experimental selves the ultimate advice is to stay in the present moment since only that experience is certain. Qohelet suggests in chapters 11–12 that whatever good fortune comes should be enjoyed while it is there. For example, he suggests in Ecclesiastes 11: 8 'for if a man lives many years let him rejoice in all of them'. Montaigne, for his part, states,

> when I dance, I dance; when I sleep, I sleep; Yes, and when I am walking by myself in a beautiful orchard, even if my thoughts dwell for a time on distant events, I bring them back for another part to the walk, the orchard, the charm of this solitude, and to myself.[54]

As both men value wisdom they stress, each in their own way, that wisdom here means the ability to spectate, to understand what is seen and to add up experiences, not a rote learning of the views of earlier intellectuals. Moreover, one person's own past experience cannot itself dictate meaning; meaning has to be constantly updated, an act which requires the autobiographer to value the present as the only space available for the process of social commentary.

Images of Selfhood

The picture of selfhood set up through this exercise in intertextuality is one of the 'philosopher' – the reflective actor. Both selves are old men who can comment on a lifetime's experiment in living and developing selfhood. The material contents of the books are different since the actors concerned come from very different cultural contexts, but they do cohere on certain points:

- personal experience and personal evaluation are highly valued
- there is something of a hermeneutic of suspicion concerning life itself. Is it really good to be alive?
- there is considerable doubt that the answer to that question is a yes made up of fame, personal glory and status.

In both works little prominence is given to any concept of a deity as one who reveals true meaning to humans. Rather it is within the framework of the world as an ordered place that humans themselves must work towards a realistic social commentary. Qohelet expresses this view in the language of the lot or portion that God has given to each one, as in Ecclesiastes 5: 18 'the days of his life which Elohim has given to him for this is his lot' and in Ecclesiastes 9: 9 'for this is your lot in life'. It is within the allotted time span that humans must seek meaning. But referring to the predetermined nature of human affairs does not end the discussion of what it means to be human and to have a good life, rather it is a beginning for the elaboration of meaning. Asserting that life conditions are allotted to each human being does not move the focus from human engagement with the lot to any personal deity who does the allotting. Yet, since Death is the real controller of life, it may be that the transcendent power hinted at reflects more the objective judge of human social discourse than the creator of human lives.

Autobiographical Selves and Social Commentary

Thus the pursuit of narrative criticism, which has led the way through the topic of narrative fiction into the area of autobiography, brings the reader back to that initial place where attention was focused on a conscious investigation of narrative structures in the search for meaning in text. It can be shown that Ecclesiastes is a work of autobiographical 'fiction', which produces a critique of aspects of the social and religious worldview of its time. In this context the book recounts the thoughts of a self who provides a social commentary on his own society. This commentary includes a critical evaluation of the role of the 'I' himself, seen as sage and teacher. The wise have no better fate than the foolish, since all their understanding cannot keep them from the common experience of loss of selfhood consequent upon physical death. Since neither body nor intellect can suffice for an eternal existence the commentary is a negative one. But, at the same time, that life, which is both physical and intellectual, set within the limits of temporality *taḥat ha ššemešš*, is in itself a thing of value. It may be arguable whether kings benefit their subjects, and it may be suggested that the young and the poor may be as valuable, socially, as kings, if not more so. But the ordinary functions of human existence and of the family as a social group, are not, ultimately, denied.

Notes

1   See the work of E. Christianson, *A Time to Tell* (Sheffield, Sheffield Academic Press, 1998), where there is a thorough discussion of the role of narrative frame and main text. See also G. Salyer, *Vain Rhetoric* (Sheffield, Sheffield Academic Press, 2001), whose study of Ecclesiastes focuses on narrative critical approaches to the text.

2   W. Booth, *The Rhetoric of Fiction* (Harmondsworth, Penguin, 1983), p. 17.

3   Ibid., p. 123.

4   Ibid.

5   Ibid., p. 135.

6   Ibid., p. 154.

7   Ibid., p. 155.

8   Ibid., p. 206. Booth discusses Trollope's use of an intrusive narrative voice in *Barchester Towers*, which indicates to the reader some of the outcomes of the plot.

9   Ibid., p. 339.

10 Ibid.

11 This is such a key term in Ecclesiastes that it has been discussed at great length by commentators. M. Fox gives a treatment of recent comment in *A Time to tear down and a Time to build up* (Grand Rapids, Mich., Eerdmans, 1999), ch. 2. Fox himself opts for a meaning of the absurd in life, allowing him to make a connection with some modern European writers. This intepretation is discussed in Part III.

12 *Taḥat ha ššemešš* highlights the particular nature of this ancient writer's approach to matters of life and its meaning. The transcendent can only be arrived at via that which is seen and experienced. Time and space are defined by their function as boundaries of human existence. The term balances with the 'I' of the autobiographer; the personal voice can only reflect validly on the material world and its possibilities.

13 Traditional knowledge here applies to the use of proverbial forms in the text. It is a matter of debate whether the writer knew these proverbs to be in existence or whether he created them out of a knowledge of a common proverbial style. As they stand they fit, in chapter 7, into the mood of the autobiographer. C.-L. Seow, *Ecclesiastes* (New York, Doubleday, 1997), presents arguments for this material being that of the writer himself. See, for example, pp. 242f.

14 Booth, *Rhetoric of Fiction*, p. 228.

15 Ibid.

16 See T. Perry, *Dialogues with Kohelet* (University Park, Pa., Penn State University Press, 1993). Perry accounts for the competing voices in Ecclesiastes by arguing for a dialogue between two voices, one of which puts one side of an argument and is responded to by an appropriate answering voice.

17 F. Jameson, *The Political Unconscious: Narrative as a Socially Symbolic Act* (London, Routledge, 1996), p. 47.

18 Ibid., p. 77.

19 Ibid., p. 79.

20 Ibid., pp. 81–2.

21 Ibid., p. 84.

22 Ibid., pp. 85–6.

23 Ibid., p. 152.

24 Ibid., p. 286.

25 This is to engage the view that narrative has a role in copying daily life and thus offering the reader a chance to reflect at a distance on the deeper meaning of human affairs. Here the particular focus is on social matters. This approach follows the general proposals of C. Walhout, 'Narrative Hermeneutics', in R. Lundin, C. Walhout, and A. Thiselton, *The Promise of Hermeneutics* (Carlisle, Paternoster, 1999).

26 L. Marcus, *Auto/Biographical Discourses* (Manchester University Press, 1994), p. 167.

27 J. Olney, 'Autobiography and the Cultural Moment', in J. Olney (ed.) *Autobiography: Essays Theoretical and Critical* (Princeton, Princeton University Press, 1980), p. 20.

28 Ibid., p. 21.

29 Ibid., p. 22.

30 Ibid., p. 23.

31 B. Mandel, 'Full of Life Now', in Olney, *Autobigraphy*, p. 55.

32 Olney, 'Autobiography and Cultural Moment', p. 35.

33 Ibid., p. 45.

34 L. Renza, 'A Theory of Autobiography', in Olney, *Autobiography*, p. 295.

35 G. Whitlock, *The Intimate Empire* (London, Cassell, 2000).

36 Ibid., p. 20.

37 Ibid., p. 21.

38 Ibid., p. 53.

39 Ibid., p. 86.

40 P. Jay, *Being in the Text* (Ithaca, NY, Cornell University Press, 1984), pp. 28–9.

41 L. Marcus, 'The Face of Autobiography', in J. Swindells (ed.) *The Uses of Autobiography* (London, Taylor and Francis, 1995), p. 17.

42 Booth, *Rhetoric of Fiction*, p. 226.

43 D. Fewell, 'Introduction, Reading and Relating', in D. Fewell, *Reading Between Texts* (Louisville, Ky., Westminster John Knox, 1992), p. 17.

44 T. Beal, 'Ideology and Intertextuality: surplus of meaning and controlling the means of production', in Fewell, *Reading Between Texts*, p. 31.

45 D. Penchansky, 'Staying the Night: Intertextuality in Genesis and Judges', in Fewell, *Reading Between Texts*, p. 77.
46 Programmatic language is in the style of Graham Ogden who speaks of Qohelet's programmatic question. See G. Ogden, *Qoheleth* (Sheffield, Sheffield Academic Press, 1987).
47 M. Montaigne, *Essais*, trans. J. Cohen (Harmondsworth, Penguin, 1958), Book 1/26, p. 49.
48 Ibid., Book 1/28, p. 91.
49 Ibid., Book 2/17, p. 196.
50 Ibid.
51 Ibid., Book 1/19, p. 35.
52 Ibid., Book 3/13, p. 344.
53 Ibid., Book 3/13, p. 354.
54 Ibid., Book 3/13, p. 396.

Chapter 4

Narrator as Character

The previous chapter explored narrative fiction under the heading of social commentary. Within this framework autobiography forms a particular kind of social commentary. For Montaigne and Qohelet this is an idiosyncratic perspective on the world as experienced by one human being. This approach offers a profile both of the character of the self who recounts the story and of the world so reviewed. There is a symbiosis at work here. The self is created by experience of the world, while the images of the world are formed from the view of a participant in this reality, a self. Thus the concept of social commentary incorporates both the 'I' of the speaker and the story which is narrated. With regard to Qohelet this entails a social commentary formed via the literary figure of 'King Solomon', on the one hand, and the interests of a wealthy, educated elite in Hellenistic Judah, on the other.[1] It is the first part of this link between self and world, between character and story, that will be examined in this chapter.

The Personal Voice

The autobiographical character may be said to exemplify the 'personal voice'. This is a subjective, limited voice. Whatever the apparent objectivity of the commentary – and Qohelet moves from his own experience to evaluation of traditional, 'universal' views on the world order – it is in fact thoroughly tied to the particular subject who is producing the account. For Qohelet acts as a critic of existing thought and as an exegete of wisdom traditions expressed in proverbial form.[2] A recent volume on the role of the modern biblical exegete, as subjective and personal, may be brought into play here.[3] I. Kitzberger notes that 'what is at stake in personal voice criticism is *nothing less than the self of the critic*'.[4] This comment can be applied to developing the profile of Qohelet as a character. It is through his critical voice that his self can be perceived. As already noted, Qohelet sometimes seems to be two, opposing selves, pessimistic and optimistic by turns. This should not be surprising for 'The "I" of each person, and thus of a critic alike, is always multi-dimensional'.[5] Insofar as Qohelet is a critic of life experience and its traditional explication alike, the textual world of Ecclesiastes is formed by the interaction between a personal voice and its subject matter. Thus, 'in narrative-critical terms, the story-world purposed by the text and the story-world brought to the text by the reader influence, inform and transform one another in a dynamic fashion'.[6] In Ecclesiastes Qohelet is both a reflection of a particular story-world and a 'reader' of it.

Here the narratively embodied self operates as two parallel voices. With the repeated use of the phrase 'I myself said in my *lēb*', Qohelet becomes both speaker and hearer as the spoken word is reflected upon in the inner self. Thus the personal voice is not a singular affair but one that contains elements of dialogism.[7] As D. Patte argues, 'a personal voice is always *a construct that took shape with the help of others.*' 'Since any formulation of my personal voice is a construct shaped by an Other with whom I am in conversation, even if this other is myself', all such constructs must be carefully assessed for trustworthiness or objective value.[8]

In autobiographical fiction the content of the character of the self who narrates is supplied by the personal voice. The character of Qohelet is constructed by speech insofar as the 'I' who speaks recounts his own acts of observation and evaluation. Character is synonymous with voice here, since, in the main sections of the book, it is only through the speech of the narrator-as-self that the lineaments of the main character of the work are established. What Kitzberger and Patte indicate is that such a 'personal voice' has a right to be listened to and taken seriously, as a source of social commentary, while, simultaneously, it is itself under critique for the reliability of its operation in the production of that social commentary.

Speech and the Self

Since the basis of personal voice criticism is the act of speaking it is necessary to look more closely at the speech act involved. In Ecclesiastes Qohelet has no existence as a character outside of first person speech. The 'I' attached to a verb is the means by which Qohelet's personhood emerges. It is through the act of speaking to the self that this 'I' operates. Although this language structure is most noticeable in Ecclesiastes it is visible elsewhere in Hebrew narrative. R. Alter notes the use of self-reflexive speech in 1 Samuel, where an aspect of David's thought is recounted under the title 'David said in his heart' – a linguistic parallel to Qohelet's speech formulas. Alter regards this usage as part of a 'bias of stylisation in biblical commentary to dialogue before all else',[9] and as a technique for expressing inner aspects of a character's profile. 'When an actual process of contemplating specific possibilities, sorting out feelings, weighing alternatives, making resolutions, is a moment in the narrative event, it is reported as direct discourse.'[10]

These observations lead into a closer evaluation of utterance as a means of developing characterization. H. White has noted that 'the act of expression is itself a constitutive event for the speaker'.[11] It is the 'polarity in consciousness between interiority of thought and the exteriority of language which makes possible self-reflection'.[12] The event of self-reflection, it can be argued, is that which creates a 'person' from a human being. When a particular individual not only frames ideas internally via formal language patterns but can then utter such concepts in such a way that both that person and other human beings may hear and grasp what the human person intends, then the utterer is constituted as a character with content. White argues that for 'language to take itself as its own object, there must exist, in language, signifiers whose function is to embody this self-reflective capacity'.[13]

For White these signifiers are frequently pronouns, especially the pronoun 'I'. The word 'I' becomes the signifier for the self as a whole. Whatever is attached to the 'I' constitutes the details of that self. It is in the act of utterance, therefore, that a self both expresses and creates selfhood. In Ecclesiastes this process is very evident. The 'I' who speaks does so to offer a personal commentary on the world order experienced, but that act of commenting also constitutes 'Qohelet' as a particular and individual expression of 'I'-ness. 'The self has gained access to the possibility of self-signification only by the displacement of the self as an object by the sign [I].'[14]

White's ideas have developed from his use of Austen's 'speech act' theories, which posit locutionary, illocutionary and perlocutionary types of performative utterance.[15] E. Bruss has also developed Austen's and Searle's work, this time linking it to the autobiographical genre as such. Bruss claims that literature can be placed alongside linguistics with regard to 'the kind of action that text is taken to be'.[16] 'Just as speaking is made up of different types of action carried out by means of language, the system of actions carried out through literature consists of its various genres.'[17] Autobiography is one genre, with its own specific form – form, here, relating to the immanent material properties of a text. In autobiography the author has a dual role, acting both as organizer and presenter of the material and as its subject matter. It is assumed that the events recounted in the autobiography are closely connected with the actual facts of what happened in the life of the self, and the autobiographer appears to believe what he asserts.[18] It is possible to fit Ecclesiastes into this format to the extent that it exhibits its own form of these basic genre rules. The narrator is a character within the text, serving a dual purpose; the text assumes a link between Qohelet and a real king in Jerusalem, and the autobiographer/narrator asserts a belief in what is narrated. The royal guise thus appears to support the serious nature of the comments drawn from human experience.

Bruss continues by pointing out the linguistic markers through which the genre achieves its shape. These include person or title/space/time/modality and mood.[19] In Ecclesiastes, as has been shown, the pronoun 'I' is a major title for the narrative voice. The location of that voice is 'here', that is *taḥat ha ššemešš*, part of the here and now of human experience, balanced by a time span, which is immediate and post-dated at the same time. These pointers dramatize the close contact the reader is meant to have with the autobiographer, Qohelet. Under the heading of 'performatives', Bruss notes the relevance of terms such as 'create' and 'describe'. For Qohelet both are significant. Qohelet 'creates' by 'description'. What he creates is a profile of memories under scrutiny. This is achieved via descriptive acts governed by verbs of observing and perceiving more deeply. Here an important element is the translation value of *àmartî*. This tense implies a completed act and because of the overall gap between the narrator's present stance and the time of starting on an exploration of life, it is best understood as past completed action.[20] So Qohelet creates, for the present time of the reader, a connection with an 'I' who has gradually come to own himself via the expression of selfhood in life events. Here tense is significant in the carrying out of autobiographical purpose.

This gives depth to the narrator as character but also means that the views of this 'I' need to be seriously considered by the reader. They are not random, one-off thoughts; they surface as a result of owning and comparing a number of stages of life experience. The combined effect of these linguistic features is that a sense of intimacy is created between the autobiographer and the reader. Here Bruss' comments on James Boswell's journal may appropriately be applied to Qohelet. 'The intimacy is genuine, since we are overhearing Boswell speaking with himself. His identity is necessarily composed of more than one voice. It has the unity of a process rather than a single role or image.'[21] Thus also in Ecclesiastes, the voice of Qohelet is at least two, sometimes contrary, voices, and the reader engages with the process whereby these personal voices interact and produce a fuller image of the biographer.

The performative role of language is linked here to the perlocutionary, defined by Austen as the persuasive effect of speech on the hearer, with a consequent stress on the social function of language.[22] The perlocutionary role of the pronoun 'I', attached to the past complete tense, is to persuade the reader that this indeed is an autobiography. As Bruss comments, auto-biography is constituted as a genre by a culture[23] which accepts the rule of the genre set out above. The reader takes seriously the existence of such an 'I' and moves to interact with this self as a 'you' to whom an 'I' speaks, in the guise of dialoguing with himself. This pattern is further endorsed in Ecclesiastes by the link between the frame and the narrator. The initial editorial bridges a potential gap between frame and narrative by use of the phrase *àmār qohelet*. The same verse and tense are repeated in the *àmartî* of the narrator. Both meanings, says and said, are conveyed in Hebrew by the one tense. Thus the time bound self-examination of the 'I' of Qohelet, with its focus towards the past as cause of present opinions and self-construction, is one with the time of the reader (any reader) as a self who meets Qohelet within his/her own time frame and 'I'-ness.

Verbal Dynamics

The personal voice of Qohelet is established by performative utterance in which the act of speech constructs character in a direct manner. The mode of speech, which is critical to this process, is the verbal structure of such self-signification, the places where 'I' is further defined by terms such as 'see' and 'say'. Here the narrator becomes an actor and by the actions performed the narrator develops into a character. Thus, in chapter 1, the name 'Qoheleth' is introduced by the editorial frame in verse 1 and owned by the internal narrator as '*aṅi Qohelet*' in verse 12. Already, by verse 2, some flesh is put to this frame via the verb '*åmār*'. Qohelet is one who speaks, above all, as indicated in the opening gambit of the work, '*dibrê qohelet*'. The entire text, then, consists of the sayings of a first person narrator. The simple third person use of *åmār* is developed further once the 'I' of Qohelet speaks directly. Having reviewed his experience Qohelet expresses his views and marks them with the phrase 'I myself spoke in my *lēb*, saying' (verse 16). Qohelet not only speaks but hears his own inner speech and through that process of speaking and hearing moves to a unified opinion on life. It is this act of speaking that holds together a poetic description of cosmic order and the evaluation that all is *hebel* in that first chapter. The leitmotif of 'I' as one who speaks or says, introduced in this opening sequence, repeats constantly to the end of the book and denotes the typical move of the text from observation to opinion.

Parallel with speech and occupying an equally important position is the act of 'seeing'. In chapter 4, for example, the narrative voice stresses the power of sight, 'and I myself turned and I saw'. This motif is repeated in verse 4, introducing another set of experiences, and again in verse 15. The rehearsal of the content of Qohelet's experiences, and of the nature of the human environment, is punctuated by the narrator's act of seeing. This is an action that starts off as simple observation but shifts towards the concept of perception or understanding, since the seeing leads to commentary on the value to be attached to the social world, as in verse 7, 'and I turned and I saw *hebel taḥat ha ššemešš*'. In chapter 4 this is characteristically a mix of *hebel* and *rå yôn rûaḥ*.[24] *Hebel* is treated as an evaluative term in Ecclesiastes, but here it introduces a story sequence which deals with a man who has no dependants to benefit from his efforts but who works ceaselessly, none the less. The placing of the story within the overarching evaluation of its meaning emphasizes that observation of action is intimately tied to comment on what happens. Whereas speech per se leads to a self-reflexive being, adding insight opens up the content of that reflectivity to the reader and helps to shape the narrator as person. The narrator is thus one who uses the products of experience, held in the memory, and, through interpretation, creates a set of attitudes and values. These constitute a self-expression and a consistent way of operating.[25]

Overall, in the twelve chapters, seeing and saying dominate as key verbs and so furnish a foundation for the narrator to become a character. In chapter 1: 12 further levels of action such as ruling are added to this core activity, and in chapter 2: 4 acquiring greatness. In chapters 1 and 2, indeed, the context of 'I' as ruler and as a great person flesh out the basic profile of the one who sees and says. Thus a further list of verbs is drawn in, all expressing the activities suitable for a king, namely making, building, planting, buying, gathering, having and getting.[26] The narrator looks back on the carrying out of these actions and passes a spoken judgement on such activity. It is all *hebel*. The experiences of wealth and status are at one with the self-definition of the speaker as 'I' the king, and it is specifically to these royal eyes that the deployment of material advantages appears doubtful.

On a wider front, acts referred to in phrases such as 'I gave my *lēb* to seeking out' (Ecclesiastes 1: 13) and 'my *lēb* guiding by wisdom' (Ecclesiastes 2: 3) expand the content of the self. The person is one who not merely sees and speaks in a swift and single movement but whose seeing and speaking are considered and deliberate acts to which the 'I' has turned or applied itself.[27] In this framework 'testing' and 'finding' also have their places, as found in chapter 7.[28] As the world is explored through interaction with it in the guise of human experience, so also the self is tried out experimentally and owned in the event of passing judgement.

Narrative Voice and Judgement

G. Ogden has described the use of a 'programmatic question' to structure Ecclesiastes.[29] In this view stress is placed on the asking and answering of a direct question. The roles of both the questioner and the respondent are contained within a single self. It is the first person narrator who enquires as to the gain or advantage (*yitrôn*) of toil under the sun. It is the same Qohelet who answers with the word *hebel*. In this paired question and answer the 'I' of the narrator is established. It is a self whose identity is rooted in the act of evaluation. The question does not represent an idle or superficial query but rather expresses a deeply felt attitude to human existence. It is in this act of asking and replying that the narrative 'I' creates itself, in the very act of evaluation through dialogue.

An example of this process at work can be found in Ecclesiastes 2: 20–23 where the phrase 'and I myself turned' introduces a separate element in the text, in which Qohelet expresses the already grave doubts he has about the value of his *āmal*. He reiterates this doubt by outlining the view that someone who has used good skills such as wisdom and knowledge to make advantages for himself will still have to leave the products of his efforts to another who has not made any effort to gain an advantage. Qohelet sees this as *hebel* and *rā' rabbah*.[30] Then comes the question – so what has a man from his toil? The answer is only the pains of effort and worry, with no permanent enjoyment. The questioning voice meets its balancing response of '*hebel*'.

In this section Qohelet's self-expression encloses an experience of the world outside the self. His self is constituted both by curiosity and the need to critique life, and by the response his 'I' makes in the light of that curiosity. To this extent it is in the act of passing judgement that Qohelet establishes his selfhood. Qohelet is a 'doer', someone who moves from one action to another, within the narrated speech patterns of the text. In these movements of the 'I' Qohelet shifts from being a narrator of a personal voice to a character as such.

This approach to characterization establishes Qohelet as a character through 'doing', specifically through his own performative utterances. The self so constructed is a literary figure, more especially a linguistic one. Whether Qohelet emerges as a rounded character here is arguable, since the basis of characterization is a set of actions, which do not necessarily imply that a coherent person exists beyond the speech acts. Taking the surface level of the narrated text, the self as 'doer' raises the possibility of evaluating Qohelet through the concept of 'traits'. This perspective on characterization is based on Greimas' actantial account of plot and characters.[31] In this mode characters are subordinated to plot.[32] As S. Rimmon-Kerman remarks, 'since action seems more easily amenable to the construction of "narrative grammars" … it is convenient to reduce character to action'.[33] The act of reconstructing a character from a text therefore requires the attribution of 'traits' such as turbulence, independence, excess, ugliness, to a named character. The character represents these traits in the movement of the story line, and is constituted by them. Cohesiveness is imparted by the repetition of elements, by similarity, contrast and implication.[34]

When this evaluative system is applied to the characterization of Qohelet some particular images emerge. Qohelet is frequently pessimistic and frustrated, as the use of *hebel* (whatever its exact meanings in the text) indicates. He is also curious and energetic, engaged in seeking and testing. He is assertive, easily willing to submit his idiosyncratic evaluations of life to the reader. He is sometimes optimistic, endorsing the value of physical benefits for human existence. Among these traits there is some cohesion – searching and testing, asserting an opinion, for instance. But there is also open-endedness since the acts of investigation range over a variety of material with separate aspects juxtaposed in a random fashion, as in chapter 8, for example, where proverbial material and human experience are mixed together.

The chapter opens with several disparate proverbial sayings related to human wisdom (verses 1 and 2). This is followed by a comment on the role of the king and the proper response to royal command. This would appear to be based on court experience and its only verbal contact with the first verses is the inclusion of the term 'wisdom'. This section opens out into a more general statement about the time and purpose of events, in which it is not certain that the reference is back to events connected with a royal command. Verse 10 does start a new train of thought, related to the fates of the righteous and the wicked. The connection back might be the issue of proper time and purpose since Qohelet speaks of the fate that will eventually vindicate those who fear God, while bringing judgement down on the wicked. The reason for these comments appears to be the experience of attending the funeral of those whom Qohelet can declare to be wicked. But the next section seems to reverse the certainty of the proper fates of the wicked and the just and is joined, by a total leap of thought, to commendation of enjoyment of food and drink. This may be due to frustration on the previous front of knowing times and structures in human affairs. Finally the chapter ends with the contrast between human efforts to gain knowledge and the frustration of these efforts by God's planning of created existence.

In this passage from the text Qohelet exhibits some of his usual traits such as searching out knowledge and assessing experience, but within this pattern he jumps around among a range of materials, which can feed the expression of his views. As the characterization of Qohelet is explored in greater depth a more rounded picture of him emerges, since he can be shown to have depth of character. This is linked with his taking into account many variables, trying to fit a single pattern to experience, but falling back from a simple solution to meaning in the face of so many uncertainties, of the tension between positive and negative appraisal. The reader engages with the narrator-character, accompanying him in his mental leaps, seeking to picture the experiences which took place in Qohelet's life. Such a focus on one character leads to the issue of whether or not Qohelet could be called a 'hero'.

In the context of characterization as 'doing' this entails a quest, for actantially a hero is a character engaged in quest. 'The trajectory in an independent story is often a search or "quest" undertaken by the hero in order to solve or cancel the problem or deficit presented at the outset. The hero is the subject of the quest.'[35] Furthermore the object sought after is not always physical.[36] In this view characterisation serves the development of the plot. This is marked by the identification of an object for a search, at the start, the carrying through of the quest and its (successful) conclusion. According to Fokkelman, the story 'begins by establishing a problem or deficit; next, it can present an exposition before the action gets urgent; obstacles and conflicts may occur that attempt to frustrate the *denouement*, and finally there is the winding up.'[37] The characters operate within and are defined by this plot trajectory. The character of 'hero' is key to the progression of events towards a goal and central to the creation of meaning in events.

E. Christiansen has taken this motif of the 'quest' seriously, arguing that Qohelet's search is for wisdom. This is an intellectual pursuit, but since the quest engages the whole of life experience it is not simply a mental search. 'There is a language element that suggests that we understand the quest, at least in part, as a physical journey, one which leaves the participant(s) exhausted and in dire need of rest.'[38] Christiansen suggests that there are two parts to Qohelet's quest.[39] In the first part he seeks understanding of life through materialist experience and fails in his quest. In the second part, the older man gazes on his younger self with the eye of longer living. He condemns the folly of a frenzied search for wisdom and states the truth about the quest for an understanding of life. 'He admits his failures and his inability to know. He is certain that he is ignorant ... That hard won ignorance forms the

basis of his strategy in the latter half of the book.'[40] Christiansen argues that
the new understanding is that valuing knowledge is replaced by practical
living and enjoyment of life.[41]

In this perspective it is possible to describe the narrator-character as a hero
– a tragic hero in part one, the first seven chapters of the book, and a
'triumphant' hero in the second part. This is in line with Christiansen's
argument that Quest A fails while Quest B succeeds in achieving its goal of
acquiring wisdom. Here 'wisdom' contains two opposing aspects. There is
the wisdom that entails complete mental control of the patterns of human
experience and the wisdom that is fleshed out as an accepted lack of the first
wisdom mode.

Taking the concept of 'tragic hero' in greater depth and considering more
the 'being' than the 'doing' of such a character, can it validly be argued that
Qohelet fills such a role? Cheryl Exum describes the context of the tragic hero
as 'a dimension that reveals the dark side of existence, that knows anguish and
despair, and that acknowledges the precarious lot of humanity in a world now
bewildering and unaccommodating'.[42] This 'tragic' atmosphere can certainly
be identified with Ecclesiastes. It is carried by terms such as *hebel*, *rāʿ*, *inyān*
and *rå yôn rûaḥ*.[43] At best these terms indicate a world of ambiguity, of
unexpected and negative consequences for human living. At worst they
identify a hostile, evil, impossible environment, in which human beings must
still attempt to wrest positive, pleasant experiences out of material conditions
that are intent on negation of meaning. It can be argued that, for Qohelet, the
effect of this is catastrophic. He is forced towards the view that stillborn
children are better off than those who have made it into life under the sun, a
view shared with Job.[44]

Yet Qohelet does not totally give in to this. The very act of describing it
as *hebel* shows him retaining his identity and powers of evaluation. Qohelet
may be said to struggle against the evidence brought by his experiences. A
central feature of the tragic story is the heroic struggle against fate.[45] This
struggle may itself be a cause of catastrophe. Exum describes the guilt of the
tragic hero as the result, possibly, of 'a transgression ... innocently performed,
a simple misjudgement'.[46] This can easily be applied to Qohelet as a definition
of his whole quest. His 'I' states confidently in chapter 1 that he set out to find
meaning in life, and, in chapter 2, that this could be found through exploring
physical pleasures and material advantages. But this very search is fated to
fail to achieve its goal. The fate that prevents it may be defined, neutrally, as
passively awkward or, pessimistically, as actively evil and obstructive.

Thus Part A of the quest, as viewed by Christiansen, is worked out through
this 'tragic hero' theme. However, Part B shows Qohelet achieving peace
and contentment. Here the hero is not 'tragic' but 'comic', that is he acts as
the central figure in a story which ends positively. As W. Whedbee puts it,
'whatever trials and threats the hero must endure, comedy usually ascends
from any momentary darkness and concludes with celebration.'[47] Yet, it
cannot be said that, in Ecclesiastes, 'all live happily ever after'. Qohelet

achieves his quest by abandoning it in its earlier form. A realignment of his self is required, specifically from the absolute horizons of intellectual knowledge to a more limited evaluation, even of events *taḥat ha ššemešš*. By accepting lack of wisdom Qohelet gains wisdom. There is a considerable paradox present here. There may even be an element of the self as a 'counter hero'. This is fleshed out via Qohelet's own 'I' who sees and says. A poor wise youth can save a city yet poor and youth are, in the traditions of Qohelet's world, opposed to wise. Thus it is the 'little person' who makes the beneficial impact on human society rather than the 'great hero' represented by the all-powerful royal character in chapter 2.

Character as Being

This discussion sets the scene for a move from 'doing' to 'being'. Christiansen remarks that the failed quest leads to frustration, even to illness.[48] This is an occurrence that finds an echo in F. Zimmerman's account of Qohelet as a neurotic personality. Here doing opens into the essence of being, of a long-term personality profile. Zimmerman notes that Qohelet's days are filled with pain,[49] that he appears to suffer from sexual impotence,[50] has a problem with women,[51] is obsessed with his own thoughts[52] and has a fixation with time.[53] All this points to a man who suffers from obsessional doubt. 'He is a pathological doubter of everything, stemming from a drastic emotional experience, a psychic disturbance ... His doubt comes from a parapathy, a disease of the mind which he shares with many neurotics.'[54]

In this description Qohelet is not defined by acts of speech but by an underlying state of health. Whether or not the reader agrees with this interpretation it establishes Qohelet as a character who *is*. It is as such a person, one whose whole being is not revealed directly in the text, but is hinted at, who is more than words alone, that the 'I' who speaks can be further explored. The means used to conduct this investigation is the reading tool focalization. T. Todorov remarks that 'the phenomena that compose the fictive universe are never presented to us "in themselves" but from a certain perspective, a certain point of view'.[55] The character(s) who provides the major input as the focalizing agent in a narrative may be the narrator him/herself but may equally be another character.[56] In Ecclesiastes it is Qohelet, the narrator and the character narrated, who offers a point of view to the reader. 'Acting as the narrating subject of the text, its teller, the character who narrates also functions as a subject of narration because he or she is an actor in the story ... the character operates as an actor in one realm of time (story) and as the narrator in another (narration).'[57]

The story in Ecclesiastes is the report of the ideas and comments of Qohelet. These amount to advice, which is offered in Qohelet's name to the reader of the text. It would have been possible for a third person narrator to have told the story as one with access to Qohelet's experiences and reactions.

The unification of this material with the first person voice of the main actor in the story allows both for a more intimate relationship between the narrative voice and the audience and for a more dramatic telling of the determined search for understanding. This focalization also highlights the problems associated with human knowledge and understanding of the most basic structures of human existence. The focalization works here through the key, repeated words that Qohelet uses. These include the view that life should be profitable in some way for the humans engaged in living.

Yitrôn anchors this concept of gain into the material world of commercial profit and loss accounting.[58] If a human being adds up the columns of work done and consequent gains, the whole should show that a human person can improve the nature of existence from that of mere subsistence. But is this the case? If life is viewed as *ámal* or labour is there any *yitrôn*? And all this is in connection with what happens *taḥat ha ššemešš*, within the boundaries of human sight and activity. The ultimate focalizer is the word *hebel*, a term on which there is much disagreement among readers of the text.[59] However, there is agreement that this word throws into doubt the possibility of anyone producing a simple and positive answer to the questions about the value of life and work. The term appears to signify the ambivalence of meaning in terms of life experience and its shifting forms; the best that can be extracted here is the transience or mystery of life, the worst is utter absurdity and total void.

The focalization of meaning through the voice of one character and such a demanding issue as the overarching meaning of life raises a further point concerning the characterization of Qohelet. It was pointed out in Chapter 2 above that the deity has a very small part to play as a named character in Ecclesiastes. It is appropriate, here, to suggest that Qohelet, as the prime source of information in the text, takes over a divine standpoint. He thus offers an evaluation of life that stems not just from temporal existence but from the very source of existence itself. M. Sternberg argues that biblical narrators tend to stand in the place of divine omniscience with regard to the stories they tell. 'Where the general model of omniscience in literature dispenses with one of the basic perspectives by virtually equating the author with the narrator, the Bible introduces a new perspective by dissociating God from the characters and aligning him with the narrator.'[60]

If this concept is applied to Ecclesiastes Qohelet as narrator presents the divine viewpoint. This is supported by Qohelet's claims to have seen *all* that happens and is done in the world of human affairs, as well as by his royal guise in chapters 1 and 2.[61] Qohelet's view of *hebel* as defining the nature of existence would lead then to ambiguity or absurdity being part of the divine character, as indicated in the comments made by W. Brown, referred to in Chapter 2 (p. 27).[62] This view of the deity links also with the book of Job, especially chapters 38–41 where, from a human position, it can be seen that God is in charge of the world but is an ambiguous and volatile figure.[63] Balancing a God who is uncertain and chancy is Qohelet's view that human actions should focus on practical living, knowing that a full understanding of the universe is beyond human understanding. This attitude can be likened to the 'Fear of the Lord is the beginning of wisdom' approach to be found in Job 28.

But, against the view that Qohelet's self in some way accesses the nature of divinity it has to be noted that Qohelet's knowledge and evaluation are always limited to what is under the sun. In chapter 3 he raises the question of a vertical axis to human existence by introducing the concept of *'ôlām*. Human beings can conceive of eternity and so are linked with the deity. But they do not visibly achieve the living condition of eternity and so are no better than animals. Here is a specifically human assessment. Caught between the divine and the animal layers of existence human beings swing, now to the divine, now to the earthy. They are neither divine nor of the earth exactly, but lack true spaces for being because of the tension between the divine and the material aspects of their species. This is, for Qohelet, an unhappy or evil affair.[64] It is specifically attributed to divine causality in Ecclesiastes 3: 11. Unlike in the book of Job God does not appear directly to answer this human evaluation of divine activity. Therefore, the 'I' who narrates can only say 'maybe' there is a possibility that the human spirit (*rûaḥ*) ascends to God. But it remains an open-ended statement, not proven and therefore possibly illusionary.[65] This maybe colours Qohelet's own characterization, since his being is so much attached to his sayings. To this extent his profile is contingent and undefined since the knowledge needed for an absolute assertion of the value of a human character is (not yet) available.[66]

Narration, Characterization and Social Commentary

Thus Qohelet offers, in Ecclesiastes, a personal interpretation of meaning in life. It is his 'I' who speaks and by speaking creates a self who is an actant. This is not only at the level of verbal acts but also at the level of activity within a physical environment. As Christiansen states, *hālak* and other verbs of motion are key terms in the text, implying the event of a journey, which is not only on the mental level but also a physical quest for the material face of human reality.[67] Speaking opens out to doing and doing to being. As a character rooted in existence Qohelet has a personal opinion to offer. The content of this opinion refers also to being, to the self who can enjoy the domestic setting of living and 'rest' there at the heart of a family existence. The only essential actions for living are the basic eating and drinking that have their place in that domestic site. There is no absolute value attached to a labour that goes beyond these basic needs. Much toiling for gain is *hebel*.

So also is any extreme activity, summed up by Qohelet in chapter 7 as a blueprint for moderation, the vocabulary of which is that of the poles of wickedness and righteousness. The *tṣādiq* may still encounter death while the *rasha* may survive long in his wicked ways (Ecclesiastes 7: 15). This is a warning to the keen observer not to put too much effort into a righteous lifestyle while, at the same time, not excelling in wickedness either. Whereas the 'I' of chapters 1–6 engages in many experiments and tests of living, these comments in chapter 7 mark the start of a different 'I'. This self also observes the imbalance of reward with input in society and in life, as in chapter 8: 10–15, but now there is an acceptance that the human being cannot expect to understand all that happens and make of it a fully complete and rational explanation. This is *hebel*, but it no longer agitates the 'I' who narrates it in so vibrant a manner. It is accepted that 'fate' controls the life span and gains of all creatures and that no one can change their awarded advantage through their own unaided efforts. 'I turned and saw under the sun that the race is not to the swift and that the battle is not to the strong, and also that bread is not to the wise, and also not riches to the intelligent and also not favour to the skilled, for time and chance happen to all of them' (Ecclesiastes 9: 11).

So social commentary melds with the autobiographical self, whose actions are measured and whose focus is in existence as such. This 'I' emerges, in chapter 12, in the closing acts of speech, as one whose activity comes finally to rest and to silence. This appears to be in the context of old age or infirmity and death, which is in some ways still an evil or unhappy affair. But now there is little energy left to debate the twists and turns of the search for understanding. All mental and physical activity cease finally in the face of the arrival of the time when a self will say, there is for me no pleasure in them (Ecclesiastes 12: 1). This is still *hebel*. But now there are no more speech acts, no more narration, no further expansion of the character as a living 'I'.

Notes

1   Scholarly opinion in general favours a non-Solomonic origin of this text and places its date in the third century BCE. This makes it a text of Hellenistic Judaism, a text from the province of Judah, which had no king. References to wisdom teaching and to amassing wealth point to the source of the text in the elite classes of Judah. E. Tamez' book *When the Horizons Close* offers a clear example of how interpretation of meaning in Ecclesiastes can be connected with establishing this dating for the text.

2   Whatever opinions are held about Qohelet as the creator of fresh wisdom poems and sayings (either that he is such a creative writer or that he is quoting existing material in order to give a fresh commentary on it) it is clear that Qohelet does not take a positive view of the wisdom teaching that he utilizes. Simply to assert that there is stable spatial and time order does not offer hopeful evaluations of human affairs. Thus, in chapter 1, the poem on spatial order is framed by phrases involving *hebel*.

3   I. Kitzberger (ed.) *The Personal Voice in Biblical Interpretation* (London, Routledge, 1999). This volume introduces the production of meaning in texts largely from a reader's own context and interests, with no attention to ancient cultures and with a free play regarding the text itself.

4   Ibid., p. 5.

5   Ibid., p. 7.

6   Ibid., p. 5.

7   This is to take dialogism in the Bakhtinian sense of the heteroglossia of texts, reflecting the social nature of all language.

8   D. Patte, 'The Guarded Personal Voice of a Male European-American Biblical Scholar',
       in Kitzberger, *Personal Voice*, p. 12.
9   R. Alter, *The Art of Biblical Narrative* (London, Basic Books, 1981), p. 69.
10   Ibid., p. 68.
11   H. White, *Narration and Discourse in the Book of Genesis* (Cambridge, Cambridge
       University Press, 1991), p. 28.
12   Ibid.
13   Ibid., p. 33.
14   Ibid., p. 37.
15   A full account of key terms established by Austen is found in J. Austen, *How to do Things
       with Words* (Oxford, Oxford University Press, 1975).
16   E. Bruss, *Autobiographical Acts* (Baltimore, Md., Johns Hopkins University Press, 1976),
       p. 4.
17   Ibid., p. 5.
18   Ibid., pp. 10–11.
19   Ibid., pp. 31–2.
20   The Hebrew *qal* form indicates simply completed action but the entire frame of
       Ecclesiastes and the interior sense of time past under review establish the personal voice
       here as one that speaks looking back, and describes reflection completed in the past.
21   Bruss, *Autobiographical Acts*, p. 92.
22   This is established with regard to Austen, *How to do Things*, ch. ix.
23   The argument here is that the person 'I' and the defining and describing of such a person
       are both qualified by what a given culture already thinks personal identity involves. This
       argument is found also in D. Bjorklund's work, *Interpreting the Self* (Chicago, University
       of Chicago Press, 1998), ch. 2.
24   *Rå yôn rûaḥ* is another difficult term to interpret, both with regard to the source of its
       imagery and to its final value in Ecclesiastes. M. Fox's book, *A Time to tear down and
       a Time to build up* (Grand Rapids, Mich., Eerdmans, 1999), provides a treatment of
       Qohelet's range of key terms that links them to the absurd.
25   That is, autobiography expresses a personal identity, but this also offers a model of being a
       self, which a reader can follow in his/her own affairs.
26   These actions are expressed by the Hebrew verbs in chapter 2: 3–10.
27   The Hebrew verbs used by Qohelet for self conscious action link 'focusing' with 'seeing'.
       Thus there is a gathering back into oneself of one's observations, and an interior pondering
       of these resources, leading to the expressing of a personal opinion.
28   As in chapter 7: 23, 29. Here the observer sets out from a base in the self to make sure of
       what is indeed happening in the human world. The term 'find' then indicates the result of
       such an enterprise and once again expresses a personal opinion arrived at after the scrutiny
       of events carried out by an 'I'.
29   G. Ogden, *Qohelet*, (Sheffield, Sheffield Academic Press, 1987).
30   *Rā' rabbah* is a third problematic term used by Qohelet. Meanings vary from
       'unhappiness' to 'evil'. The latter meaning implies a hostile universe actively thwarting
       human attempts to progress in life. The question remains, is this extremely pessimistic
       perspective what the ancient writer intended?
31   Greimas' semiotic perspective implies that characters in narratives are only structurally
       significant in terms of what they contribute to the plot. So it is possible to locate each
       character with regard to their role in the plot sequence, thus identifying character
       stereotypes.
32   S. Rimmon-Kenan, *Narrative Fiction* (London, Routledge, 1999), provides an outline and
       discussion of the contribution of structuralist theory to reading methods for narratives.
33   Ibid., p. 34.
34   Ibid., p. 39.
35   J. Fokkelman, *Reading Biblical Narrative* (Louisville, Ky., Westminster John Knox,
       1999), p. 78.

36 Ibid.

37 Ibid., p. 77.

38 E. Christiansen, *A Time to Tell* (Sheffield, Sheffield Academic Press, 1998), p. 221.

39 Ibid., ch. 8, where this issue is discussed in great detail.

40 Ibid., p. 243.

41 Ibid., p. 247.

42 C. Exum, *Tragedy and Biblical Narrative* (Cambridge, Cambridge University Press, 1992), p. 1.

43 At their worst, most pessimistic interpretation these terms point to the total meaninglessness of human life and to any effort to improve life as a waste of energy in the face of evil, frustrating forces.

44 See, here, Job 3.

45 Exum, *Tragedy*, p. 10.

46 Ibid.

47 W. Whedbee, *The Bible and the Comic Vision* (Cambridge, Cambridge University Press, 1998), p. 7.

48 Christiansen, *Time to Tell*, p. 241.

49 F. Zimmerman, *The Inner World of Qohelet* (New York, KTAV, 1973), p. 3.

50 Ibid., p. 19.

51 Ibid., p. 32.

52 Ibid., p. 40.

53 Ibid., p. 47.

54 Ibid., p. 8.

55 T. Todorov, *Introduction to Poetics*, trans. R. Howard (Minneapolis, University of Minnesota Press, 1981), p. 32.

56 M. Toolan, *Narrative: A Critical Linguistic Introduction* (London, Routledge, 1988), pp. 67–9.

57 S. Cohan and L. Shires, *Telling Stories* (London, Routledge, 1988), p. 109.

58 The meaning of 'profitable' is linked generally to the concept of pleasure, as in chapter 2 with the experiment in living involving houses, gardens, food and drink. But in this instance the meaning is more numerical, to do with the financial surplus left in a person's account at the end of business transactions.

59 The real crux of interpretation with regard to Qohelet's personal voice is always the meaning of this central term. All is *hebel hebalim* thus remains an inconclusive result to personal experience.

60 M. Sternberg, *The Poetics of Biblical Narrative* (Bloomington, Indiana University Press, 1985), p. 131.

61 A king as observer is a useful tool for arriving at a comprehensive view on life, since the scope for experience of a royal observer is broad. It includes the mobility of military campaigning and the royal court as a draw to visitors from far afield, as well as being the centre of a justice system.

62 W. Brown, *Character in Crisis* (Grand Rapids, Mich., Eerdmans, 1996).

63 The God who appears to Job in the whirlwind is such a deity. The power of God allows him to control nature in all its violence, and to know all the actions of wild creatures and all the secrets of time past, but this deity rejoices in aggression and is not to be tamed to meet human expectations of justice and balance.

64 The meaning here depends on the translation of *inyān* and *rāʿ rabbah*, either as totally negative terms or as more nuanced towards optimism.

65 The key here is chapter 3 with its questions about *ʿōlām* and the ultimate destiny of the human spirit. Should this be read as indicating that there may be some future, indeed, or as a vain thought with no real content? See here, C.-L. Seow, *Ecclesiastes* (New York, Doubleday, 1997), pp. 158–76.

66 Only absolute parameters create an absolute meaning for component parts of the bigger picture. God and human beings are topics interwoven in a religious text. In Ecclesiastes

God provides the wider order but the possibility that that order confines human beings leaves Qohelet's 'I' with an uncertainty about the human fate within the divinely ordered universe.

67   Christiansen, *Time to Tell*, pp. 221–7.

Chapter 5

Story as Social Discourse

In pursuing the topic of the life of a self as a form of social commentary attention has now to be devoted to the second part of the equation set out at the beginning of the last chapter. This involves the view that the profile of a social world can be formed from the perspective of a participant in the reality, namely of a self. In relation to Ecclesiastes this means that Qohelet's 'I' speaks a world into existence. This symbolic universe is clearly linked to the milieu of ancient society within which the text originated, but offers a version of that social context as experienced by a narrator who speaks his personal voice pictures of his surroundings *taḥat ha ššemešš*.

If a focus on the narrator leads to characterization, then a focus on the setting of that self leads to story and plot. Strictly speaking Ecclesiastes gives no evidence for the usual plot structures. There is no dramatic encounter of particular characters, leading to complex episodes with a final conflict, followed by a closure of the original situation.[1] However, it is possible to argue for Ecclesiastes as story – the story of one man's progress through adult life as enacted through his observations of the social context of that life. This progress is marked by the introduction of one who embarks on his rule, in chapter 2, and who, at the end of the account, speaks as an elder to the young, in the shadow of death and silence. At this level what marks the plot sequence is the progression from the younger king to the older sage via a sequence of scenes from life, including the private and public faces of society.

This plot line is parallel with a variant story sequence, this time one of intellectual form, the search for wisdom and understanding. Here there is an initial problem posed by the story: the problematical *hebel* nature of human experience. The same concept frames the end of the narrative, thus raising the point that there is a closure to the story but this is circular. It is not clear that the initial tension has been eased. In between these points the plot structure involves a testing out of the problem through the quest of the 'hero' for wisdom, carried out through a series of experiments in living and via an exploration of the importance of inherited learning, which is manifested in poems and proverbial sayings.[2] Frequently, this search, or series of searches, ends in frustration, with *hebel* as its marker. But each time Qohelet picks up his quest again and sets off on the next stage of his journey through time and place, for the borders of his search are the times of human seasons (chapter 3) and the cosmic order (chapter 1). The sun above boundaries human existence while dust indicates its final destiny. Life is made up of days (*yamim*) in which a person can engage in social discourse.[3] But as night closes day so, eventually, death closes life, and according to the mood of chapters 11–12, this comes about more swiftly than a person expects, while the search for meaning is still in its midst.

In telling these stories which make up the overall narrative, Qohelet is offering a social commentary on two levels. The story is about a social world, its very heart is a commentary on human beings in their historical context. By choosing these particular scenes Qohelet brings a particular symbolic society into being. On a second level, Qohelet's search for wisdom provides a narrative commentary on that same, created social environment. Thus this is not autobiography from 'cradle to grave', accompanied by details of dates and career, but a 'random' view of a life, which is the same event as a quest for the understanding of life. Qohelet's 'I' is an autobiographer whose narrative produces a *bios*, which sheds light backwards both on 'Life' and on the nature of a 'Self'.

Words

It is obvious to state that Ecclesiastes is made up of words, but this statement does touch upon an important focus for story, that of the link between continuous text and its individual verbal components. This has been introduced already, in the last chapter, where the importance of the root *āmār* was explored. Qohelet is constructed via his own speech patterns. So, in considering the nature of story in Ecclesiastes, it is sensible to consider words, which in turn build up to an account of events, set in time and place contexts.

It is relevant here to approach words as signs, set into chains, which construct meaning. As Cohan and Shires state, 'the term "fiction" ... directs our attention to a story's medium of telling: language'.[4] In language words as signs 'combine a concept and a written or visual image as well as a spoken one.'[5] Thus language does not simply name things at a surface level, but rather symbolizes the reality so named. 'The sign itself is the *relation* between signifier and signified, it holds them together as a unit of meaning'.[6] Beyond this level words build up, in grammatical structures, to language as a tool for the expression and manipulation of complex patterns of meaning. In the process they themselves take on an existence in their own right.

> The paradigms of a language maintain its operation as a system by keeping its conventions stable and continually recognizable to users of the language – so stable and recognizable, in fact, that one is rarely conscious of the elaborate grid of similarity and difference which this system of paradigmatic marking constructs for language use.[7]

G. Steiner, in *Real Presences*, discusses the tension between words used as tools for the human expression of meaning and words as themselves expressions of meaning. 'The chain of signs is infinite ... inhabiting language, bearing on language or the grammar of sense as it is instrumental in a painting ... Both the act of interpretation and that of assessment, hermeneutics and criticism, are inextricably enmeshed in the metaphysical and theological or anti-theological question of unbounded saying.'[8] A response to this tension between unbounded saying and the ultimate significance of expressivity is to be found in the movement towards creating canons. In this balance of infinite events of expressive acts and the boundaries of word usage, meaning emerges in a new way. 'Ritual, liturgical, canonic codes of saying, as in prayer ... and in sacred or revealed texts, strive to close, to circumscribe, word and world by means of taboo, of reiteration, of apocalyptic finitude.'[9]

For Steiner, it is through this interaction of speech acts and chains of circumscribed meaning that human beings can explore the phenomena of human existence. At one end human speech patterns process events. 'What is meaningful in history is gathered into the dynamic, elucidative custody of the rational sentence.'[10] At the other end language opens out into the transcendent deity of Jewish, Christian traditions. 'In the western sphere, the conceptualisation of God was at the outset and during its history in action that of a speech-act, of a grammatical absolute manifest in the tautologies of God's definition.'[11] As language examines the interrelationship of the material world with its transcendent sources it entails dialogue, both essentially and in terms of the structure of debate. One aspect of this is self-reflexive speech, as a human person understands his/her own existence through hearing its utterance. 'We do address ourselves in constant soliloquy. But the medium of that soliloquy is that of public speech.'[12] Steiner here provides a possible perspective for reading Ecclesiastes. Qohelet is an example of a human being engaged in this process of creating dynamic language, whose words open out onto the public world through the framing narrative, which allows the reader to engage in an act of overhearing a self creating identity through words.

Words and Qohelet's Story

So words have two facets. They are pieces which can be moved around and juxtaposed to create meaning in longer phrases and sentences. They also have a 'life of their own' within which 'the word', according to Steiner's theories, underpins and boundaries the many words of a text. There is a canonicity to words; they have boundaries and yet exceed them. In Qohelet, as already mentioned above, a few key words help to define the quest for wisdom and its consequences with regard to meaning. Words shape the social world of the story and allow its discourse. Thus, for instance, *àmal* (toil) proposes a life of engagement with the material environment, and makes possible the question 'What is the advantage of such an engagement?' On another level the term has an introductory role vis-à-vis the material aspects of the social world which is linked with the autobiographer's enquiry. *Àmal* here brings together bodily realities such as food, drink and sexuality with mental activity, the anguish of a self seeking to explain social existence to itself. Beyond these immediate material contacts toil draws to itself the existence of sons, commercial ventures, building programmes, courts of justice, city life, wars and dangers.[13] Thus *åmal* controls a wide range of social experiences and allows them to be placed alongside one another and so evaluated.

From *åmal* it is possible to move to *hōkmâ*, another key word, which appears as a focus for action in Ecclesiastes 1: 13. The goal of Qohelet's endeavour, in this story, is to have wisdom. It is to accompany his greatness and to be a sign of his superiority over previous rulers. Thus *hōkmâ* symbolizes wealth or possessions; it is wisdom as a material reality. But this term is equally itself governed by *hebel* and *rå yôn rûaḥ*, leading to its value as vexation and sorrow (*kāås*, *makob*). The social issue that arises is whether *åmal* and *hōkmâ* go together, whether effort in living produces an understanding of life. But, in chapter 2, although *hōkmâ* exceeds folly in value, in its nominal form, when it is used adjectivally (wise man, fool), it has only equal weight with folly. This is so since, incarnated in human existence, both qualities fail to survive and go to the grave. A similar tension can be seen later in the text. In the proverbial teaching of chapter 7 the *lēb* of the wise is better than the *lēb* of fools (verse 4). This theme is continued in the view that wisdom is better than an inheritance (verse 11) and preserves the life of the one who has it. But this must be balanced against the argument that wisdom cannot be attained (verse 23). The word *hōkmâ* thus stands, in Qohelet's speech, for that which is good per se and desirable for human beings, but which also involves frustration and failure. Its owning means sorrow, and its depths cannot be plumbed by human beings. In the middle range of vision, that of the world of daily reality, wisdom operates as a socially beneficial quality, and seems to offer a more absolutely good goal. But pushed to its extremes, at the boundaries of the human world, wisdom loses its power of signification for human beings, according to Qohelet's personal voice.

This is because both *åmal* and *hōkmâ* are governed by *mot*. What is the ultimate tool of judgement of meaning in life for human beings? It has to be death, since the goal of human existence is death, not as a goal sought for its goodness but one owned as a real, externally imposed boundary. Take, for instance, Ecclesiastes 5: 13–16. Here the linguistic focus falls on 'naked' and 'empty'. A human being is to be separated from that which s/he adds to the self by living. Death and birth weigh equally in this perspective. Nothing can be added permanently into the human self – and this is *rå*. Likewise, in chapter 9, the defining language for death is evil or unhappy. One fate comes to all, and this is the boundary marker of death. So to be a 'king among beasts' but dead is of less worth than to be a dog and alive. The lowest form of life is still of greater worth than death itself. The language of the text stresses this approach to the social world; the dead have no more – for ever – any share – in life *taḥat ha ššemešš*. *Mot*, then, colours the value attached to *hōkmâ*. Wisdom is only acceptable if it is linked to mourning and sorrow. What matters is to know and understand that the day of *mot* is better than the day of birth.

What is critiqued within this play of words is the social scenes of human existence and the language to carry out this task itself creates social discourse. *'Amal, hōkmâ, mot* all obtain meaning as terms linked to human acts of body and mind. In this context *yitrôn//hebel* provide a 'canon' for exploring meaning. They are the specific linguistic markers, which continue to surface throughout Ecclesiastes. As such they balance one another as two poles, gain and emptiness, within whose borders other words can be situated. *'Amal* and *hōkmâ* would appear to align with *yitrôn*, but in fact drift towards *hebel*. *Mot* is *hebel* since it empties out positive value from potentially pleasurable social existence.

But, paradoxically, it is ultimately the only source of *yitrôn*. For it has to be embraced as the final and transcending social act of daily life. It is in the light of *hebel/mot/yitrôn* that Qohelet can find a space for the happiness he seeks in life. Under the certain knowledge of death the 'I' who speaks can utter a commandment, a direct injunction to the reader, in Ecclesiastes 9: 7–10. Go. Eat, drink. Enjoy life in a spirit of enjoyment and a merry heart. These material conditions are to be viewed positively and as approved by *hōkmâ* and achieved by *'amal*. This is because, semantically, they are one with *sheol*, which is the final goal of 'go' and where there are no material or mental activities. Here the key word is *ki* – for or because. Go to enjoy because you will go to *sheol*. The enjoyment is shadowed by this reality as *hebel* reappears in this word sequence, attached to life (all the days of your *hebel*).

'Amal, hōkmâ, mot thus signal the reality of events in the social world of human beings. At the same time they also, as words, gain their life within the language patterns of the text. Here they exist as the speech acts of the 'I' whose views are aired and realized through a complex story world in which speech leads to a social discourse, which is itself the narrative, the self-narration of Qohelet.

Events

In the speech patterns of Qohelet words, formed into sentences, constitute the events of the book. All action operates within symbolism, the sign system of a text narrated by an 'I', whose presence is contemporaneous with the reader. Even the acts of that self are subject to this construction of meaning. They are words narrated by a voice, which describes them post eventu. 'I turned ... then I saw ... it was.' Thus canonicity is created by the autobiographical self, as the multivalent events of human life are brought within the boundaries created by one personal voice. Yet the events themselves continue to have their own value, of equal weight with this personal opinion. As W. Spengemann asks, 'how can the self know itself? By moving inquisitively through its own memories and ideas to some conclusion about them?'[14] He argues for an approach to autobiographical story in which the guiding impulse is the 'conviction that the retrospective narrator can see his life from a point outside it, that his view is not subject to the limiting conditions of the life he is recounting'.[15] Thus autobiographical story is a social discourse in which a human being not only enacts a version of his/her own significant encounters with the world at large, but also reaches out to the limits of social actions and their signification. 'When time rather than the eternal is the ground of reality, the ever moving, never-vanishing present becomes the alpha and the omega, the point upon which all times concentrate and from which all times radiate'.[16]

This perspective assumes that the momentary present imposes its shape on the recollection of the 'I' who narrates, while itself being shaped by the contiguity with other 'presents' and by the overarching speech patterns of the narrating self. P. Ricoeur notes the relevance of Heidegger's existential analysis in the creation of the narrative of a self. '*Dasein* is the "place" where the being that we are is constituted through its capacity of posing the question of Being or the meaning of Being.'[17] This essential 'being-within-time' (*innerzeitigkeit*) underpins particular 'present moments' in the narrative. 'The words "future", "past" and "present" disappear, and time itself figures as the exploded unity of the three temporal extases.'[18] Thus, although the 'I' of Qohelet travels, on one level, through a series of chronological sequences, at the same time he is contemporaneously exploring the boundaries of the 'beingness' of a self.

In relation to Ecclesiastes this perspective can be linked with the auto-biographer as one who speaks and so acts his account of self and world. Bruss suggests that a focus for 'readers of autobiography is the arrangement and the process of narration in the text … in autobiography the structural display of the text is stipulated to be a demonstration of certain of the capacities and habits of the man about whom we are reading'.[19] It is valuable, then, to consider the topic of selection. Selection describes the situation in the narrative when the narrator does not treat all the events of a life equally. In Ecclesiastes this entails the selection of some events of an adult human life, a choice made through one person's critical choice of what constitutes the meaning of life itself. 'The series that we see is a radical selection, and when we understand what it is that governs the writer's choice, we will have found the main point of access into his linguistic work of art.'[20] Fokkelman's account of selection is based on the basic story format of a plot line with a clear beginning, middle and end. But he argues that the data selected are not to be seen as simple features on a linear scale. 'They have been carefully attuned to each other, which is not surprising as they themselves are deliberate products of selection.'[21] The writer is guided by a particular vision, in the case of Qohelet that is the personal voice of an autobiographer. 'The writer "sees" what would be a meaningful whole within the material he is working on, and how to delineate this whole.'[22]

In Ecclesiastes this plot trajectory relates the beginning and end of a movement towards the understanding of existence. This search is installed as the main action of a king over Jerusalem. 'I gave my heart to search out and to seek by wisdom concerning all that is made under the heavens.' Within the trajectory of pursuing wisdom a king acts out his royal power and makes use of his wealth to create a pleasurable environment. But this stage of practical living closes in chapter 2, with the perception that although wisdom is better than folly the ultimate content of wisdom is to know that a wise person is not better off than a foolish one. An initial stage of the plot has thus come to a conclusion, but more scenes open out, each of which is oriented towards meaning-in-existence, more especially to the value to be attached to what appear to be the valuable material goals of human endeavour. Each stage of the story, each individual short scene, ends with a similar movement in which the perception is that it is hard to locate any absolute advantage to human existence. Finally, the entire plot sequence closes with the same critical analysis.

That life is *hebel* is both the beginning and the end, then, of the story line in Ecclesiastes. All the individual events are selected to meet that pattern. Wealth in its various guises, family and sons, the public life of a city state, all are brought to bear on the central soliloquy of the 'I' who narrates. And all are critiqued with reference to that aspect of a living self, whose viewpoint holds them together in a single story. This fairly simple plot sequence is expanded in chapters 1, 3, 7, 10 and 11, to include traditional literary sources of social meaning, such as poems and proverbs. These elements, too, contribute to the creation of story as social discourse in Ecclesiastes. The two poems in chapters 1 and 3 raise, particularly, the issue of the role of space/place and time in the creation of narrative meaning.

Order

Ordering a story involves setting short sequences into a broader frame, frequently one of time. This entails the use of sequential ordering which, in turn, conveys order-in-meaning to the reader. As Toolan states 'time itself, in the sense of the systematic measurement of the distance between, for example, past states and our present one, is itself a structuring and structuralist notion'.[23] This structuring involves stating a relationship between particular states or changes of state, which relies not on real time, but on a linear verbal representation of time.[24] In this setting 'order', according to Genette, refers to the relationship between the assumed sequence of events in the 'world' under narration and the use of temporal markers in the text itself.[25] This can involve flashbacks (analepsis) and predictions (prolepsis). Through these devices a narrator can fill in gaps in the telling of a story (analepsis) or indicate to readers where the story will go (prolepsis) before the actual event.

Used with regard to Ecclesiastes the term 'story' indicates the auto-biographical account uttered by Qohelet. This is told within the framing editorials, which define the story as that of a Qohelet who is king in Jerusalem (Ecclesiastes 1) and who by Ecclesiastes 12 is spoken of as having been king. Thus the speech is put into the past; this was how he used to speak. The temporal order of the story is from present to past, but, probably, the past time should be viewed as the major ordering tool and the use of the present time as a dramatizing technique. The framing temporal order is picked up in the mid-career of the said king in Ecclesiastes 1: 12, with the 'I' who speaks naming himself as one who 'has been king'. Thus the present of the speaker still involves a past, which allows the narrative 'I' to explore the meaning of what has been experienced in that past.

Within that time frame there is yet another as Qohelet describes his own past acts and thoughts as a present and future reality, as in Ecclesiastes 2: 1. 'I *said* Come now, I *will* make a test.' The result is then judged from a future time as a past event, 'This *was hebel*.' So a complex ordering of times shapes the message of the text, playing on past, present and future. This interplay is more obvious from a reading of the English text, as indicated above. Hebrew narrative only distinguishes between a complete action and an incomplete one, without specifying past/present tenses. It remains for the reader to adjust the text to the rules of English usage. However, something of the juxtaposition of times can be traced in the move from completed action to incomplete action and back to finished act in the verse set out above. The final word, according to Qohelet, lies with a completed act, indicating the possibility of evaluating events across time.

A similar complexity of time usage can be found in chapter 3. Verse 16 begins 'I *saw* ... there *was*.'[26] But the 'I' who speaks then adds ' I *said* ... God *will* judge ... for he *has* appointed a time. I *said* ... God *is* testing.' This last verbal form introduces a sequence of thought, which is the narrator's overall assessment of the seeing and saying in the past and the application of a future state, namely a judgement by Qohelet on the human world, which stands in a continuous present. Verse 19 asserts that the fate of beasts *is* the same as that of humans; all die and are from dust and return to dust. The focus of meaning here is the levelling of all created beings to a common source which also defines their destiny. Time involves circular motion.

More generally each scene involving human activity is introduced in a past tense, but these are equally present in the synchrony of the reader's appropriation of the narrative. Occasionally this sequence is broken by a command directly addressed by Qohelet to the reader, as in Ecclesiastes 5. 'Guard your steps when' (verse 1) and 'Pay what you vow' (verse 4). Chapter 9 repeats the motif of direct, present tense advice, concerning a practical lifestyle, while chapter 11 sums up the entire work through the commandment form, 'Rejoice, young man ... Remember also your creator.' These direct injunctions are timeless in the sense that they enter into the space of every reader in any given time. They are always immediately present and demand a response, an involvement in Qohelet's own experience. The 'I' who speaks urges other selves to model their present and future actions on his past experience. This urging becomes a given present in the reciprocal sequences of actions involved in both speaking one's own past and listening to its current meaning, on the one hand, and, on the other, overhearing a past 'I' reflecting on his own past.

These sequential orderings of action on the part of the autobiographer shape the social world of the text which is inhabited by kings, by their households, by wicked and righteous persons, by wise and foolish, by rich men who lack sons and men with sons who lack wealth. These are all characters who existed in the time of Qohelet's past experience and whose actions form the basis for his subsequent critiques of life and its meaning. And, on the level of that current judgement of the present tense 'I', they all pass into a single evaluative commentary where the poles of time collapse into each other, as in Ecclesiastes 7: 14, where the opposing *yamim* of prosperity/adversity are evened out in their common making by God. The effect of this is a current and continuous present state in which human beings cannot make any progress to a different timescale, symbolized in the phrase 'what *will be* after him'. The effect of ordering in time, then, tends to bring the 'I' of the reader back to the present tense. Past and future lack any true value. As the narratival use of time moves across all three periods it is only the present that is a source of meaning in life. And, since the present is all that can be understood, the imperative mode urges the reader to grasp the material existence offered in the contemporary environment, before the future takes over and dispossesses the self of social identity. Even the identity involved in existing as the past in a future self's remembrance will disappear, as in Ecclesiastes 2: 16, where there *is* no lasting memorial (*zĭkarōn*), because/in days to come/all *will have been*/long forgotten. Here 'is not' is fleshed out by the isness of the future act of forgetting.

Qohelet's Language of Time

Thus the concept of time plays a major part in the structuring of thought in Ecclesiastes. Externally, the narrative is framed as an expression of thought, located in a particular past figure. This fixity of a single time setting in the history of Israel is balanced by Ecclesiastes 1: 4, which opens out the narrative voice to a wider range of human existence in the concept of *dôr* (generation). *Dôr* is frequently used, in legal passages, to imply the timeless nature of the legislation, as in the Passover codes in Exodus 12. But here the term is more limited. A generation comes and a generation goes and/but the earth remains forever. The link is ambiguous here, but should probably be translated as an opposition between the short span of humans and the eternal cosmos. This is reinforced by the fact that verse 11 refers to 'no remembrance' of former things. Remembrance, linked to generation in Exodus 12, refers to a cultic act which has force throughout all Israel's history. Thus, from the start, the tension between all that is *taḥat ha ššemeš* being open to human beings and yet mysterious and hidden is built into the text, and focused through the narrative 'I', for these are all the *dibrê* of Qohelet.

Within the narrated, autobiographical account there is frequent reference to *yom* as the basic measure of a human existence. This *yom* is within the poles of the day of birth and the day of death. Thus *yom* equates with life as night balances death. This theme of day may be treated as chronologically linear, as in days of youth and days of age, or former days and what is yet to come. This usage represents ordinary human experience. Day and night are the normal measures of activity when there is no major artificial lighting, and the movement from former to latter, from youth to age, is part of the structure of the human organism. But *yom* can also be addressed as the day of adversity//prosperity (Ecclesiastes 7: 14), indicating a further layer in which time runs simultaneously. All days are evaluated with regard to their contribution to the *yitrôn/hebel* boundaries. At this point time turns to meet itself. In Ecclesiastes 1: 10, 'anything new' has already been in the ages before us. Experienced afresh in each stage, time is in fact one reality which underpins all human perception.

This comment leads to another very significant use of time in Ecclesiastes. Chapter 3 dwells on the development of time as the root of human experience. Verse 1 speaks of every *zĕmān* and every *ēt*. Here the narrator moves from day to season as the definition of time. In the poetic material that follows, *ēt* is the tool by which all human activity, broken into pairs of opposites, is defined.[27] This measurement also comes under scrutiny from the *yitrôn/hebel* frame. Here time appears to be 'time-as-meaningful', as the narrator deals with the appropriateness of particular times and acts. Social discourse is expressed via this pairing of temporality and human affairs. In this usage Qohelet's use of season is balanced by his references to days as the portion given to human beings. Thus days (so many of them) provide the context for human existence as that time which has been allotted for each person. A human being has only that time which is measured out to him or her. This repeats the focus on present time as the only time which has any force for human society. Neither past nor future are 'grasped' by a generation of human beings and, even more significantly, the possibility of experiencing time as a whole escapes human control. In Ecclesiastes 3: 11 Qohelet speaks of the concept of *'ôlām* (eternity), which can be imagined by the intellect, but which cannot be enjoyed by any actual human person. This concept implies a union between time and human existence. It can be conceived that the human person could live forever, but this thought can never be proved from actual experience.

Here Qohelet places the deity as the boundary of human affairs. It is *Elohim* who is in charge both of *ēt* and *zĕmān*, and of *'ôlām*, as these concepts are understood within the human intellect. *Elohim* is the one who is co-existent with time in its fullest sense, whose works are 'from the beginning and until the end' (verse 11). This fits with other, infrequent, references to God in Ecclesiastes. God is constructed as the existence which is always present and from within which that which is *taḥat ha ššemešš* emerges. Thus God operates as creator and giver of gifts as well as judge of human activity. The consequence is that human beings should 'fear from before him' (verse 14), reverencing the one whose existence transcends the seasons and the days and is co-existential with eternity. This symbolic order offers a secure environment for human affairs, but it is not necessarily so evaluated. In this passage beauty and eternity as human realities are linked with happiness and the enjoyment of drink and food. Yet all this is 'so that' human beings cannot find out what God has done. Chapter 5 spells out the cultic aspects of human conduct in the setting of this 'fear God' motif. Human vows are honoured by a God, who holds the makers of vows to account. But this view of order is held in tension with Ecclesiastes 3: 18. God is testing human beings to show them that they are but beasts. In Ecclesiastes 4, the results of this tension can be seen. There is an absence of divine retributive justice and so it is better to be 'not yet' than to be born into human time. And it is from the concept of time as ordered into days and seasons that this negative assessment emerges.

Patterns of Duration and Frequency

It is useful, at this point, to refer back to Genette's narrative analysis in which duration indicates the length of time a scene lasts in a narrative while, according to Toolan, 'by the term "frequency" we denote the business of repeated textual telling of a single story incident'.[28] There are several interesting ways of applying these theoretical perspectives to the book of Ecclesiastes. It would be possible to argue that the whole of the section narrated by an 'I' is one scene, for instance, since, as has been argued, past and future sequences collapse into the present tense. Duration would, then, bring about a contemporaneity which links the adult life of one man and the narrative of a self. Equally, it might be noted that this one long scene involves many very short scenes where minimal action is reported. An obvious example of this is the scene of the public works in Ecclesiastes 2: 4–8. Houses, vineyards, gardens are all sketched in quick succession, as the context for a large household and its possessions.

This in turn situates the royal head of this household as a man at the pinnacle of human social power. Even shorter scenes occur frequently, as in the beginning of Ecclesiastes 5, where going on pilgrimage is sketched in seven verses, or, even shorter, Ecclesiastes 5: 8, where one verse creates a whole social context, that of the balance of power in an area and its oppressive weight against true justice for the poor. The balance between the variety of short scenes and the longer, overarching narrative allows for the emergence of social commentary within the autobiography. Since many, independent events are united via a single voice, a consistent line of critique regarding human affairs can be traced.

This critique links with the topic of frequency. It cannot be said that any one scene in Ecclesiastes is repeated exactly, though similar motifs recur, such as a man and his sons. However, there is reiteration at a more global level. Not only is *hebel* repeated constantly at the end of sequences, drawing them all to a whole, but also the frequent use of *taḥat ha ššemešš* repeats aspects of Qohelet's thought while covering a variety of social settings. In Ecclesiastes 4, for instance, verse 1 uses 'under the sun' to introduce the theme of oppression. This leads Qohelet to pronounce that the dead are better off than the living and the unborn better off than both. This evaluation closes in verse 3 with *taḥat ha ššemešš*, governed this time by *rāʿ*. This short scene is one example of what goes on in human society; it is set alongside many other such scenes, all of which are parallel pieces of evidence for a common human experience. In Ecclesiastes 9, also, scenes are punctuated with the theme of human experience. In the first section 'under the sun' joins up the experience reflected on in verses 1–2 with the overall evaluation of this in verse 3a, and opens the way for a parallel version in verses 3b–6. In the first part the focus is on the righteous/wise and good and bad, and in the second part this moves to evil human beings, the dead and the living. But all are treated as part of a *taḥat ha ššemešš* paradigm, which allows for the same message to be reiterated across the text.

Being in Time: Time and Being

The effect of both duration and frequency structures in Ecclesiastes is to focus the reader's attention on human existence itself and on experience as a time-bound reality. Ricoeur comments that 'from an Augustinian point of view, the future and the past exist only in relation to a present, that is, to an instant indicated by the utterance designating it'.[29] So, within the narrative of Qohelet's 'I', past and future take meaning from their relationship to the present moment of performative utterance. Qohelet conceives beingness in time with regard to his own experience of living across time and synthesizing a variety of events encountered in that life span. It is through the cross-referencing of these two facets of human existence that social discourse comments on the value of human endeavour. Qohelet sees what happens but then, more deeply, perceives a universal significance to events. This personal perception takes voice in the frequent usage of the phrase 'then I said'.

Thus, in Ecclesiastes 2: 1, Qohelet examines the effect of his activities in time and finds them lacking in permanent significance. This leads him, in verse 12, to a further stage of activity, this time of reflection on what *hōkmâ* consists of, and this in turn leads to a further 'moment' in which wisdom gives insight. But this too is illusionary. Verse 15 introduces the final moment in this time cycle, when the abstract messages gained from a period of reflection are applied to the thinker himself. Thus Qohelet as a self gains nothing from the engagement with the material world over time. Being in time is underscored by a necessity, 'the wise, too, must die' (verse 16).

Qohelet searches for the meaning of existence via meaning in and through time. His speech thus creates an understanding that human identity is founded on action within time. But this action 'looks forward' to the time when the autobiographer will own this truth within his conscious thought, and will produce a commentary on his beingness and so on existence itself. Ricoeur comments, with regard to Heidegger's *Being and Time*, 'if therefore we admit that the question of time is first of all the question of its structural wholeness ... it remains for us to find in Care's Being-ahead-of-itself the secret of its completeness.'[30] Only with the closure of the sequence of being and time can meaning emerge. In Ecclesiastes this closure is found with *mot*. For it is with the boundary marker of death that the true quality of human meaning is revealed, even though this knowledge is problematic for the autobiographer. Ricoeur notes of Heidegger's thought that, 'the end of Being-in-the-world is death'; 'ending as dying is constitutive for Dasein's totality'.[31] For Qohelet it is only within this understanding of being in time that authentic wisdom can be uttered.

At this point some of the problematic introduced by the concepts of *hebel/mot* is eased. The social world of material activity within time swims back into focus as a source of gain for human beings, both physically and intellectually. This wholeness is achieved by a complex interaction of movements over time. For Heidegger's thought, 'Temporality is then the articulated unity of coming-towards, having-been, and making-present, which are thereby given to be thought of together.'[32] The true nature of existence, then, can only be revealed by time, while time itself is brought into a unity within the self-expression of a human personal voice, and this is manifested in the narrative of Ecclesiastes.

Place and Context in Ecclesiastes

A second aspect of the framing of a text is that of place setting. In Ecclesiastes Qohelet's 'I' ranges, as narrator, over several contextual levels of human existence, involving cosmos, community and personal being. For M. Bal the context of narrative action is a significant focus for a story. With reference to 'place', 'the term refers to the topological position in which the actors are situated and the events take place'.[33] In Ecclesiastes these positions are illustrated by the cosmic *tahat ha ššemešš*, by Jerusalem and the *Qahal*, and by the self and the body. 'Space' is a term parallel with place and expresses the manner in which particular places contribute to meaning. Bal refers to the concept that, in the story, 'where space is connected to the characters who "live" it, the primary aspect of space is the way characters bring their senses to bear on space'.[34] For Qohelet this is true of his gaze. The autobiographer looks out carefully at the places found within the human environment, and especially within social groups, at home and in the wider culture. His vision is on a horizontal plane, he is on an equal level with these places which he examines. But the places become themselves productive of 'inner vision' and so become 'actors' in the autobiographical narrative's construal of meaning. They then function as 'spaces', as places which are not passive but which contribute directly to meaning in a text.[35] The meaning to which they contribute is mostly, of course, *hebel* or *rā'*.[36]

Qohelet's gaze can travel upwards, too, to the sun itself and so to the cosmic boundary of the human world. But this boundary, though ordered, is not without problems. In Ecclesiastes 1 the poem on spatial order identifies the movement of sun, winds, waters, but none of these fixities of space convey comfort. Rather their recurrent motion functions as an oppression in which 'there is not any new thing under the sun' (verse 9). The human gaze cannot penetrate the recurrent cycle of the world order and cannot bring about any creative act within the cosmic field of human affairs.

At the same time, Ecclesiastes 1 situates the 'I' who speaks in Jerusalem and in the *Qahal* (assembly).[37] This provides a social context for the auto-biographer which he himself owns later on in chapter 1 and develops in the next chapter. Jerusalem functions as the symbol of royal authority and power. Solomon, in the books of Kings, built up his power base in Israel by establishing Jerusalem as the centre of government and of cult. Such was the reputation for wisdom of this Israelite king that foreign rulers engaged in debate with him.[38] He is also presented as gathering people together for the dedication of the Temple and as speaking to the deity on their behalf.[39] This regal background is implied, presumably, by the description of Qohelet as 'son of David'. This ensures that his social commentary is even more worthy of attention since it is the advice of a great king, in a world where kings and their elites formed the highest social and religious authority.[40]

The universe and society form a backdrop for Qohelet's speech. They reappear inside his utterance in the repeated phrase *taḥat ha ššemešš*, and in references to kings and city life. But the focus is on Qohelet as an 'I', a self who speaks his own identity. It is this 'I' that is the most significant space within the narrative. Qohelet's self is constituted by speech, but that speech indicates the existence of an intelligence, situated in a physical body. Here it can be noted how often *hōkmâ* is viewed as a possession to be owned by such a bodily person, and its contents linked with the products of physical sight and inner reason. A considerable part of Qohelet's selfhood, then, is made up of his powers of reasoning. S. Smith has described the self in post-Enlightenment Western Europe in a manner which sheds some light on Qohelet. 'The self is neither constituted by, nor coextensive with, its class identification, social roles, or private attributes.'[41] 'This self is conceived to be persistently rational. As such it is an ahistorical or transcendent phenomenon and remains autonomous and free.'[42]

There are aspects of Qohelet's self-presentation which fit this model. These include his distance from events – present and past – and his projections from individually located events to generalized moral meaning. Since all that happens in connection with human life is *hebel*, Qohelet finds life itself problematic, only death seems to provide stability. Here it can be noted that, with regard to the growth of a Cartesian self in European culture, F. Barker argues that the separation of self from body context to inner knowledge led to a 'death drive'.[43] This is partly due to the fact that, in this move, the self becomes self-conscious. There is an 'I' and an 'Other' in relationship. 'For the subject [apprehends] itself as Other, which is the gesture of the Cartesian subject as it recounts the fable of its own existence, to construct the legends, the readability of its own life.'[44]

In such a perspective the self can experience a gap between inner and outer levels, between self and body. 'The autobiographical subject may find body to be the home of a stranger who is not at home in the body, who is in fact homeless.'[45] And if this is read as referring to a living human body certainly Qohelet has problems with owning bodily existence as meaningful for the self when it has no gain attached to it; so it is better not to be born, not to have a body. But the stating of one pole of human selfhood eventually swings back. 'The Cartesian text can even refer, eventually, to a mind–body composite as the total self.'[46] And so with Qohelet, once he has negated the body as a marker for self-identity via *mot* and dust, he can come back to that physicality in its rudimentary material form of food and nurture, and can assert the pleasure which bodily expression can give to the self.

Here Qohelet owns his own social context as a member of a city elite, with the resources suitable for commercial enterprise and for enjoying a 'good table'. Thus his 'I' returns, in its expression, to the king and assembly context, and from that stance offers a last, ambiguous advice.[47] Here cosmos, city and person, as places of meaning in the text, come together in providing meaning. 'Youth' identifies a person as body, with the characteristics of energy, enthusiasm and some years to live. But the youthful self is addressed by a voice which stands for community tradition. This voice urges both 'rejoice' and 'remember' as the action suitable for a self to engage in. Here physical action is encouraged, but also critiqued. The powers of the intellect must colour personal identity. God, the source and end of human destiny, is aligned with storm and the forces of nature. Darkness and storm in nature are balanced by silence and stillness at the community level of a human household – and eventually by the funeral procession. The natural world as the setting for human life is shadowed by the fact that life is only an allotment of days and by a sense of 'eschatological terror' among other creatures. Yet some aspects of human activity escape the fate of an individual human self. The cord, bowl, pitcher and wheel are artefacts which survive their makers, who return to the dust from which they are made, being themselves artefacts. The focus at the end of this passage is once again on death and selfhood. The individual 'I' has no abiding context within a body, but without the body is obliterated, as spirit and dust return to their separate spheres.

Story as Social Discourse

This exploration of story and meaning has covered a great deal of ground, from words and events to time and place. Yet the story of this 'I' of Qohelet is essentially circular, from *hebel* to *hebel*. It is also a contemporaneous account, even though it covers different time periods, as measured by verbal signifiers. These observations bring the reader back to an assessment of Ecclesiastes as a narrative which both creates a self and also critiques self identity, constantly checking out the value of human existence through the exercise of reflective reason. This creates a social commentary made by a personal voice. But the thinking involved in this commentary in turn depends on images of society, of living in time and place, for its content. The last chapter focuses this within a community context. This is a direct social commentary uttered by one human being for the benefit of others who, as yet, lack his experience of world and of society.

Notes

1   That is, Ecclesiastes does not demonstrate the structural features associated with story form in any obvious way. There are never two active characters on stage together, except insofar as Qohelet himself constitutes speaker and responder. There is a problem set out in chapter 1, but this is not the usual tension between good and evil as these forces are likely to impact on a person's fate, as that character's actions are narrated. Yet good and evil, gain and *hebel*, are central elements of the autobiographical recital.

2   Qohelet's search for wisdom goes beyond foundational knowledge. Such information is offered in traditional styles such as poems and proverbs, but Qohelet critiques the message of this traditional communication, pointing out the flaws in its content, seeking new ideas. The pondering on *'ōlām* offers new perspectives, as does the reversal of the value to be attached to poverty and youth. This search is an arduous one for Qohelet, one in which he finds few advantages for human beings.

3   *Yom* is used as a basic marker for the limits of human existence. See here Ecclesiastes 2: 23, 'all his days' is the equivalent of 'his whole life'.

4   S. Cohan and L. Shires, *Telling Stories* (London, Routledge, 1988), pp. 109, 3.

5   Ibid., p. 10.

6   Ibid.

7   Ibid., p. 13.

8   G. Steiner, *Real Presences* (London, Faber and Faber, 1989), p. 59.

9   Ibid., p. 87.

10   Ibid., p. 91.

11   Ibid., p. 88.

12   Ibid., p. 137.

13   As evidenced by Ecclesiastes 6, 2, 3 and 9.

14   W. Spengemann, *The Forms of Autobiography* (New Haven, Conn., Yale University Press, 1980), p. 32.

15   Ibid., p. 6.

16   Ibid., p. 107.

17   P. Ricoeur, *Oneself as Another*, trans. K. Blamey (Chicago, University of Chicago Press, 1992), p. 60.

18   Ibid., p. 61.

19   E. Bruss, *Autobiographical Acts* (Baltimore, Md., Johns Hopkins University Press, 1976), p. 13.

20   J. Fokkelmann, *Reading Biblical Narrative* (Louisville, Ky., Westminster John Knox, 1999), p. 76.

21   Ibid., p. 77.

22   Ibid.

23   M. Toolan, *Narrative: A Critical Linguistic Introduction* (London, Routledge, 1988), p. 48.

24   Ibid.

25   A story line goes from A to B in terms of its component events, but the narrator may choose to tell it from the end point, from B. Or a narrator may jump around in the story, starting from a time part way through and looking back, but then picking up a forward movement. A narrator may also tell the story by starting early on, offering a picture of events much further down the line, and then returning to that earlier point in events.

26   The RSV English edition wording is used here.

27   Although some of the pairs of opposites balance each other easily not all do so, which has led scholars to suggest problems with the Hebrew text, especially with regard to verse 5. C.-L. Seow, *Ecclesiastes* (New York, Doubleday, 1997), pp. 158–62, offers an account of the text which views these paired opposites in a coherent light.

28   Toolan, *Narrative*, p. 61.

29   P. Ricoeur, *Time and Narrative*, trans. K. McLaughlin and D. Pellauer (Chicago, University of Chicago Press, 1984), vol. 3, p. 19.

30   Ibid., vol. 3, p. 64.

31   Ibid.

32   Ibid., vol. 3, p. 70.

33   M. Bal, *Narratology* (Toronto, University of Toronto Press, 1997), p. 133.

34   Ibid.

35   Ibid.

36   That is, potentially positive social situations turn out not to have a fully joyful meaning in terms of their after-effects.

37   Jerusalem and *Qahal* are to be treated separately although the site of the cultic assembly ought to be Jerusalem once Solomon's temple was in operation and while there was a temple in the city, at any time. However, *Qahal* indicates the people who constitute the worshipping group, and in Torah this people was a wandering crowd. Likewise, in the biblical exile, the assembly for worship could still happen, but without the Jerusalem cult centre.

38   See I Kings 10 for the visit of the Queen of Sheba, and I Kings 5 for the overtures of Hiram, King of Tyre.

39   See I Kings 8.

40   This is a general social reality in the ancient Near East. The city state was centred on the king, who was in turn linked with the city's gods. This pattern of royal control is critiqued in Ecclesiastes 9, but, perhaps, valued in Ecclesiastes 5: 9.

41   S. Smith, *Subjectivity, Identity and the Body* (Bloomington, Indiana University Press, 1993), p. 6.

42   Ibid.

43   F. Barker, *The T P Body: Essays on Subjection* (London, Methuen, 1984), p. 110.

44   Ibid., p. 56.

45   Smith, *Subjectivity*, p. 128.

46   Barker, *T P Body*, p. 56.

47   The last words of Qohelet are of course the riddle in chapter 12. The meaning of this poetic piece is not entirely clear, but it does appear to carry an admonitory force, warning that youth and energy are transient realities.

PART II
NARRATIVE AND CULTURE

Chapter 6

Readers as Selves
and the Exploration of Social Worlds

In this middle section of the present book the focus begins to move from text as a fixed, self-contained reality, to text in its relationship to a reader. The basis for this shift of attention is the argument that a text without a reader is a dead thing; only when a reader interacts with text does the material have meaning, the meaning it has for a given reader. 'As the reader passes through the various perspectives offered by the text and relates the different views and patterns to one another, he sets the work in motion, and so sets himself in motion, too.'[1]

With regard to autobiography this means that the 'I' of the autobiographer finds its further significance in the 'I' of the reader. As the narrator operates as a self so also the reader is here interpreted as a self, and a further content for the term 'selfhood' is achieved by the interaction of these two selves. The 'I' of the narrator addresses his/her words to a particular audience, the self (or selves) designated as the hearers within the text. In Ecclesiastes the narrative of Qohelet is addressed partly to self and partly to the imagined young man of Ecclesiastes 11 and 12. Insofar as Qohelet debates the meaning of life (*ámal*) in his own animated thoughts he can be said to be narrating for his own self as audience. He is both the 'I' and the 'Other' of a dialogic process of reflection. The results of his thoughts are then addressed outwards to a posited hearer – the young man who has not yet had the benefit of lived experience to provide a rationale for action.

In addition to these levels of readership, Qohelet is introduced by a framing narrative, which adds a further dimension to the topic of narrator/narratee. Qohelet is here presented as king over Jerusalem and as a source of guidance for the *Qahal*. In this guise the narrator speaks to an implied narratee which is that same *Qahal*, centred in Jerusalem with its royal traditions. This opens out further still, in chapter 12, to whichever, later, assembly hears the words of Qohelet and attempts to find religious significance in them. At this point the narrator/narratee relationship moves across to the reader-at-large in his/her interaction with the reported sayings of Qohelet.

George Steiner

In *Real Presences*, George Steiner discusses the link between reader and text in its most philosophical form. Key to this discussion is the link between a single self and others. Autobiography can be placed here as a very particular signal of the way in which a self cannot find expression without an other, in dialogue. For Steiner the root of this understanding lies in the sphere of religious thought. 'It is the religious thinker and the metaphysician when they give to their findings the persuasion of form, who instruct us that we are monads haunted by communion.'[2] It is possible to consider Ecclesiastes as evidence in support of this view, to the extent that Qohelet operates as a monad whose speech none the less deals with social discourse and reaches out to the reader in an act of communion.

Steiner then considers the two halves of this social communion. On the one hand is the literary work, which provides the starting point for evaluative acts. 'The poem, the picture, the composition is the *raison d'être* ... of the interpretations and judgements which it elicits.'[3] On the other hand is the human person who engages in an act of reading and thus contributes to textual value. 'We bring to our readings, to our visions, to our hearings of aesthetic ... intelligibility, both expectations and incomprehensions. The ways in which we situate in reference to ourselves the pastness of a text ... constitute the dynamic unsayabilities of the very experience of meaning.'[4] Here Steiner moves beyond the symbiosis of text and reader as productive of a meaning in an immediate act of reading, to the mystery of meaning-in-itself. Only when a dynamic act of reading takes place does the possibility of meaning per se occur. For, by its impact on the reader, its entering into the personal space of the reader, a text awakens the reader into his/her own consciousness of being a person in a social world.

Steiner addresses the particular contribution of autobiography: 'The self portrait is the expression of [the writer's] compulsion to freedom, and of his agonistic attempt to repossess, to achieve a mastery over the forms and meanings of his own being.'[5] It can be argued that this comment is applicable to Ecclesiastes since, by delineating his 'I', Qohelet defines himself as a personal voice who frees himself from the daily round of activity to consider the ultimate goals of such action. And in so defining his self, Qohelet offers readers the chance to mirror his action and to seek the meaning of life, as extracted from the values expressed in their lives. The freedom so gained is the intellectual ability to view a life from a longer perspective and so to discover its boundary markers. 'Responding to the poem ... we re-enact, within the limits of our lesser creativity, the two defining motions of our existential presence in the world: that of coming into being, where nothing was, where nothing could have continued to be, and that of the enormity of death.'[6] This remark offers a link with the progress of Qohelet's thought, since he, too, fixes the effective boundaries of meaning as life and death.

Qohelet's personal voice offers the reader the chance to reflect on the balance between birth and death. In his account *mot* outweighs generation, and life, as a concept, collapses into death. The funeral rather than the birth day party is the key to meaning in chapter 7, highlighting sober awe before the finality of death as better than superficial hilarity over a successfully born baby. Qohelet's even more radical move to arguing that 'not to be' is better than 'to be', with 'have been and are no longer' as its mid-term, can be used in line with Steiner's commentary cited above. It erases, or places under grave suspicion, the first of the two defining motions, that is coming into being, and puts only one defining moment before the reader, that of cessation (or absence) of existence.

Yet Qohelet finds the mystery of *mot* impenetrable in chapter 3's debate over the significance of *ʿōlām* as a reality for human beings. He can be certain only of the fact of death as an end to human social discourse. The reader is left uncertain of the final meaning to be gained by these autobiographical narratives. There is 'a sense in which we do not know what it is we are experiencing and talking about when we experience and talk about that which is. There is a sense in which no human discourse, however analytic, can make final sense of sense itself.'[7]

Steiner's view proposes that the relationship between reader and text works on two levels. The first level is the immediate delineation of meaning for a person, the reader, whose viewpoint is created by the influence of the text on a self. At the second and deeper level, lies the path to understanding life and world, to seek meaning in itself. Both of these levels are fruitful with regard to a reading of Ecclesiastes. Here a reader encounters a parallel self, an 'I', whose selfhood is created through performative utterance. The reader is thus invited to take up the views and values of this personal voice of the autobiographer and so to form his/her own personal voice. The immediate area of meaning related to this task is that of material realities, notably wealth and possessions. But the debate over money, houses and sons leads to a critique of the less material reality of wisdom. This in turn moves to the issue of life as a final mode of possession, and here the major problem with the concept of meaning-as-possession emerges. Life evades human control, both life chances and the amount of and possession of time for living as such. Since life as a possession cannot be maximized by human beings its intrinsic value is queried. Death replaces life as that which has a fixed and permanent value in human affairs, but *mot* is not something a human being possesses, rather death 'owns' human beings. These movements within the text deepen the self-reflectiveness of the reader, leading to an exploration of meaning itself, as this is evidenced through the ideas of life and death.

In these movements of thought the reader is encouraged to follow the directives to which Qohelet's thought leads, especially to 'go' to 'enjoy' while time and opportunity are available, as urged in chapters 11 and 12 of Ecclesiastes. This command is addressed first of all to the young man, but then to all members of the *Qahal*, since Qohelet's *dibrê* are offered to all who would seek religious meaning through reading the ideas of an ancient personal voice within community traditions. This guidance for an individual narratee has as its shadow side the transient nature of life, while the community tradition to which it belongs, as manifested in the books of the Old Testament, contains a largely positive attitude to existence. There is therefore some tension between Ecclesiastes and other Old Testament works.[8] Qohelet's view that all tends towards *mot*, with its corollary that there can be no totally positive critique of life as a valuable human commodity, places this book on the margins of belief for the narratee who is a member of the assembly.

Paul Ricoeur

Part of the exploration of reader/text relationships is concerned with the meaning of the term 'self'. Qohelet, as a character, is an example of a self, just as an individual reader is another example of selfhood. Since Qohelet speaks in the first person self interchanges with 'I'. It could also be argued that a reader is another 'I' as a self. But this matter is complex because Qohelet's 'I' becomes a 'he' within the editorial framing and is addressed by a reader's self as 'you'. It seems that the concept of selfhood is linked with a network of relationships between I/You/s/he. At the heart of this is the ambiguity of Qohelet as a self. His frequent phrase 'I said in my heart' (translatable as 'I said to myself') raises the question of the actual relation between the 'I' who can refer to 'my' self. Already a single personal voice contains both a self and an 'other', held together by being-in-dialogue. It is at the point of dialogic meeting between this self and its other that readers can enter into the selfhood of Qohelet and can also begin to work out their own concept of selfhood. If Qohelet's 'I' is formed by 'hearing' himself speak, even if interiorly, then a reader's 'I' is also formed by listening in to the thoughts being uttered.

Paul Ricoeur's study *Oneself as Another* explores the boundaries of identity within the concept of the *ipse* (self).[9] Two foundational points are significant here. Ricoeur states an issue of critical enquiry. There needs to be an understanding of how the self can be at one and the same time a person of whom we speak and a subject who designates himself in the first person, while addressing a second person. This theme involves the possibility of shifting self-designation from the first to the third person and the experiencing of a third person who, in discourse, appears as someone who designates himself as a first person.[10] Second, Ricoeur argues that 'there is no self alone at the start; the ascription to others is just as primitive as the ascription to oneself. I cannot speak meaningfully of my thoughts unless I am able at the same time to ascribe them potentially to someone else.'[11] Key to the concept of selfhood in these two lines of thought is the shifting of the centre of meaning between an 'I' and an 'other', whether within one character in a narrative or between textual character and reader. In this way the reader can be viewed as essential to the fuller meaning of the narrative 'I'. It is the reader as other whose dialogic engagement with the narrator provides the basis for a wider meaning of the selfhood of an 'I'.

At the heart of this manner of addressing issues is the concept of a semantic self. This concerns a selfhood created through speech: selfhood being manifested by a personal voice. This mode of identifying the self is clearly important for any treatment of Ecclesiastes. The self created via this linguistic tool is constituted by the 'I' of the narrator, who speaks to himself as to another, and a reader whose selfhood emerges from being addressed as a 'you' by the narrative voice. The link between narrator and narratee is particularly clear in the context of the 'framed Qohelet' whose utterances are the subject of the editorial offering to the assembly. Here the reader's interaction with the text receives extra weight since the text is re-uttered, in a public act of reading, as part of the selfhood of the community. By engaging with Qohelet a reader relates to the whole social world of the group who would define its self as the recipients of the book Ecclesiastes. In this act of reading a reader not only meets as one self with another on an individual level, but also meets with the communal self of the social world which identifies itself as addressees of Qohelet. This is not without difficulty, since the three stages of editorial comment in Ecclesiastes 12 show both a unity of the group self with the 'I' of the speaker and a distancing from that personal voice because of the unease produced by reading the sayings of that 'I'.

In this discussion there is a movement of content for the word 'I' which is inherent in the definition of semantic selfhood. Although, according to Ricoeur, there is something fixed and central to selfhood, understood via an 'I' who speaks, there is also ambiguity. 'I'–'you' roles can shift as an 'I' shares the nature of a 'you'. The 'I' as a signifier of meaning both unites social discourse and blurs its boundaries. On the one hand, 'I' denotes Qohelet, as opposed to any other personage. On the other hand, Qohelet as 'I' is balanced by Qohelet as 'you', in his self-address. When linked to the social world of readers Qohelet is a 'he', whose selfhood can be delineated and investigated. Thus 'I' can be a concept which does not have one absolute meaning, but stretches to include the literary voice of Qohelet and the interpreting voice of the reader-commentator.

Narrative Identity and the Self

Ricoeur moves the discussion along via two further aspects of self-identity, the first of which is that produced by narrative criticism. The point of contact here is that of characterization. A reader builds up an impression of a character across the temporal span of a narrative by noting the habitual patterns in the character and the constancy of his/her actions. It could seem that self here equals 'same' (*idem*), but this would work against the dialogic tendency of selfhood. A character may well change over time and 'act out of character'. Thus it is better to say that sameness is balanced by selfhood, that actions converge towards a focused profile, although this is not without the possibility of change and otherness. These comments can be applied to the profile of Qohelet. He is not always the same, but speaks rather with two personal voices. On the one hand he urges the ambiguity of life and on the other endorses the value of material pleasures. Yet, overall, his thought does converge to a profile of a self, constructed by speech acts, and expressed in the shifting relationship between *åmal/mot: hebel/yitrôn*.

Ricoeur notes the relevance of the term 'role' in narrative identity. He argues that two roles are available to characters – agent and sufferer. 'The sufferer appears as beneficiary of esteem or victim of disesteem depending on whether the agent proves to be someone who distributes rewards or punishments.'[12] In Ecclesiastes, Qohelet is the main character so it can be argued that he fills both roles. In Ecclesiastes 2, for example, he is an agent, engaged in building works and the construction of a pleasant material environment through the labour of others. In other passages in that chapter he is a sufferer, since he cannot work out the advantage for an agent of such activity. Also the shadowy figure of the deity as agent relegates Qohelet to a sufferer. It is God who gives life and fortune, who is creator and judge. Here Qohelet becomes a type of self-as-sufferer, one who merely experiences the social world of life *taḥat ha ššemešš*. In some ways Qohelet is in charge of the affairs of his self, and in others not. It is this mixture of roles which is offered to the reader of Ecclesiastes and in which a reader partakes. The reader as self is an agent insofar as s/he controls the text by reading it and evaluates the worth of its narrative voice. A reader is, at the same time, a sufferer who must listen to the particular words already uttered by the 'I' of the autobiographer.

The various interpretations of self and narrative identity connected with these roles of agent and sufferer align with Ricoeur's view that 'the mediating function performed by the narrative identity of the character between the poles of sameness and selfhood is attested to primarily by the *imaginative variations* to which the narrative submits this identity'.[13] Qohelet is formed as a self via playing a variety of different roles in which he features as agent and as sufferer. Yet the site of these various roles is a single body. Qohelet is a king and/or an upper class sage.[14] It is within this physical setting that Qohelet experiences himself as an 'I'. This is obviously the case in Ecclesiastes 2. His frequent references to himself as a *lēb* also remind the reader of the bodily contextuality of selfhood in this text. Ricoeur notes that 'literary fictions are imaginative variations on an invariant, our corporeal condition, experienced as the existential mediation between the self and the world'.[15] In turn each reader has his/her own bodily context and it is through that material and social setting that the text is encountered. This process produces a variety of responses to meaning in the text, as the imaginations of readers situated in a variety of social worlds engage in the act of reading. The variety of responses will be the major concern of the next chapters on the cultural exegesis of Ecclesiastes.

Moral Identity and the Self

The view that selfhood is dialogic, that it involves a self and its other, is extended via narrative identity to selfhood expressed by social roles that selves carry out. This shift leads easily to issues of ethics and morality. 'Literature is a vast laboratory in which we experiment with estimations, evaluations and judgements of approval and condemnation through which narrativity serves as a propaedeutic to ethics.'[16] If the roles of agent and sufferer are central to selfhood then issues of power and justice emerge as aspects of the self. Since 'I' can also be 'you' or 's/he' the self cannot be identified with 'my' life and interests. Any definition of the ethical 'good life' needs to incorporate the concept of reciprocity as part of selfhood. The autonomy of action of an 'I' needs to be balanced with respect for a 'you'. Conflict is thus built into moral life and into the idea of selfhood. As an 'I' of action Qohelet builds palaces, buys slaves, but as a self-reflective 'I' he tells his own 'you' that all this is *hebel* and not *yitrôn*. As narrator to an assembly as narratee, Qohelet offers the meaning that the obvious social goals of readers of his social elite are not advantageous to the self.

It is in the conflict between possession as provider of meaning for the self and as lacking in provision of such meaning that the moral self of the text appears. This conflict opens up a new profile on the social world of the assembly: one in which the reader, as sufferer, finds his/her own identity challenged by the 'I' of the autobiographer. It is one in which the world of current social activity is brought under suspicion of not being a 'good life'.[17] So, moral vision does not consist of pleasure through possession. Rather, the content of morality tends towards *mot*. It is death that offers a moral identity to selfhood in Ecclesiastes. As Ricoeur comments, 'by giving it [death] in imagination this or that death fiction has a role to play in the apprenticeship of dying'.[18] Qohelet gives to *mot* a special face by placing it equal with *yitrôn*. In this approach death becomes a moral quality, which is to be embraced by the narratee as expressive of the true weight to be given to human existence.

Ricoeur's study is significant for the creation of a link between the narrator and the narratee since both figures can be defined via the concept of selfhood – a self-identity located inherently in the dialogue of speaker and hearer. His view that 'utterance equals interlocution' involves both self-utterance and utterance to the other.[19] Qohelet's focus on his self through the action of *âmartî* is taken up by the editor's *dibrê* and so forms a foundation for a reader's own act of speech in response.

Mikhail Bakhtin

At the heart of this approach to the self is dialogism, a structure which makes a social tool of language. It is possible to bring to bear here the ideas of Mikhail Bakhtin. 'We are taking language not as a system of abstract grammatical categories, but rather language conceived as ideologically situated, language as a world view.'[20] Since language cannot be disassociated from the social world it transpires that the mode of discourse is heteroglossic, made up of many voices. Bakhtin argues that 'character' in a novel is essentially tied to the issue of speech. A human being, in a novel, 'is first and foremost and always a speaking human being. The novel requires speaking persons bringing with them their own unique ideological discourse.'[21] From a Bakhtinian perspective a self is a speaking identity which involves several different 'others'. Among these others are, for instance:

- others' utterances in a *single* language
- others' 'social languages' in a single *national* language
- different national languages in the same *culture*.[22]

With regard to reader and text, the concepts of narrator//narratee do not each form a singular selfhood. Instead, through heteroglossic shifts 'a word, directed to its object, enters a dialogically agitated and tension-filled environment of alien words, value judgements and accents'.[23] The proper pattern here is not 'word … object', in which each concept remains individually formed, but rather word/object, where the two key terms in the phrase mutually form each other. The spoken utterance, in its own act of formation, encounters and is affected by the other.

This argument is clearly relevant to the formation of Qohelet as a self in Ecclesiastes. Introduced by the editor, Qohelet is a third person 'object' who is constituted as a self by the dialogism of his personal voice where 'I said' meets 'I turned and said'. The narrated word constitutes the object of the act of reading; the reader acts as subject, an 'I' encountering the 'he' of the narrator. When a reader adds his/her own voice to this process then a social discourse of selves in dynamic relationship occurs. The addition of the voices of several editorial words in chapter 12 increases the heteroglossia of the text, contributing a note of ambiguity to the ultimate meaning to be taken from the book.

Wolfgang Iser

Wolfgang Iser's views take these reflections further. The focus falls on the 'I' of the reader in the dialogic process of production of meaning. As readers addressing text 'we do not grasp it like an empirical object, nor do we comprehend it like a predicative fact, it owes its presence in our minds to our own reactions, and it is these that make us animate the meaning of the text as a reality'.[24] The reader thus becomes part of the meaning of the word, as indicated in Bakhtin's thought. The relationship between narrator and narratee implies that a reader exists within the text itself. 'The concept of implied reader designates a network of response-inviting structures, which impel the reader to grasp the text.'[25] This remark of Iser links with the idea of literature as social discourse outlined in an earlier chapter. The life-world of the text invites the reader to engage mimetically with it. By engaging in the social world of the text readers produce a social meaning for the linguistic structures of the text. By extension, literature operates as a form of cultural anthropology. For Iser the ambiguity of existence 'has its roots in the decentred position of man: he is, but he does not have himself'.[26] So there is a need for images that can bridge the unbridgeable. Literature, understood as social fiction, reflects the human condition of a constant search for selfhood, but also is itself shaped by the existing identity of social worlds. 'The extent to which literature expresses our social and historical self understanding is also the extent to which it helps us to gain insight into the nature of our imagination'.[27]

Applying this line of thought to Ecclesiastes leads to an appreciation of the way in which the 'I' of the autobiographer invites the individual 'I's of readers to interact. That invitation refers to the interaction of selves, but this is a social matter since narrator and narratee are definable as both individuals and selves. Qohelet's selfhood is rooted in his self-dialogue and the implied reader is an individual who can also address his/her self as an 'other'. The subject matter for this self-dialogue is that of the daily round of social and economic tasks. Qohelet and the reader are individuals who examine the value of communal activities. At the same time the role of Qohelet as an 'I' is that of religious and philosophical critic. Qohelet offers a model of philosopher self which the reader is invited to copy, adding in his/her particular and individual philosophical responses. The selfhood offered in Ecclesiastes is thus inherently dialogic, through the heteroglossic acts of individuals who are selves whose profile is linked with an 'I' who does, who sees and who says. This model of implied reader develops from the autobiographical nature of the text and raises echoes of the *Essais* of Montaigne. Here also cultural anthropology acts as an umbrella term to hold together the random thoughts of an 'I' who is self aware and who speaks about the self and social experience, and a reader who engages in constructing a parallel personal voice through reading and finding value in Montaigne's attitudes.

The Role of a Reader

It is now possible to make a move to a direct focus on the reader as such – a move which can be introduced by a reference to Jane Tompkins' stress on 'the idea of the reader as a means of producing a new kind of textual analysis', bearing in mind that this stress 'suggests that literary criticism can be seen as part of larger, more fundamental processes such as the forming of an identity'.[28] A rationale for this view is provided in the ideas of N. Holland, that people deal with texts in the same way that they deal with life experience.[29] The reader can be described as an actor in the text world, alongside fictional characters, fulfilling the role of participant observer. Tompkins notes that there are a variety of approaches to the content implied by this comment. 'Whereas for Poulet this means allowing one's consciousness to be invaded by the consciousness of another, to Iser it means that the reader must act as co-creator of the work by supplying that portion of it which is not written.'[30]

The particular locus of reader-response criticism is the individual self of the reader. 'The practical goal ... is to achieve knowledge of the self, of its relation to other selves, to the world and to human knowledge in general.'[31] Discussion of the concept of selfhood returns, therefore, to a stress on an 'I'. In Poulet's definition a reader is an 'I' who happens to have as objects of his own thought, thoughts that are part of a book.[32] As a reader 'I am a self who is granted the experience of thinking thoughts foreign to him'.[33] This treatment of the gap between reader and text, as connected also with the interaction between these two realities, widens the concept of selfhood with regard to a reader. The reader is an 'I' who includes an 'other'. 'Whenever I read, I mentally pronounce an "*I*" and yet the *I* which I pronounce is not myself.'[34] But from the narrator's perspective the narratee is a s/he who can be addressed, according to S. Fish, as a you: 'Reading is an activity, something *you do*.'[35]

This brings the discussion back to a view of selfhood as that which is expressed through I/you/s/he language. Qohelet can now be described as a self whose identity is expressed not only through *his* two voices, nor through those plus the editorial additions, but also through the voice of any reader who acts as 'you' to Qohelet's 'I'. A constant in all these debates concerning a self, either as speaker or hearer, narrator or narratee, is the weight to be attached to words themselves as bearers of meaning. This was addressed at the start of this chapter via the opinions of George Steiner. It will be useful to return to this matter, this time through the thoughts of Denise Riley.

Words as Selves

Denise Riley's study *The Words of Selves* focuses on the way in which a writer is dependent on words and how words can take over the author's job of expressing meaning, coming into the conscious mind in their own patterns and times.[36] When this happens the writer is being written by that which is 'outside of self'. The conscious self does not have absolute command of what is written, nor does the literary 'I' fully reflect the truth of a person, but can produce lies. 'Calling out, calling myself and being called are all intimately related incarnations of the flesh of words.'[37] There is a tension between the hegemony of language and the controlling writer.[38]

In Ecclesiastes narrator and narratee are products of words, they are selves 'written' by the text. Qohelet is written as self by his key terms – gain and loss, value and absence of meaning. His self is one that weighs and evaluates meaning. The young man addressed in Ecclesiastes 11 and 12 is made in the same mould, exhorted to be a weigher and measurer of life and not simply an actor in events. The Qohelet of the editorial frame offers a positive and negative gloss on these positions. Qohelet was wise and taught many things to people, but then these teachings are hard, like nails hammered in. Finally, the narratee is encouraged to silence and stillness, to 'draw a line' under Qohelet's 'I' and to leave it alone, seeking no further layers of meaning. 'Get on with living', the editorial voice seems to advise. Thus the second of Qohelet's own two voices comes into its own at this ultimate boundary of Qohelet's voice of self, within Ecclesiastes.

It is thus through words that both Qohelet and his readers are created 'living' selves. A reader can only delineate a personal identity and a version of selfhood by engaging with the evaluating words of Qohelet's self. A reader can claim to have understood Qohelet's personal voice and can argue that s/he demonstrates the tendency inherent in that literary 'I' by his/her own engagement in social discourse. This personal voice of the reader is created not by the reader alone, by a taking charge of 'dead' words. Rather, the literary words of this autobiographical fiction produce 'live energy' in the reader. When the reader then recontextualizes the words of the text within his/her own time and place, a new strand of selfhood comes into existence, one that brings together both the individual and social aspects of self-identity. It is not the self of Qohelet, but it is an aspect of a 'Qoheletic self'. Cultural exegesis develops, in this way, from a reader's response to text. It could be argued that the reader is a middle term here between an autobiographical 'I' and a cultural 'I'.

It is as if the reader 'tries on' Qohelet intellectually, just as a person tries on an item of clothing. Words can thus become 'mere fashion', as Riley notes with disapproval. 'Sign up under some popular slogan of identity and you have indeed bought the T-shirt.'[39] This perspective, that language is variable and superficial, runs counter to Steiner's view that words, properly managed, lead to meaning-in-itself. Riley argues, however, that words can have a longer term and more authentic role in the creation of selves. 'Repetition is never an inert affair, despite its mechanical fidelity. Say it, read it, echo it often enough and at short enough intervals, and the word suffers a mutation, its thingness abruptly catapulted forward.'[40] Thus a reader, by response, allows life to words so that they develop and change. The Qohelet who utters words to his self includes, by derivation, all the I/you/s/he voices whose integration into the autobiography is an act of putting on a 'Qoheletic self'. This extension of selfhood through a readership transforms a work of ancient social fiction into a living, dynamic force for the emergence of social meaning.

Disclosing Human Possibilities

The interaction of text and reader brings a story into the present moment and provides it with a future. This future provides the afterlife of texts, as they pass from reader to reader, moving into new periods of time and new social worlds. Within this context the story gains the function of disclosing human possibilities, as John Barton notes.[41] Barton suggests that biblical narratives be read as if they were icons. This mode of reading does not promote the search for meaning behind the text, but allows for the projection outwards of a story to grasp and gather in the reader. 'The lines of perspective in the story seem at first to converge behind it, giving it a satisfying aesthetic shape and a satisfactory closure. It is only as we read it more deeply and grasp its "point" that we realize that they really converge on us, the readers.'[42] A critical point here is the concept of 'closure'. If a narrative plot comes full circle it offers little encouragement to a reader to add in further events and consequences. But if the text ends on an open note, the reader is forced into direct interaction with it. Barton notes here the endings of *The Tempest* and the book of Jonah, in both of which the audience is directly addressed by the closure of the story. 'Instead of the curtain falling between us and the actors when the play ends, the action moves as it were in front of the curtain and transports itself from art to life.'[43]

If Barton's views are applied to a reading of Ecclesiastes it can be seen that this story also opens itself out to the readers. At one level this is happening throughout the book, as has been discussed in earlier chapters. But at the end, too, there is an openness of text to a reader's additions. The last scene of Qohelet's reflections ends on ambiguity. The riddle of life cannot be fully explained by the autobiographer, who none the less proffers death as its likely solution. The actual death envisaged in the narrative has not yet come about, as it is the inevitable end to which the young man is moving, but which he does not comprehend. The time of youth stands 'before' all the events related in this passage; its meaning, however, is drawn precisely from that 'before'. The reader, too, stands in the time of 'before' but is encouraged by Qohelet to contemplate 'that which will be hereafter'. Thus the narrative discloses to the reader a final image of meaning-as-existence, which invites the reader to take up the challenge of death as negation of being. This move is endorsed by the following editorial comments, which further urge the reader to take the story seriously since these are the words of a great and wise man.

Barton's arguments reinforce, from a biblical perspective, the importance of the role of the reader in finding meaning in texts. At the centre of this relationship are the words of the story, which Riley described as having lives of their own.[44] But this life only comes to be within the understanding of human persons.

> what this comes down to is that 'openness' is a kind of literary *metaphor* for the way in which biblical narrative ... operates on the reader who is prepared to be open to it. In the biblical narrative, possibilities are disclosed when the reader acknowledges the correctness of the verdict 'You are the man!', when the story strikes home into the reader's own heart and mind.[45]

Notes

1   W. Iser, *The Act of Reading* (Baltimore, Md., Johns Hopkins University Press, 1980), p. 21.
2   G. Steiner, *Real Presences* (London, Faber and Faber, 1989), p. 140.
3   Ibid., p. 151.
4   Ibid., p. 166.
5   Ibid., p. 205.
6   Ibid., p. 209.
7   Ibid., p. 215.
8   This is to regard the books of Hebrew Scriptures as shaped by a common identity as part of a canonical collection serving a faith community, as a source of authorized teachings about religious tradition.
9   P. Ricoeur, *Oneself as Another*, trans. K. Blamey (Chicago, University of Chicago Press, 1992). The play of terms dealt with by this volume is clearer in the French title, *Soi-Meme comme un autre*.
10 Ibid., pp. 34–5.
11 Ibid., p. 38.
12 Ibid., p. 145.
13 Ibid., p. 148.
14 The reader can take up the fictive character of Qohelet as a king in the first two chapters of the book or can go behind that figure to the sage of the third-century Hellenistic Judaism whose viewpoint emerges from chapter 3 onwards. These characterizations are pinned together by the editorials of chapter 12.
15 Ricoeur, *Oneself as Another*, p. 150.
16 Ibid., p. 115.
17 See D. Clines, *Interested Parties* (Sheffield, Sheffield Academic Press, 1995). Clines deals with the ideology of readers and writers. With regard to writers he pursues a policy of mirror reading the work to search for the social and cultural interests served by the text. Using his method here would lead to identifying the social concerns of an elite upper-class male.
18 Ricoeur, *Oneself as Another*, p. 162.
19 Ibid., p. 44.
20 M. Bakhtin, *The Dialogic Imagination*, trans. M. Holquist (Austin, University of Texas Press, 1998), p. 271.
21 Ibid., p. 332.
22 Ibid., p. 275.
23 Ibid., p. 276.
24 Iser, *Act of Reading*, p. 129.
25 Ibid., p. 34.
26 Ibid., p. 213.
27 Ibid.
28 J. Tompkins, 'An Introduction to Reader-Response Criticism', in J. Tompkins (ed.) *Reader-Response Criticism* (Baltimore, Md., Johns Hopkins University Press, 1980), p. xi.
29 Ibid., p. xix.
30 Ibid., p. xv.
31 Ibid., p. xix.
32 G. Poulet, 'Criticism and the Experience of Interiority', in Tompkins, *Reader-Response Criticism*, p. 44.
33 Ibid.
34 Ibid., p. 45.

35   S. Fish, 'Literature in the Reader: Affective Stylistics', in Tompkins, *Reader-Response Criticism*, p. 70.
36   D. Riley, *The Words of Selves* (Stanford, Calif., Stanford University Press, 2000). This is a writer's self-reflection on the work of writing, viewing words as tools of the trade. Words are sometimes controlled by the writer, but sometimes find their own creative existence by springing to the mind of an author 'unbidden'.
37   Ibid., p. 111.
38   Ibid., p. 71. This relates to the spontaneous activity of words in a writer's consciousness.
39   Ibid., p. 153.
40   Ibid., p. 158.
41   J. Barton, 'Disclosing Human Possibilities: Revelation and Biblical Stories', in G. Sauter and J. Barton (eds) *Revelation and Story* (Aldershot, Ashgate, 2000).
42   Ibid., p. 57.
43   Ibid.
44   Riley, *Words of Selves*. See Riley's introductory chapter, which rehearses themes of self-conscious scrutiny of the connection between 'selves' and 'words', thus exploring the linguistic expressions used by a human self to express the contents of an inner self.
45   Barton, 'Disclosing Human Possibilities', p. 59.

Chapter 7

Cultural Exegesis
and the Language of Selves

In the previous chapter attention was shifted from a focus on the text as a literary product to a wider perspective, which includes the reader as productive of meaning within the subject of literature. Words cannot be evaluated without a consideration of the social ownership of language and literature. As A. Easthope remarks, 'the text persists, if it does, within the (hopefully) interminable process of human history, which ensures a constant spillage of meaning beyond any given reading'.[1] From text as inclusive of reader, as narrator paired with narratee, a move is now made to cultural aspects of text production and, therefore, to meaning as carried by social and historical processes.

Culture is a term with many possible meanings, as noted in earlier chapters, but these are always connected with the social world of human activity. T. Eagleton notes that the term emerges from the Latin root to cultivate, and so carries agricultural meaning. It 'at first denoted a thoroughly material process, which was then metaphysically transposed to affairs of the spirit'.[2] For Eagleton, the idea of culture includes both material existence and the world of human thought, while not attaching itself to either completely. 'The idea of culture, then, signifies a double refusal: of organic determinism on the one hand, and of the autonomy of spirit on the other. It is a rebuff to both naturalism and idealism.'[3] In addition, culture may describe what exists, as well as evaluating modes of human social discourse and finding them wanting. Under the label of 'high', culture turns to the aesthetics associated with social elites; as labelled 'low' it signifies the art, music and reading matter that emerges from the manual working classes. In general, culture parallels human society. It is 'the unconscious *verso* of the *recto* of civilised life, the taken-for-granted beliefs and predilections which must be daily present for us to be able to act at all'.[4]

To speak of cultural exegesis is to suggest that a given text has its place within the cultural boundaries of human social groups and that one mode of finding meaning in text is to explore the ways in which readers in different times and places have interpreted it. For the book of Ecclesiastes this means considering its place in Christian and Jewish canons of sacred texts and how its being placed before readers as a carrier of religious meaning has led them to explore its possible message for their own time and place. Carrying out this exercise includes picking up the ideas about Ecclesiastes which have

already been put forward, insofar as it has been treated within literary critical
boundaries. The work has been construed as an example of autobiography
in which an 'I' narrates his 'story'. Any definition of the narrative self so
produced must include the 'I' of the reader who encounters the book, to
whom the material therein is addressed as to a 'you'. One critical issue here
is whether the text or the social context of the reader is the dominant half of
the relationship. Wofgang Iser argued for a 'co-temporaneous' interaction of
these two contributors to meaning.[5] It is true that both text and reader, narrator
and narratee, are products of a cultural context, a social world. But does that in
fact infer the overarching nature of culture, as it holds together both text and
reader? Eagleton would argue that this is so, but Easthope would nuance this
view by suggesting that text still has a specifically literary part to play in the
social construction of meaning.[6]

On the one hand stands the 'empirical' search for ultimate literary
paradigms, to which particular pieces of literature give content, and, on the
other, the impossibility of producing any formal literary tools for examining
text which can be agreed by all or many critics. Easthope explores the current
tension between these modes. 'Twenty years ago the institutionalised study
of literature throughout the English-speaking world rested on an apparently
secure and unchallenged foundation, the distinction between what is literature
and what is not.'[7] Since then that paradigm has been challenged and has fallen
into crisis. In its place has risen 'cultural studies', which not only addresses a
canon of high literature but also takes popular publications seriously as proper
subjects for study.

Easthope moves beyond an account of the historical shift in literary to
cultural study to suggest a new paradigm, which incorporates text and cultural
context in its methodology. Easthope proposes as themes for a new paradigm
– institution, sign system, ideology, gender, subject position, the other.[8] These
blend text and cultural context in approaches to reading. Sign system, for
example, refers to the signifier/signified in the text, whereas ideology denotes
meaning which is socially constituted.[9] If the term 'ideology' indicates
the social realm, 'gender' moves the commentator to pin down specific sub-
groups within society, and 'subject position' goes even further, drawing in
individual rather than broader social consciousness, promoting a position
for the transcendent and self-sufficient individual, to which it relates the
reader.[10] 'Other' breaks down the individual as self to several voices, as in the
methods posited by Freud, and stresses the concept that meaning consists of
paired items, as in the Derridean pairs of speech/writing, life/death.[11] Finally,
institution brings readers back to the overall social setting within which these
other tools operate.[12]

Easthope gathers these terms together by stating that

each term has an autonomous definition and covers its own space yet each relates
to others, becoming imbricated with it to strengthen analysis of a specific area or
problematic. No equal weighting among the terms is intended but crucially no term

is originary or foundational ... This is appropriate to a cultural analysis taking as its object the dissemination of textuality and acceding to the necessity for viewing totality as constituted according to different times which are nevertheless relative to each other, not independent.[13]

Applying Easthope's terminology to Ecclesiastes it can be noted that the book reaches the reader by virtue of its belonging to a fixed collection of religious texts inherited from earliest Christianity and Judaism. In ideological terms, therefore, it is a 'high' text, part of a cultural aesthetics. This ideological stratum is heightened since the work is in itself a piece of elite reflection on an elite social world in antiquity.[14] As to gender, the viewpoint of Ecclesiastes is that of a male, individual thinker whose importance is underlined by being linked with royalty. However, under the heading of 'other' the reader can note that the dominant security of a royal male voice is challenged by the other voice of the autobiographer, that of insecurity, of an ambivalent balance between *yitrôn* and *hebel*. It is thus possible to look at the text as part of the third-century BCE world, while also applying Easthope's criteria for reading literature culturally.

But the traces of these positions are handed on in the text to the reader who will reread the material from different social perspectives, from within individual or sub-group identities. How, for instance, would a feminine response to the book operate? Is there any space for a womanist reading, since, for example, chapter 7 contains such negative views of woman as seducer and as trap? How does the theme of subject stance balance against a text that can be read as autobiography? This might offer the reader deeper social insights with regard to meaning-as-existence, but if it involves admittance to the private wisdom thoughts of a privileged person will that always work? What happens when the reader is not from a privileged elite and cannot align with the narrator? Suppose that this form of existential questioning with its emphasis on money and status appears to be out of social reach to a reader of a more 'popular' kind. Would such a reader agree with the high value placed on an acceptance of *mot*, with its apparent downplaying of material pleasures? A reader who does not have great opportunities for abundant material pleasures may well feel that the whole debate is useless. Could such a reader find in Ecclesiastes a narrative self with which s/he would want to identify? It is necessary to consider in more detail, here, matters of ideology and historicism, in order to examine the content of the term 'cultural exegesis'.

Ideology and Historicism

These two topics are not fully distinct from each other. Both deal with the material context of words as communication tools for human beings who live within a social world. They are the signs (visible shapes) of the activity of social discourse, which itself is defined by belonging to a particular social context. Whereas historicism 'is the critical movement insisting on the prime importance of historical context to the interpretation of texts of all kinds',[15] the word ideology 'usually designates a way of thinking which is systematically mistaken, a false consciousness'.[16] Thus a historical focus on the role of language highlights the way in which the cultural context through which texts have been handed on in a society is key to the shaping of meaning. This approach is best developed by considering the role of past events and their connections with present reality. An ideological focus looks at the main structures of ideas in which words are embedded. Although this involves suspicion of their value, as noted by D. Hawkes, quoted above, the approach can be used more broadly to cover any self-conscious social explanations of the human world. Postmodernist thinkers, for example, infer that the autonomous subject exists only within an ordered ideological structure. 'If there is no experience without representation, then the media of representation must be prior even to our experience of our selves.'[17]

Both approaches to exploring the cultural framework of literature converge, when Western European culture is the subject, on key historical stages of thought and key thinkers: in topics such as empiricism, idealists, Marxists, postmodernists.[18] Between them these movements in the history of ideas shape the reception of texts in Europe from the Enlightenment to the present day. Empiricism prefers texts whose contents are scientific, proven. Idealists privilege abstract ideas over material examples. Marxists stress rather the concrete channels within which ideas are carried and re-expressed. Postmodernists prefer variety and flexibility, relativity both of ideas and of material expressions, which prevents the emergence of any overarching systems of written words as ultimate explanations of meaning. Within postmodern times the development of feminist thought and that of post-colonialism expands the significant other voices to include those of persons other than male, white, middle- and upper-class Americans and Europeans.

... And the Language of the Self

For present purposes what is relevant in the fields of historical and ideological investigation is how major ideas impact on the language of the self. Empiricism focuses on the knowledge gained by a single subject, rational search for meaning. The Enlightenment arose from a cultural suspicion of the value of an *ancien régime* thought system.[19] As Hawkes notes the 'potential of rational analysis and empirical investigation for exposing and eliminating customary falsehood, gave ... great appeal for progressive thinkers for centuries', from the time of Hobbes onwards.[20] The stress was on the value of the autonomous individual rather than on buying into a collective worldview. This movement tends to a concept of the self as rational being, an approach taken further by Kant and Hegel. The process begins with a Cartesian, thinking self, moves to the transcendent ego of Kant and progresses to Hegel, who collapses the gap between spirit and matter. For Hegel spirit is the dominant reality and needs to be so perceived. 'Once the spirit has achieved full self-consciousness, once it has learnt to recognise the external world as its own alienated and objectified form, the opposition between subject and object will be abolished.'[21] Here an ideological viewpoint is tied into a form of historicism since history is the process via which spirit achieves its own self-identity.

In contradiction of this perspective Marx argued for a dialectic, but one that focused more on material expressions as the living content of selves. This view was carried further by post Marxists who insisted on a strict materialism in which subject and object still form an antithesis which needs conjoining, though with a different emphasis on the process by which this is achieved. 'There is thus a mutual determination between the inherited objective circumstances in which people unavoidably find themselves, and their ability to impose their subjective will on this material environment and alter it', according to Hawkes.[22] In addition, he argues, there is a need to bring the alienation of subject and object to an end. 'Just as, for Hegel, alienation would be transcended when Spirit recognised matter as its own alienated self, so for Marx alienation will be abolished when human beings understand that the "market forces" which shape their lives are nothing but representations of their own alienated activity.'[23]

Both Hegel and Marx see the operation of spirit and matter in history as productive of a 'true self'. By contrast postmodern thinkers attack both positions as 'totalitarian'. This can be seen in the work of Foucault, for example, who argued, according to Hawkes, that 'when we try to shape the flux of events into a coherent narrative ... we impose upon it the ostensibly unified, apparently conscious form of our own subjectivity. In fact, however, the subject is neither unified nor fully conscious; it can only come to appear so when it is artificially removed from the objective context that generates it.'[24] For a postmodern view there are many versions of what it means to be a self, but with the focus on the variety of local and particular selves within a global social world, rather than on any single universal form of achieving self identity. For Foucault, for instance, there is no ideal sphere: the appearance of autonomy for an individual will is a deceit. Human beings are actually constituted by the here and now of personal voice and not by any further possibilities of existence such as a transcendental self.[25] History does not reveal some ultimate condition of existence covering all human beings, rather it reveals only the particular instances in which human beings have existed. History can be used, however, to create an illusion of authority to substantiate the use of power, as in religious claims, in colonialism and in patriarchy. In this context the 'other' comes to have a special role. It is that by which 'we' define ourselves across time.

A further version of self-definition through the concept of the other is that produced by Freud, who claimed that all history is case history.[26] In psychological theory an individual self exists by virtue of separation from the mother, who is now viewed as the other present in the depths of the psyche. Irigaray has developed this theory in terms of male/female perspectives and Lacan has developed it with regard to the uncanny. It is at the boundaries between the 'I' and the other that the self emerges, in all these theoretical systems. Thus the liminal becomes important as an existential marker. Death itself is such a liminal point, linked to the uncanny, and so offers a site where selfhood finds its content. This offers a clear link with the views of Qohelet, as expressed in the main sections of Ecclesiastes.

And Qohelet

The following emerge as central themes from this short survey of European cultural schemas:

- the role of rational investigation as constitutive of the self in action
- the self as product of a search for ideal/spiritual identity
- the self as emerging from individual engagement with the material circumstances of human life
- the self as a variety of individual existences, with the focus for 'I' being not what is the 'same' but what is 'other'.

These themes are an inherent part of Western European 'high' culture which, in turn, impacts on 'popular' culture since thinkers increasingly include aspects of 'low' culture in the resources utilized for producing meta-theory. All of them turn, ultimately, on a belief in the reality of a concept of individual selfhood: 'The belief in an autonomous self is one of the fundamental characteristics of the western "metaphysics".'[27] This belief has been operative in cultural theories since the Enlightenment, although it has been challenged, more recently, by Nietzsche's extreme scepticism. The contemporary European social world holds a tension between the search for a cultural rooting for self/selves and an absolute despising of this search, since selves do not own themselves but exist in a passing temporal and material phase. One mode of examining Ecclesiastes culturally, then, is to situate the text within these European parameters and to read it from this ideological gaze.

By contrast it is possible to read Ecclesiastes from within a postcolonial perspective, using postcolonial theories. In a sense these theories are still a European phenomenon since they would not have existed without European expansion and the creation of empires with their concomitant colonies. Since Christianity was a cultural artefact within the development of colonialism colonies have the profile of social worlds in which European religion has become part of cultural identity. But the ongoing development of meaning in these cultural entities does not have to follow Western European approaches. Since a book like Ecclesiastes is now 'owned' by postcolonial social worlds they can make such a work culturally relevant to their particular needs, as distinct from what a text may come to mean for a European society. As G. West states, the Bible 'plays an important role in the lives of many, particularly the poor and the marginalised. The Bible is a symbol of the presence of the God of life with them and a resource in their struggle for survival, liberation and life'.[28]

West argues that it makes a significant difference, when reading a biblical text, whether the poor and marginalized, in postcolonial contexts, are viewed as primary interlocutors.[29] West develops his point through a reading of two interpretations of Mark 10: 17–20, one being that of the present Pope and the other being the product of seven workshops held with lay readers in South Africa. Pope John Paul's commentary skips over the issue of why the rich man could not give away his goods and whether he should do so. The workshop members focused on the practical matter, omitted by the western reading, of the fact that wealth comes to some through the exploitation of others. 'The significant difference between these readings is who the primary interlocutors are. The Pope has chosen to read with other trained ... readers in a place of privilege and power, whereas I have chosen to read with ordinary African readers in places of poverty and marginalisation.'[30]

There is an echo here of the comment made above about the significance of textual voices which debate issues of gain and advantage for poor readers who have not much access to these concepts in material terms. In Ecclesiastes a postcolonial reading might not pick up on the *yitrôn* themes as ambiguous but might have a greater focus on maximizing what there is to be had. Since *mot/hebel* are the usual condition of *åmal taḥat ha ššemešš*, then, if there *is* an increase in food/housing/health this should be seized upon and celebrated as a sign that death and nothingness cannot destroy a human being's sense of self-worth.

Qohelet as Authority Figure

In the first line of cultural interpretation referred to above, Qohelet speaks as another male, intellectual, western self. The nature of such a voice may be taken, for instance, from the writings of George Steiner. In *Grammars of Creativity* Steiner relates literary shifts to the underlying presence of Jewish, Christian and Islamic religions in the region.[31] On page 62 of his study he notes the literary effect of texts such as Ecclesiastes on later literature. It thus seems reasonable to use Steiner to establish a cultural paradigm for a 'high' reading of Qohelet.

For Steiner the stress falls on the atmosphere of decline lying over European culture at present. 'There is, I think, in the climate of spirit at the end of the twentieth century, a core-tiredness. The inward chronometry, the contrasts within time which so largely determine our consciousness, point to late afternoon in ways that are ontological.'[32] Steiner attributes this to social and political events: 'for the whole of Europe and Russia, this century became a time out of hell.'[33] The question that follows is whether there is any hope for the future. Or is the future tense under suspicion of nothingness?[34]

Steiner comes to focus on existentialism as both negative and positive. 'Existentiality is a compelling potential in the singular energies and inherence of a nothingness (*nichtsein*) which is simultaneously a *sein* or being there.'[35] In this line of thought End and Beginning form a continuous concept in which beingness takes the lead and where nothingness can be negated, in the annihilation of nothingness in any truly creative act.[36] For Steiner these views lead to the conclusion that being is inherently twinned with non-being. 'All phenomenality is alternative, to other possibilities of substantiation and, more radically, to "insubstantiality", which is to say inexistence.'[37] Key interpretive attitudes emerge concerning the ambivalence of life and death, of something paired with nothingness as constitutive of a full concept of beingness.

Putting on such a pair of spectacles, how would a reader find meaning in Ecclesiastes? S/he might note the similar interests of the two literary voices of the critics, ancient and modern. Qohelet evaluates the meaning of social existence in another 'high', male culture and finds it unproductive of happy meaning. In his life he has witnessed injustices and oppressions, though not quite of the same ferocity as those of Steiner's Europe. Qohelet has been led by experience of his culture to examine existence as a meaningful reality. Steiner talks of hope and the value of the future tense, also of the philosophy of nothingness. Qohelet speaks in more phenomenological terms of pleasure and gain, and their meaningfulness as an expression of existence. But this can be paralleled with Steiner's 'future'.

The future tense proves to be an illusion, in Qohelet's view. What the future holds is loss and the ultimate form of this is death and ashes. Thus Qohelet can argue that it is better never to have been than to live facing this annihilation of life-as-gain understanding. But the role of *mot* is ambiguous, since knowledge of death as goal turns into wisdom. By owning this to be truth a self can move beyond decline in the present tense. The point of nothingness turns into the point of coming into being. The selfhood so constructed offers a meaning for beingness as enjoying life here and now.

So, putting on another male, elite approach to life, albeit academic rather than royal, the reader can view Qohelet as a 'fellow traveller' of the paths of existence. The key overlap is that cross over between something and nothingness within the boundary of meaning-as-existence. In this reading, the ancient autobiographer is drawn within the sphere of a modern literary critic and a form of selfhood is thus created, which covers philosophical and literary explorations of traditional cultural norms. The ambiguity of Qohelet's position is felt to resonate with contemporary ambiguities over values and cultural explanations of existence. The modern critic takes on the role of a *hakam* and Qohelet 'becomes' an academic critic.

In the reading of Qohelet given above he serves as a kind of 'authority figure', one whose understanding guides elites in their approach to the exercise of power. A parallel context for Qohelet as an 'authority' exists within the area of Christian religious teaching. In this setting the biblical canon operates as a privileged resource for guidance over the relations about God, world and human existence. W. Brown's commentary on Ecclesiastes fits into this cultural use of biblical texts.[38] Brown's aim is to provide a commentary on the ancient text which will make it a resource for teaching and preaching. This cultural reading is also an elite interpretation since Brown is himself an academic and is aiming his account at qualified teachers and ministers of religion in north-west America and similar societies, readers who would understand his references to the work of Flaubert,[39] and to middle-class interests.[40] It could be said that two key elements drive such a commentary. First there is the use of Ecclesiastes as part of a sacred canon which offers a 'total' understanding of the Christian Bible as divine revelation. Second there is the application of the 'old' worlds of these texts to new cultural contexts in such a way that 'old' turns into former to a latter which is the reader's own application of the text to contemporary issues.

The view that all biblical texts offer the reader an insight into divine truth sits in tension with the message of Ecclesiastes, which is so often uncertain about finding any clear meaning in life. Brown's commentary reflects this discomfort. He remarks that, as a minister, his first reaction to Qohelet's scepticism was negative.[41] Elsewhere he notes that the sage is concerned with the incapacity of the human being to prevent the onslaught of death.[42] Such extreme doubt appears 'to contravene the very ethos of faith'.[43] But the book is part of a guaranteed religious library and so cannot be thrown out. This canonical status of the text provides a bridge for Brown, who turns around Qohelet's uncertainty about daily affairs to a positive feature, by arguing that he abandons grand claims to understand revelation in preference for the meaning of everyday reality.[44] Even death can be turned around in this perspective; 'Qohelet reminds the church that faith in Christ entails facing the fullness of death.'[45] Finally, it is not life itself that is empty but the particular life of a person who is a solitary figure engaged only in work.[46]

Brown also draws on the injunctions of Qohelet to go and enjoy the pleasures of life, by suggesting that the second part of Ecclesiastes appears to be more settled in its teaching. Thus the autobiographer can be said to be using a via negativa method, starting with doubt only to move towards certainty.[47] Gradually, then, Brown can accommodate Qohelet within a religious culture which argues for the existence of a positive deity with clear purposes for human affairs. 'Only by confronting life in all its vicissitudes and death in its totalizing scope can one experience the fullness of the mystery of God.'[48] Thus death itself becomes a positive. Brown argues that the book should be read as an obituary. 'Since Qohelet prefers the "end of a thing" over its beginning (7: 4) the conclusion of his discourse discloses something of the purpose and scope of his work as a whole. Ecclesiastes is essentially an obituary of life itself.'[49] In this manner Brown encourages the Christian reader to explore the text as apparently different, as an 'other', which becomes a voice of 'sameness' and which speaks to the self of the church and helps to create Christian self identity. That which most expresses otherness, namely focusing on negativity, eventually contributes greatly to the creation of a 'believing self', by being transformed into the 'same' message.

Brown's interpretation of Ecclesiastes thus allows to Qohelet the role of being a teacher and guide for modern Christian culture. Qohelet addresses not only the ancient assembly centred in Jerusalem but also modern, Christian assemblies. This, too, is a reading from and for a 'high' culture. Those reading Brown will have the task of passing on their reading to 'ordinary' members of the congregation, but the posited reader is a specialist, a religious practitioner with a voice of authority with regard to religious truth. Whereas a 'Steinerian' reading offers a voice of interpretation in a secular 'high' culture, Brown produces something similar for a religious 'high' culture.

Self and the Other

Whereas the tendency in the interpretations dealt with above is for the production of a Qohelet whose voice can be aligned with the culture of the reader and, who can thus be read as the 'same', the following readings move to a greater focus on difference. A contemporary interest in European culture is the contribution of otherness to the construction of selves. In 'Re-visioning the Subject in Literature and Theology' H. Walton notes, Levinas's contribution to this debate. 'For Levinas, it is the desire for the other which calls the self into being as it journeys beyond its own territory into a strange land.'[50] The rise of Freudian psychology of the self has fed this perspective. Lacan, in particular, developed the theory of the child's separation from the maternal as a sense of a repressed 'other' – a chaotic substratum of the human psyche which is ready to erupt into the conscious self of an adult.[51] In these theories the body is an important element of the self, focused on the embodied experience of individual human growth into selfhood. The body is the text in which human experience is recorded and can thus be reviewed as 'inscribed' with cultural meaning.

A further strand here is the uncanny as the other, including death as an expression of the uncanny. According to H. Pyper, Freud argues that death is the ultimately unthinkable which nevertheless impinges on human consciousness. In certain circumstances primitive beliefs are triggered and these undermine our carefully constructed rational worldview.[52] Pyper links this to the poetry of Walter de la Mare, where living and dead figures often stand side by side.[53] 'We are listeners to, and watchers of, lives and events which we cannot participate in. In turn we are listened to and watched by others whose purposes we do not fathom.'[54] By analogy, Pyper links these poetic themes with reading the New Testament. The text and its meanings are voices 'other' to our experience; exploring the meaning of self through engagement with biblical texts entails a respect for that difference. It can be suggested that this view can be used with regard to Ecclesiastes. The voice of Qohelet invites a response from a listener, but there remains a gap between the speaker and the listener. They operate in two separated worlds. This gap reminds the reader of the inherent separations within the human person, offering a paradigm of the inner strangeness of the self to itself.

F. Segovia, in *Decolonizing Biblical Studies*, also deals with the strangeness of one voice to another. He argues that, since all texts are socially constructed, they do not carry one single voice, but that there are 'dissenting voices, suppressed voices, contradictory voices within the text'.[55] The task of a reader is to discover texts as 'others'. 'Intercultural criticism calls for help in dis-covering the reality of texts as *others*' and 'in dis-covering the reality of these "texts" as *others* in their own right – as realities from different social and historical contexts than one's own'.[56] Segovia builds up a paradigm for a postcolonial reading mode from the base of cultural difference in which the empirical search for a single voice is finally abandoned and replaced by an attention to the constant play of many voices. The 'emphasis is placed on the din of texts and authors as such, the cacophony of voices in the ancient agora or forum, coming from every direction and going every which way'.[57] The reader has to 'shop around' among these voices, thus the key symbol here is the *mercado* (marketplace) and the only boundary for the construction of a self is that of fluidity, polyvalency, polyglot speech.[58] Implicit in this shift is the move from a 'high' culture approach to a more 'popular' format, where many divergent cultural expressions can be regarded as authoritative.

It can be argued that Segovia's stress on the marketplace leads to the commodification of culture and so of the self. The reader as consumer is urged to buy a version of self identity without deeper discrimination as to the quality of the merchandise. However, the disadvantages attached to Segovia's postcolonial theory of reading have to be balanced against the disadvantages of a reading method that looks for a single voice of truth. The empirical search for true selfhood, the project of a post-Enlightenment Europe, often makes no distinction between absolute truth and the voice of a male, white, western 'I' who identifies the 'you' of the text as 'the same as me'.

What effect would this shift of paradigm have on a reading of Ecclesiastes? There is no longer any need to make 'of two voices, one', for instance. Qohelet's contradictory voices can stand as different. Qohelet is an 'I' whose selfhood is inherently fragmented and whose conscious voice is under pressure from other internal voices, those of his own others. Here the ambitious king is deconstructed by the rigorous sage, as noted by Brown.[59] The enthusiasm of the younger self is challenged by the scepticism of older age. Here is an 'I' who values family life and an 'I' who denies any lasting value to female partners and to sons. The fullest extent of the self and the other, of the uncanny and of death, is found in the closing scenes of Qohelet's narration. In the riddle of chapter 12 it is the household that crumbles and falls silent. If this is read as an analogy for the body, then that body is inscribed with cultural meaning. It is a self bent, weak, failing, which encounters the uncanny as the mourners gather in the street and a sense of terror pervades consciousness. Thus age deconstructs the selfhood of youth.

Cultural Exegesis and the Language of Selves

A. Milner notes that 'if there is any one theme that has guided the development of cultural studies since the 1960s it has been the progressive dissolution of a notion of a single culture and its supersession by *cultures* in the plural'.[60] The view that there exists a single voice with a single 'gaze', of which writers were the creators and readers the discoverers, has been identified as that, not of a universal social world, but of a particular temporal and spatial culture which creates itself by its engagement with textual material. In this process such an 'I' can claim selfhood as its own, denying existence in speech to other 'I's. The present polyglot state disturbs the harmony and peace of a monolithic selfhood but gives life to many more voices of selves, albeit in a chaotic and noisy competition for attention. In the empirical mode, too, a speaker must clamour for attention and, since only one voice can ultimately be truth, an 'I' needs to shout louder than others to seize hegemony. If the postmodern and postcolonial modes of reading accept cacophony, they do not regard this as deafening. The competing voices of others offer an 'I' the challenge and the excitement of engaging with the unfamiliar and the strange in a watching and a listening that is a journey towards construction of a selfhood in which spirit and matter are both at work.

In the final section of this book it is these notions of cultural exegesis that will be examined more closely, through particular lenses. The hub of this activity is still the figure of Qohelet whose autobiographical speech is inscribed in the text of Ecclesiastes. But now attention turns from that text to the texts of those who are readers of the work. What contributions to the profile of an autobiographical self are made by readers who watch and listen from different cultural positions? If there is any common ground to be found here it may be that Milner's comment on Lukacs is helpful. 'The novel as a form is thus for Lukacs originally organised around the problematic hero in pursuit of problematic values within a problematic world.'[61] The ambiguous, enigmatic Qohelet will now be explored through three fields of cultural discourse, drawn from European and postcolonial stances.

Notes

1   A. Easthope, *Literary into Cultural Studies* (London, Routledge, 1991), p. 33.
2   T. Eagleton, *The Idea of Culture* (Oxford, Blackwells, 2000), p. 1.
3   Ibid., p. 4.
4   Ibid., p. 28.
5   This viewpoint stresses the intimacy of the link between reader and text.

6   The Bible and Cultural Collective, *The Postmodern Bible* (New Haven, Conn., Yale University Press, 1995), offers a commentary on this matter from a biblical studies perspective.
7   Easthope, *Literary into Cultural Studies*, p. 3.
8   Ibid., p. 129.
9   Ibid., p. 130.
10   Ibid., p. 131.
11   Ibid., p. 134.
12   Ibid., p. 135.
13   Ibid., p. 137.
14   This is in keeping with the line of approach to reading texts established by D. Clines, *Interested Parties* (Sheffield, Sheffield Academic Press, 1995).
15   P. Hamilton, *Historicism* (London, Routledge, 1996), p. 2.
16   D. Hawkes, *Ideology* (London, Routledge, 1996), p. 4.
17   Ibid.
18   This list uses the paradigm set out in Hawkes' study of ideology. It is clearly a pointer to intellectual movements, which were complex and multi-layered, rather than a comprehensive account of the development of European thought.
19   This comment refers to the interlinking nature of intellectual ideas and economic, social and political structures. The challenge to stable and hierarchical patterns of society connected with an aristocratic power centre, which took place in the Enlightenment, fed into political unrest.
20   Hawkes, *Ideology*, p. 42.
21   Ibid., p. 77.
22   Ibid., p. 93.
23   Ibid., p. 100.
24   Ibid., p. 102.
25   Ibid., p. 138.
26   Ibid., p. 122.
27   Ibid., p. 158.
28   G. West, *The Academy of the Poor* (Sheffield, Sheffield Academic Press, 1999), p. 9.
29   Ibid., p. 15.
30   Ibid., p. 32.
31   G. Steiner, *Grammars of Creativity* (London, Faber and Faber, 2001), for example Chapter II.
32   Ibid., p. 2.
33   Ibid., p. 3.
34   Ibid., p. 9.
35   Ibid., p. 97.
36   Ibid., p. 98.
37   Ibid., p. 104.
38   W. Brown, *Ecclesiastes* (Louisville, Ky., Westminster John Knox, 2000).
39   Ibid., p. 26.
40   Ibid., p. 9.
41   Ibid., preface.
42   Ibid., p. 13.
43   Ibid., p. 33.
44   Ibid., p. 12.
45   Ibid., p. 75.
46   Ibid., p. 51.
47   Ibid., p. 18.
48   Ibid., p. 21.
49   Ibid., p. 104.

50 H. Walton, 'Re-visioning the Subject in Literature and Theology', in H. Walton and A. Hass (eds) *Self/Same/Other* (Sheffield, Sheffield Academic Press, 2000), p. 12.

51 Ibid., p. 13.

52 H. Pyper, 'Listeners on the Stair. "The Child as Other in Walter de la Mare" ', in Walton and Hass, *Self/Same/Other*, p. 73.

53 Ibid., p. 72.

54 Ibid., p. 79.

55 F. Segovia, *Decolonising Biblical Studies* (Maryknoll, NY, Orbis, 2000), p. 59.

56 Ibid., p. 104.

57 Ibid., p. 95.

58 Ibid., p. 110.

59 Brown, *Ecclesiastes*, p. 11.

60 A. Milner, *Literature, Culture and Society* (London, University College Press, 1996), p. 131.

61 Ibid., p. 90.

PART III
CULTURAL EXEGESIS

Chapter 8

Ecclesiastes as Provider of Religio-cultural Boundaries

In the previous chapter attention was paid to W. Brown's commentary on Ecclesiastes. The point was made that this commentary is so framed that it enables a reader to incorporate Qohelet the sceptic into a positive framework of religious thought, within a Christian context. Qohelet the individualist is thus transformed into Qohelet the giver of advice for an assembly of Christian readers and teachers. This focus makes Qohelet into a voice for an intelligentsia, someone who speaks of the 'same' selfhood as twentieth-century readers. Thus Qohelet's autobiographical self provides a context for religio-cultural boundaries. The present chapter intends to explore this cultural reuse of Qohelet further. The religio-cultural boundaries in question are those of modern Western European culture from the nineteenth century to the second half of the twentieth century.

Interpreting the Self

The context for this discussion is the autobiographical self, an 'I' who speaks and tells a personal tale, who offers a mode for readers to explore their selfhood. As D. Bjorklund states, 'as human beings we are self-reflective creatures. We ponder not only our own qualities and traits but also the nature of selfhood – trying to make sense of what it means to be human.'[1] As part of this pondering, human beings dialogue on the concept of selfhood. Thus it is sensible to ask how they explain the world, using a language of selfhood, in an enterprise that is not purely individualistic, but accepts that individuals construe their world and their experiences not randomly but as influenced by their cultural and historical perspectives.[2] For Bjorklund, reflecting on selfhood is a practical exercise based on how people comprehend and describe the self. 'Studying how people use the concept of self in everyday life leads us to the question of cultural and historical variations in ways of understanding the self. Do other groups understand the self as we do? How have our (and their) constructions of the self changed over time?'[3]

Each autobiographer wishes both to detail his/her own story and to communicate with an audience of readers who have their own life experiences. Thus an autobiography is a work in the social domain and its narrator seeks to tell the story in a socially acceptable manner. In Chapter 2 of *Interpreting the Self* Bjorklund suggests that there are typical aspects in American autobiographies that make this social bridge. She refers to topics such as:

- educational background as a plea to be taken seriously
- sense of humour and the ability to recognize irony
- virtues such as love, compassion and, especially, modesty and honesty
- telling the tale of an interesting life.

It is possible to relate these qualities to Qohelet's autobiographical self, in certain ways. He does make a plea to be taken seriously because of a wisdom background. This plea is interwoven with the claim to royal status. This ploy provides a point of cultural contact for a reader from an elite group in a different culture. There is perhaps not much direct humour about Qohelet, but he is very aware of irony, of the paradox of living. It is this mixture of resistance to, and acceptance of, the concept of the meaningfulness of life that makes it possible for readers from a different cultural context to incorporate Qohelet into a positive religious perspective. As to virtues, Qohelet does not read as loving in individual relationships, but he does have claims to modesty and honesty. Bjorklund points out that one way of being modest is to be honest. An autobiographer simply states that s/he has had major events in his/her life, and by being honest lessens the possible accusation of boasting.[4] Qohelet can be placed in this category of narrator. His whole value as a personal voice turns on the fact that he has been exposed to all that life can offer. But this is not cause for superficial pleasure, a mood Qohelet himself defines as the way of fools in chapter 7: 6. 'For as the sound of thorns under the pot likewise the laughter of the fool and this also is *hebel*.' Rather it leads the self into sorrow and doubt and to the deeper aspects of meaning-as-existence. This combination makes Qohelet an interesting self, with a worthy tale to tell. Yet the telling of doubt leaves the reader with the task of location, of identifying the face of social doubt in his/her own cultural experiences. It is the interaction between the autobiographer's doubt and the location of that social uncertainty in the reader's experience that makes the story worth reading, but provides major challenges for commentators who have the job of re-expressing a 'Qoheletic self' within their own religio-cultural boundaries.

A necessary skill for producing a compelling account of human existence is that of holding together a variety of views and experiences in an over-arching, coherent perspective of the whole of a life. Autobiographers usually manage this by using a time frame, reviewing events from a later age, as does Qohelet himself. The effect of placing events in a coherent order is to make the life so described accessible to a number of readers. 'Telling a good story, making a good impression – these are the requirements of the social situation of writing an autobiography. The act of self-interpretation in an autobiography is a resourceful act of public self-interpretation. Not only have autobiographers learnt what it means to be a self, they also are well aware of the standards by which persons evaluate themselves, and they are positioning themselves in relation to their standards.'[5] In projecting from an original auto-biographer to the modern reader as commentator on Qohelet's experience the task is also one of looking back, this time from a later age altogether, piecing together a response to Qohelet's 'I' which puts the later age in continuity with the earlier one. This, also, is an act of public self-interpretation in which the commentator reads text as another 'I'. It is this event of interactive reading which is at the heart of cultural exegesis, and one example of the process is that of modern biblical criticism in Europe, with its historical methods.

The Historical-critical Context

Modern biblical criticism is marked by its search for the meaning of a text with regard to the text's historical origins. Nineteenth-century and early twentieth-century interpretations of Ecclesiastes, in European style, belong to the broad category of biblical studies that developed post-Enlightenment. At the centre of this is the historical approach to biblical exegesis. Texts were no longer read allegorically or typologically but were examined with regard to possible origins in an actual historical society, which for the Old Testament is that of ancient Israel.[6] The source of this exegetical style lies in the growth of empirical methods of enquiry in early modern Europe. As J. Hayes argues, 'the scientific revolution which peaked in the sixteenth and seventeenth centuries has probably been of more consequence to biblical studies and to theology as a whole, than any other single phenomenon'.[7] The method of exegesis which developed from this impact is described by Hayes as stressing that the Bible is a book like others. As such it can be subject to a literary criticism in which the search for authorship leads to full acknowledgement of the historical stages through which texts have passed, together with the likelihood of multi-authorship.[8]

R. Lowth is a key figure here. His interest was mainly in Graeco-Roman literature, but he applied the categories drawn from this to biblical literature, with a particular focus on poetry.[9] 'One of the major differences between Lowth's and most earlier approaches is that some portions of the Bible which had been previously regarded as rhetorical – especially, prophetic materials – were treated by him as poetic.'[10] A little later, Spinoza noted that the literary style of the New Testament epistles was argumentative as against the authoritative tone of other biblical books.[11] The combination of such comments, made from a literary perspective, with a focus on the historical development of separate biblical texts, broke apart the unity of the Christian Bible and encouraged attention to the human, historical contexts for the development of this literature. The Bible remained of value for European cultural identity, but not as a single work imparted through divine revelation.[12]

A further stage of the growth of historical method is found in the impact of Romanticism.[13] As European culture adjusted to intellectual empiricism and to the political aftermath of the French Revolution, new emphases came to the fore in the religious field, associated with the Romantic movement, itself characterized by a sense of loss and a longing for retrieval. S. Prickett argues that

> what had been lost was religion [in the sense of] a general and collective world picture in which there was no boundary between the sacred and the secular, in which supernatural or divine power was everywhere apprehended through type, symbol and sacrament – and through a language where such apprehension was implied and taken for granted.[14]

History took on a new meaning, recognizable to modern Europeans. Whereas past and present had been a continuous reality they now had separate identities. The past formed an earlier and independent social reality out of which the present emerged as a separate future. 'The movement from typological to narrative readings of the Bible was also a movement from a static to a dynamic worldview.'[15] The term 'revolution' no longer indicated a return to the past, by a turn of the wheel, but the radical shift to a new and different future.[16]

In Germany the acceptance of a new understanding of 'revolution' led not to political events, as illustrated by the French Revolution for example, but to intellectual shifts. 'As a result the metaphor of revolution in its new sense, implying a radical and dynamic transformation of ideas, quickly became a critical commonplace in German writing.'[17] And part of the new intellectual movement was to find a place for religion among these new cultural values.[18] The Christian Bible can be situated here as a model for subjective religion.[19] As a piece of art it has aesthetic value which touches on religious experience. The historical approach pointed to a multiplicity of authors; the addition of religious aesthetics offers modern readers paradigms drawn from the subjective experience of ancient Israelite authors.

One of the high points of biblical romanticism came in the work of Johann Herder. He enunciated this view of the aesthetic nature of the Old Testament, regarding the contents as Israel's experience of the divine.[20] His thought contained a union of the pantheistic and humanistic spirit of his time with romantic and intuitive insights. His work had a great influence on H. Gunkel and his elaboration of a historical-critical method. Under this Romantic impact the Bible was re-established as culturally valuable for modern Europe. 'From being a book of uncertain provenance, doubtful authority and dubious veracity', claims Prickett, 'the Bible had been re-appropriated ... as the source of cultural renewal, aesthetic value and literary inspiration.'[21]

Form Criticism

It is within this cultural framework that Gunkel produced his theories concerning research into literary forms. He wanted to acknowledge the social context of an historical reading of the Old Testament, not so much a naming of historical authors as a consideration of the social usage of the original literary styles. Gunkel thought that Hebrew literature tended towards typical styles and that identification of blocs of material could lead the reader to recognize the original literary forms and their role in the life of the ordinary people of a land.[22] Gunkel was at work in 1862–1932, in a Germany moving from an old aristocracy and separate states to a nation, united at first under its Kaiser, then threatened in post-First World War settlements, and seeking a renewal of social and political identity in the 1930s. In this setting Gunkel's methods reflect the growth of a new intelligentsia that had ousted the aristocratic elites of the past and thought of itself as linked to the people as a whole. Hence Gunkel's ideas were shaped by a philosophical shift away from the novelty, individualism and historicism of the nineteenth century and towards a renewed interest in community, the larger social world with its social structures and institutions.[23] This philosophical shift was accompanied by the rise of psychology and the social sciences.[24] Gunkel himself wanted to take biblical ideas to a wider public, and gave lectures within the university extension movement.[25] His circle had a commitment to social issues and general welfare as well as support for nationhood.[26]

In line with these concerns Gunkel developed an exegetical method which stressed that Old Testament texts were the product of the 'ordinary people' of past times. These texts now form part of a common cultural heritage for Europeans and can be examined via literary studies. Here Gunkel drew on comparative literature such as Germanics and Classics,[27] as well as that of the ancient Near East.[28] Out of these foundations he gradually worked towards a stress on the *sitz im leben*, or social occasion with which a literary piece is associated.[29] In relation to Genesis, for example, Gunkel argued that 'the usual situation ... which we have to imagine, is this: during an evening of leisure the family sits at the hearth'.[30] Gunkel's work was thus culturally suitable for a developing Germanic consciousness of cultural identity, and made biblical criticism and biblical studies of interest to this contemporary context. Under his students Gunkel's concern for the social nature of text development moved further towards a concern with social discourse. As Buss states, Gunkel's students 'moved the focus on particularity from the individual to the group ... giving little attention to larger, including international, cultural phenomena. This move paralleled what was happening in German society after World War I, reaching a climax in "National Socialism".'[31]

Gunkel's work made a lasting contribution to biblical studies even though it was not well received in the academic theological schools of his own time.[32] In E. Kraeling's revision of Bewer's *The Literature of the Old Testament*, for example, echoes of Gunkel's language resound. 'The common folk with their songs and stories, the poets and the prophets, the historians, lawgivers and sages, all stand before us as we follow in our imagination the various phases of the great development [of Old Testament literature].'[33]

The Wisdom Tradition

The aspect of form criticism which applies more especially to Ecclesiastes is
the literary genre labelled by modern scholars, the wisdom tradition. This
particular genre is one among the broader literary categories of form criticism.
Under the term *hōkmâ* are brought together three books of the Hebrew
scriptures, smaller literary forms such as the proverb, riddle, fable and
discourse, and social contexts of life in the family and at the royal court.[34] Key
to this view on wisdom style is the concept of the sages, the *hakamim*, whose
setting is that of the royal court and through whose work an ancient oral form
of the people was preserved and institutionalized.[35] To quote Bewer/Kraeling
again, 'neither rising to the lofty conceptions of the greatest prophets nor
partaking of their glorious enthusiasm, they yet kept the true balance between
form and spirit in an age of growing legalism by their insistence on wisdom
as the true norm/guide of life'.[36] Although this view endorses the significance
of wisdom genres for the common identity of a nation, a note of doubt
creeps in, since wisdom books do not deal with the revelation of Israel's God
in Israel's history. Bewer/Kraeling reflect on the sages that 'as pronounced
individualists they addressed themselves to individuals, not to the nation'.[37]

Here arises the recurring issue of the individuality of Qohelet's personal
voice. Individuality is a problem with regard to all wisdom texts, but a much
worse one in connection with Ecclesiastes than with Proverbs. Form criticism
tends to highlight the importance of biblical literature for a nation, so how can
this gap be bridged? Two points can be utilized, for Qohelet. The first is the
Solomonic guise. 'The conviction that Solomon is the author of the book and
that the saintly and wise king wrote only words fit for edification has much to
do in overcoming the objections to its canonisation', say Bewer/Kraeling.[38]
Thus Qohelet is taken over by the role of a king whose function is to pull a
nation together and provide a central leadership – a theme not unconnected
with German Nationalism. Second, within the historical-critical framework of
levels of authorship, it can be argued that the work had been edited towards a
positive social discourse. A disciple had inserted wise additions of proverbs
and maxims and thus strengthened the reliability of this book of wisdom.[39]
Here commences a form of reading a 'Qoheletic self', which can be seen at
work many other times, the harmonization of Qohelet's awkward angles into
a single, coherent text. At its simplest level this involves the reading of the
book as a whole by one of its two voices.[40] More complex is the attribution of
the second voice to a later editor who has 'harmonized' Ecclesiastes with the
traditional wisdom tradition of the day.

Wisdom Tradition and Wisdom Schools

The basis of a form-critical approach to Ecclesiastes, then, is the formation of
a holistic interpretation in which this book is viewed as part of a 'typical type'

of wisdom teaching. This in turn is viewed as set in national history, derived from 'the people' but re-expressed through an intelligentsia, as part of national vision. This section of the Old Testament is slightly tangential to the Pentateuch and the Prophets, when the whole collection is interpreted canonically, because it is less focused on Israel's land and patron deity and more open to cosmopolitan and international literary styles. But it can still be accommodated to these themes of deity, people and land.

From this broad picture specific strands of scholarly evaluation emerged – notably the promulgation of *a* wisdom tradition and *schools* of wisdom. These proposals established a total social setting centred on the wise man or scribe. This perspective is a cultural artefact created by modern European thought using the historical-critical method. Gunkel's stress on the particular and the typical in the pattern of literary forms opens the way for considering certain life settings 'typically' suitable for individual literary styles. Hence the proverb finds its original home in the family and the village community. Later in time proverbs were gathered together by the scribal elite to produce an organized approach to life as a whole. At this point modern scholars can fairly discuss the theology of the wisdom tradition, as with L. Perdue's *Wisdom and Creation*.[41] Here Perdue argues both for the value of searching for the one central theological theme of the wisdom texts and for the identity of that theme as located in nature and creation imagery.

A further aspect of the argument for the existence of a wisdom tradition with its own social base involves putting the three Hebrew wisdom books into a linear time frame. Thus Proverbs is the normative form of the tradition, the product of the intellectual elite of the kingdom of Israel, against which Job and Ecclesiastes can be measured. If the encouraging signs of boundaries and structures in universal order, enunciated by Proverbs, supports the elite power base, the pessimism of Ecclesiastes must be viewed as antagonistic to that elite viewpoint. For J. Crenshaw using form-critical tools entails the view that Ecclesiastes belongs to a new social setting, that of a sage who turns away from his establishment roots to teach ordinary people. 'The epilogist claims that Qohelet branched out beyond the school to include the common folk in his assembly of hearers.'[42] The social doubt in Qohelet's autobiography stems from his abandonment of his own social certainty and his movement across class boundaries, from aristocracy to people.[43] Thus Qohelet is accommodated in a holistic approach to the wisdom tradition by locating the autobiographer in one particular stage of its development and in one particular social setting. It is the work of a later stage in this tradition and is in debate with the earlier normative stance of wisdom. Thus Crenshaw both applies and adapts Gunkel's form criticism.

Qohelet stands in line with traditional wisdom forms, but equally stands apart from his own cultural nexus. It can be argued from the content of Ecclesiastes that Qohelet radically dissociates himself from the traditional values of his society. But that would cut him off totally from a part in Israelite traditions as these are gathered in the canon of Hebrew scriptures.[44] The inclusion of Ecclesiastes in the Hebrew canon indicates that Qohelet is not so cut off, largely because the Epilogue provides a means of harmonizing him with national religious beliefs. In this interpretation Qohelet can never be really 'other', standing outside the normal wisdom pattern. He can be a 'self' posing as an 'other' but in the end his personal voice must be accommodated with the return to the 'sameness' of a common religious self identity. The tension evidenced in the early history of the reception of this text, in Rabbinic circles, has a continued impact in modern form-critical scholarship, more especially in scholars whose commentaries combine a historical approach with a teaching role in Christian communities. Modern historical biblical criticism allows European readers to align Qohelet with a modern social discourse which moves authority from aristocracy to democratic elites while preserving the relevance of the biblical text for Christian culture in Europe.

Historical criticism pursues significant cultural goals. The Bible of the European past was a single construct which illustrated timeless divine truths. Such a Bible ceased to be valuable as the society with which it was linked came to an end. But Europe remained culturally connected to Christianity and historical criticism proved to be fruitful in re-establishing the relevance of biblical material. A new orthodoxy of intellectual Christianity was produced through the link between Christian thinkers, communities and the rise of universities; in this worldview historical criticism with its empirical origins was adopted as itself revelatory of the Christian God. The works of Herder, Schleiermacher, Gunkel and others were bridgeheads here, adapting the historical via the romantic and intuitive. In later form criticism the Bible as a historical record of religious truth became the focus for belief, open to all literate Christians, but more especially the preserve of academic exegesis carried out by male authority figures. Commentaries on Ecclesiastes illustrate this development and the struggle to make Qohelet a meaningful self for modern Europe.

Christian Commentaries on Ecclesiastes in the Twentieth Century

The essence of such a 'meaningful Qohelet' is that his voice must be heard as an integral part of an Old Testament viewed as a sound theological source for Christian perspectives. Several permutations of this approach will be examined in connection with twentieth-century commentaries. R. Gordis, like all commentators on Ecclesiastes, begins from the apparent unease within the work itself. That is, he assumes a harmony or coherence of ideas to be the norm and so finds Qohelet's personal voice enigmatic but fascinating. 'Commentators were confused by the startling contradictions in which the book abounded, the cool skepticism of one passage, followed by apparently unimpeachable orthodox sentiments in the next.'[45] Gordis situates this paradoxical text within a framework of Hebrew thought. Tracing a form-critical exegetical line he explores the life setting of the Hebrew scriptures within a monarchical society. He notes that both Torah and Prophecy, which he locates in First Temple times, place the nation at the centre of their religious viewpoint – another trace of form-critical emphasis, as noted above.[46]

By contrast, wisdom is concerned with the individual, though still in a communal context. Wisdom goes with song and songs belong with the life of the people. 'Harvest and vintage, the royal coronation and the conqueror's return, courtship and marriage, were all accompanied by song and dance.'[47] But, by the time of the three biblical wisdom books, this context had passed. 'What remained of Wisdom is its literary incarnation ... To convey truths, Wisdom created an educational method and its own literature, which is generally couched in the *mashal*.'[48] Here Gordis follows a typical form-critical approach to wisdom texts, moving their settings from village and tribe to nation and professional sages. He sees the immediate social context for Ecclesiastes in the Hellenistic world, which he views as placing more value on the individual than the group.[49] 'Prosperity and freedom for a tiny weak people were not likely to be achieved in a world of mighty empires. All that remained was for each human being to strive to attain his personal happiness.'[50]

Gordis specifically links this with 'perennially modern and recurrent questions' about social discourse, bridging the gap between an ancient autobiographer and a twentieth-century European reader, endorsing a work ethic as the basis for personal meaning. A self is a sober, hardworking individual who is loyal to social responsibility. As for the specifically religious dimension, Gordis regards the crisis for Qohelet as the uncertainty of the nature of God. It is interesting that Gordis here specifically aligns Qohelet with Spinoza, who is regarded as one of the founders of the historical investigation of biblical literature, as noted earlier in this chapter.[51] Gordis sums up Qohelet's personal voice as an 'I' who urges the innate desire of human beings for happiness. 'It thus becomes clear that God's fundamental purpose for mankind is the furtherance of man's pleasure.'[52] For Gordis the real form-critical setting of Qohelet's 'I' is that of philosophical, reflective speech utterance, a search for meaning in the world arena. Qohelet, like Spinoza, is an honest seeker after truth and his notebook of personal jottings was not intended for public consumption as a mainline religious work.[53] The autobiographical self thus becomes that of a modern philosopher, a self-identity accessible to a 1960s audience.

Tremper Longman III also takes up a form-critical stance and argues that Ecclesiastes provides a 'framed autobiography' as its dominant form, a style evidenced by fifteen Akkadian texts.[54] Qohelet's autobiography, unlike those of the Akkadian texts, moves not to the goal of a display of great acts, but to a counterpoint to such displays. Longman regards this emphasis as bringing the main section of the book into shadow, as 'lost to despair'. 'Reading Qohelet's statements about God in context leads me to side with those scholars who characterize Qohelet's God as distant, occasionally indifferent, and sometimes cruel.'[55] For Longman, then, nearly all of Ecclesiastes is meaningless for Christian instruction. The text as a whole is salvaged by the few verses of the epilogue which express the real meaning, containing 'simple instruction'.[56] Once this is owned then a reader can return to the rest of the book and gain deeper insights for faith. Qohelet experiences the despair of a world without God while remaining a believer in divine existence.[57] This provides a parallel for Christ and his Cross, for Christians facing death as a physical truth of human existence. And such teaching is for the whole assembly, unlike the modern individual autobiography, says Longman.[58] It is the voice of the community, couched in the epilogist, which provides access to this communal 'I', who knows despair but passes beyond death to meaning. Longman is much more focused on Christian self-identity than is Gordis and struggles much more with individualism than does Gordis who, by stressing civic duty and philosophical stance, unites a secular cultural setting with traditional Christianity more broadly.

W. Brown, in *Character in Crisis*, also picks up on the ancient Near Eastern genre of a king's grand achievements and sees Qohelet's words as 'counter-speech' in this genre. This very move Brown considers to be Qohelet's communal voice. 'By stepping out of the character that traditional wisdom forged, Qohelet is able to cast question on the profile of traditional character and its formation through an unquestioning assimilation of tradition.'[59] Yet this step outside is in fact an advance for 'insiders' because here Qohelet constructs a new character through 'introspective reporting'. His 'I' urges all 'I's, as individual personal voices, to make their reflections on the moral coherence of their life and world. Ultimately, Qohelet is a preacher of joy since he urges readers not to dwell on what cannot be achieved but, by the discipline of engagement with what is, 'to keep on working, keep toiling under the sun, keep crying out for justice and right relationships'.[60] Unlike Longman's message, but like Gordis, Brown moves to the sphere of civic society and produces a religious model which supports and endorses a training for social engagement among society members.

L. Perdue notes that scholars normally place Qohelet in two different form categories – sayings and first person narratives.[61] He traces a first person profile through a number of ancient Near Eastern styles, such as righteous sufferer poems,[62] Egyptian funerary sayings,[63] grave biographies[64] and royal testament or instructions.[65] Perdue then moves on to consider the significance of such first person narratives. He notes that they represent an act of self-justification, evidence that there is something redeeming in the storyteller's life, whose meaning can be declared. The aim is to find the good in life through critical reflection on reality, and then to bring that reflection to others as teaching that life can be positive. Qohelet is situated within this framework. In Ecclesiastes there are two boundaries to human existence, the cosmos and the tomb; the two constants of creation for Qohelet's speech are cosmology and human nature. 'Philosophically conceived, human history is both shaped and limited by creation and death.'[66]

This framework contains a serious religious problem, since there is no real dialogue possible with God. Cosmos and anthropology are separate realities, as in Gordis' thought.[67] None the less the hallmark of Qohelet's self-knowledge is 'carpe diem'.[68] This marker is itself *hebel*, understood by Perdue as meaning transient, but it represents the good in human experience.[69] Ultimately, God rules over the cosmos in utter secrecy and it is a futile waste of human resources to try to bridge the gap between human and divine understanding. What is lost in such an attempt is the only gain humans have, joy in what *is* possible. And even that gain is a passing asset which cannot be retained for further exploitation. Perdue goes in an opposite direction to Brown by viewing the positive in Qohelet's personal voice as specifically individual, while at the same time relating it to anthropology more generally. This is a religious interpretation in a broader sense of an aesthetic open to all readers interested in a religious book, whether they 'practise' within a particular religion or not.

In these commentaries a common basis is the form-critical approach to text. The issue is how to situate the ambiguity of Qohelet's 'I' with regard to national literature and the norm of establishment wisdom tradition. The problem of a clash between norm and Qohelet's self is undeniable. It can be explained as one part of a wider genre, that of wisdom itself or that of royal self descriptions, but it still tends to deconstruct a positive union of life and belief, of national and religious identity. Longman manages to turn disharmony around only in the last few verses of the book of Ecclesiastes, and then only through an editorial epilogue, the voice of a community spokesperson who has found Qohelet's sayings useful. Gordis and Brown focus more on civic duty and interpret 'carpe diem' as sober, hardworking attitudes to life's ambiguity. This endorses the status quo of Christian social responsibility. Gordis has less of a problem in admitting theistic doubt than Longman, as also Perdue. Gordis, Brown and Perdue provide a basis for a secularized Qohelet, a figure who offers a modern reader an aesthetic paradigm that has echoes of a Christian cultural past. All the commentaries, however, are interested in 'sameness', in Qohelet as another self whose strangeness yields to sameness. A key focus in this approach is harmonization.

Harmony and Selfhood

The topic of harmony was referred to earlier, and defined as a special kind of cultural harmony, that of a 'Christian' commentator using a form-critical perspective on text. The effect of this harmonization is to stress the wholeness of a literary work, as part of finding a positive religious message in it. M. Fox, returning to a commentary on Ecclesiastes after a gap of years,[70] remarks on the similarity of approaches among previous commentators. They all agree on the tension within the text, but 'the traditional approach is harmonisation, the reconciling of apparently contradictory statements by showing that they use the same words differently or deal with different matters.'[71]

> The context within which these interpreters are reading these verses is not the immediate literary unit or even the book of Qohelet as a whole, but rather their own system of religious axioms. They know in advance what Qohelet-Solomon's meaning *must* be. The grand system washes over Qohelet and effaces much of his individuality.[72]

Fox himself has come to believe that the dissonances within Qohelet's speech should be allowed to stand for what they are, for 'the contradictions may reside in the world itself'.[73] But this viewpoint moves to selfhood as allowing for 'otherness', a topic to be addressed in the next chapter.

What then does the historical-critical method and form criticism provide by way of cultural exegesis? This approach contributes to a religious dialogue in which historical origins shape later meaning and a message is authenticated by the 'pure' forms of the past.[74] In its Enlightenment setting the application of historical study to the Bible 'relativised the past in such a way as to weaken its significance for the present', as Buss states.[75] This was, at that time, a breaking down of older religio-cultural boundaries. 'This negative function played a significant role in liberating human society and culture from external authority and unquestioned tradition.'[76] Partly through Romanticism and its aesthetic spin-offs, however, the historical method, linked with the social sciences and with literary history, became itself the founder of religio-cultural boundaries for a further stage of 'Christian' European thought.

This development met the need to create a basis for the democratization of European society, as well as the need to create national identities in many parts of nineteenth- and twentieth-century Europe, where new regional units were established based on people, territory and a shared language and literature. Within this wide cultural frame the historical method allowed Christian educators and preachers, in Christian assemblies, to reuse biblical texts. As has been shown, even an awkward customer such as Qohelet could be brought back into a communal fold, and a 'Qoheletic self' could be presented as a model for citizenship alongside those paradigms drawn from an Abraham or a Moses – even if as a distant and relatively lesser relation of these national heroes. In this extension of the 'Qoheletic self' the modern commentary uses the personal tale of an ancient figure as a means by which European culture can explore its own selfhood. As noted by Bjorklund, an autobiography is a work in the social domain.

Notes

1   D. Bjorklund, *Interpreting the Self* (Chicago, University of Chicago Press, 1998), p. 1.
2   Ibid., p. 3.
3   Ibid., p. 5.
4   Ibid., p. 29.
5   Ibid., p. 42.
6   This comment relates to the history of interpretation of Scriptures in Europe. Before the late seventeenth century the approach to reading was largely allegorical and typological, focusing on the static, single content of material viewed as divinely inspired and unconnected with cultural settings. H. De Lubac's work offers a thorough exploration of the systems of reading contained by this perspective. H. De Lubac, *Medieval Exegesis*, trans.M. Sebanc (Edinburgh, T. and T. Clark, 1998), vol. 1.
7   J. Hayes, *An Introduction to Old Testament Study* (London, SCM Press, 1979), p. 104.
8   Ibid., p. 106.
9   M. Buss, *Biblical Form Criticism in its Context* (Sheffield, Sheffield Academic Press, 1999), p. 111.
10   Ibid.
11   Ibid., p. 117.
12   S. Prickett, *Origins of Narrative* (Cambridge, Cambridge University Press, 1996), p. 114.
13   It is impossible to pinpoint a whole movement in a few short comments, but what is referred to here is an intellectual and cultural movement that stressed the subjective and aesthetic in human affairs. See, for instance, A. Day, *Romanticism* (London, Routledge, 1996).
14   Prickett, *Origins of Narrative*, p. 153.
15   Ibid., p. 155.
16   Ibid., p. 164.
17   Ibid., p. 181.
18   Ibid., p. 182.
19   Ibid., p. 183.
20   A. Suelzer and J. Kselman, 'Modern Old Testament Criticism', in R. Brown, J. Fitzmyer and R. Murphy (eds) *The New Jerome Biblical Commentary* (London, Chapman, 1990).
21   Prickett, *Origins of Narrative*, p. 221.
22   Suelzer and Kselman, 'Modern Old Testament Criticism', pp. 1122–3.
23   Hayes, *Introduction to Old Testament*, p. 125.
24   Ibid., p. 124.
25   Buss, *Biblical Form Criticism*, p. 223.
26   Ibid., pp. 224–5.
27   Ibid., pp. 229–30.
28   Ibid., p. 231.
29   Ibid., p. 235.
30   Ibid., p. 236.
31   Ibid., p. 287.
32   Ibid., p. 218.
33   J. Bewer, *The Literature of the Old Testament*, rev. E. Kraeling (New York, Columbia University Press, 1962), p. xi.
34   Much of the scholarship referred to here relies on the view that it is valid to talk of 'the wisdom tradition' as having a common identity composed of schools, scribes, secular context and religious outlook. This construct is part of the form-critical approach placing texts in community settings, but has the problems attached to this manner of modelling. That is, it makes a tight connection between oral traditions and written forms of literature which are insufficiently nuanced.
35   A further aspect of creating 'a wisdom tradition' is pinpointing the role of scribes as those

responsible for taking popular proverbial forms and translating them into instructive texts suitable for guiding new members of an administrative service. There is little known about scribes in the pre-exilic context, but rather more about post-exilic Judah. See D. Jamieson-Davies, *Scribes and Scholars in Monarchic Judah* (Sheffield, Sheffield Academic Press, 1991), who dates literacy in Judah to late monarchic times and thus doubts the existence of scribal schools before that date. See also P. Davies, *Scribes and Schools* (Louisville, Ky., Westminster John Knox, 1998), a study which explores the possibility of dating the growth of a canon of Hebrew Scriptures linked with the development of scribal schools.

36   Bewer, *Literature of the Old Testament*, p. 321.
37   Ibid.
38   Ibid., p. 253.
39   Ibid., p. 352.
40   M. Fox, *A Time to tear down and a Time to Build Up* (Grand Rapids, Mich., Eerdmans, 1999), p. 15.
41   L. Perdue, *Wisdom and Creation* (Nashville, Tenn., Abingdon, 1994), creates an over-arching biblical theology of the whole wisdom approach through the topics of nature and creation.
42   J. Crenshaw, *Ecclesiastes* (London, SCM Press, 1988), p. 34.
43   Ibid., p. 37.
44   Rabbinic sources show a clear lack of ease with the inclusion of Ecclesiastes in a canon of religious works. See, for instance, T. Longman, *The Book of Ecclesiastes* (Grand Rapids, Mich., Eerdmans, 1998), pp. 26–9.
45   R. Gordis, *Koheleth: The Man and his World* (New York, Schocken, 1968), pp. 3–4.
46   Gordis follows scholarship of his period in believing that the biblical material points to a growth of literacy with the rise of David and with Solomon's reign. In this model the first major writing of the Hebrew Scriptures would occur alongside the building of the first temple; this material underwent later revisions and the task of the historical critic is to sort out the levels of redaction. This is the intellectual foundation for the historical method developed in Europe in the modern period.
47   Gordis, *Koheleth*, p. 17.
48   Ibid., p. 18.
49   Ibid., p. 25.
50   Ibid.
51   Ibid., p. 89.
52   Ibid., p. 123.
53   Ibid., pp. 130–1.
54   Longman, *Ecclesiastes*, p. 18.
55   Ibid., p. 30.
56   Ibid., p. 40.
57   Ibid.
58   Ibid., pp. 17–18.
59   W. Brown, *Character in Crisis* (Grand Rapids, Mich., Eerdmans, 1996), p. 148.
60   Ibid., p. 150.
61   Perdue, *Wisdom and Creation*, p. 194.
62   Ibid., p. 195.
63   Ibid., p. 197.
64   Ibid., pp. 198f.
65   Ibid., p. 202.
66   Ibid., p. 205.
67   Ibid., p. 227.
68   Ibid., p. 237.
69   Ibid.
70   Fox, *Time to tear down*, preface.

71 Ibid., p. 15.
72 Ibid.
73 Ibid., p. 26.
74 Gunkel's system can be criticized for its suggestion that a tight connection between life setting, content and linguistic form existed in oral life. Oral forms were less accommodating to a 'pure' construct than the paradigm allows for. See, for instance, Buss, *Biblical Form Criticism*, pp. 259–62.
75 Buss, *Biblical Form Criticism*, p. 32.
76 Ibid.

Chapter 9

Ecclesiastes and the Critique of Religious Values

It has already been shown that fitting the 'I' of Qohelet into a positive religious framework is a hard task. This is partly due to that individualistic tone commentators have perceived in the wisdom tradition as a whole,[1] and partly to the particularly individualistic mode of Ecclesiastes as a form of autobiography. Qohelet's 'I' fits more easily into an interpretation of his autobiographical self as critic, even as judge, of religious boundaries and values. Whereas the historical-critical approach associated selfhood with sameness, postmodern European explorations of meaning more easily align with the individualism of Qohelet, since they believe dissonance to be normal, and understand selfhood through otherness or alterity.

The modern roots of individualism as a mode of self-depiction lie in the intellectual movements which arose from the Enlightenment. Romanticism in England, for example, encouraged a shift from the outer self, engaged in active social discourse, to the interior self, a selfhood that is the possession of a single person. This was, in some ways, an attempt to regain a dynamic view of the human person, understood as in opposition to the 'classical self', a selfhood defined as a mechanistic copying of the past, according to Day.[2] Modern literary commentators such as Abrams have, according to Day, emphasized the dynamic aspects of Romanticism, arguing for the potential of Romantic poetry to strengthen the sense of individual freedom in the face of totalizing political forces.[3] Abrams focuses on Wordsworth's shift from earlier political, revolutionary hopes to the interiorization of such aspirations. The aesthetic becomes itself creative of selfhood in a positive way.[4] 'The idea that Romanticism involved, above all else, an emphasis on the inner processes of the individual mind is an idea that was treated, in different ways, by a large number of commentators on Romanticism in the three decades or so following the Second World war.'[5]

Within this appreciation of Romanticism literary critics such as Abrams constructed a literary/aesthetic self unitive of inner and outer dimensions. Coleridge, for instance, was viewed as stating that Nature (the outer) is Thought (the inner) and Thought is Nature. This model of selfhood is constructed of two aspects in such a way that the inner predominates. Its effect is to stabilize the human inner self via nature's eternal existence. 'The temptation exists, then, for the self to borrow, so to speak, the temporal stability that it lacks from nature.'[6] Selfhood, in this context, relates to the focusing of exterior, natural elements through the subjective individual. It is not so much human society but the cosmic context of human existence that acts as an aesthetic influence on human self-understanding. Thus a path is opened up for the rise of the individual subject as against the communal self.

But this paradigm of selfhood is not ultimately a stable one. The individual subject is not a self-regulating unit. Later critics have dismantled the Romantic approach to the self. P. de Man, for instance, considers that such an aesthetic self is founded on language. To exist a self has to reveal the inner boundaries of the subjective existence. As a literary self such as Wordsworth describes his inner feelings and derives from them a concept of aesthetic selfhood he is using language as the only possible vehicle of creating that self. 'No self escapes temporality. Romanticism's claims to have found through symbolic language a means of uniting the subject, the self, in all its temporality, with a larger, often transcendental object were a delusion', states Day.[7]

At issue in these shifting models of selfhood are two facets of the operation of the self, the sensible and the intellectual. The Romantic approach, referred to above, collapses the two into a unity in which the intellectual gives voice to the sensible. De Man, however, moves beyond the sensible/intellectual divide and, by focusing on language as a self's mode of operation, deconstructs the paradigm. The instability of language takes the place of sense and intellect. The effect of the succession of models, here, is further to move selfhood into subjective and individualistic modes. It is in the very words of an autobiographer that selfhood lies, but a human speaker does not use words consistently and words are, themselves, capable of many meanings. It is likely that an 'I' cannot hold together in unity an account of his/her past and present. All that can be done is to describe how the 'I' engages with the present moment.

Qohelet and Existentialism

One philosophical perspective which has emerged from a shift towards an individualistic emphasis is existentialism. R. Gordis comments on this modern philosophical trend with regard to Ecclesiastes and Qohelet's autobiographical voice. 'From the varying formulations of existentialism extant, its essential features may be set forth as the distrust of reason and the placing of modern existence at the center of its world view ... Basically its impact derives from its preoccupation with failure, dread and death.'[8] Gordis views this approach to meaning as one with the chaos and brutality of the first half of the twentieth century in Europe. In the face of such grave disasters as two world wars all fixed systems of thought can be found meaningless. 'Existentialism offers a basis for abandoning all abstract theory, which seems to have been weighed in the scales of experience and found tragically wanting.'[9] Thus the experience of fifty years of collapse of social relations between European nations has produced a distrust of rationalism and an acknowledgement of the temporary nature of definitions of selfhood.

> As existentialism has gained in influence, a natural tendency has arisen to seek its forerunners. The great works of unconventional Biblical Wisdom, like Job and Qohelet, which find it impossible to accept on faith the teaching of traditional religion concerning God and man, express a position that seems closely akin to that of existentialism.[10]

Once again a mode of biblical interpretation is found which allows contemporary readers to situate ancient literary artefacts in their own world of social discourse. Gordis accepts that current treatments of Ecclesiastes suggest that this work concurs with the existentialists in viewing the world as absurd and incomprehensible.[11] However, Gordis finds a basic difference between the biblical book of Ecclesiastes and modern philosophies of existence. He argues that Qohelet does not have, ultimately, a meaningless approach to life, for he was a Hebrew and could not be an atheist. 'Koheleth does not doubt for a moment that there is such a purpose [for the existence of this world] known to God, though unknown to man.'[12] The biblical writers share much with modern subjectivist thought in that they cannot accept easy answers produced by conventional religion. Yet they also maintain the truth of religious values. 'In a moment of bitterness or frustration Koheleth may say, "Therefore I hate life" ... but it is not his dominant mood, which is an affirmation of life.'[13] For Gordis, Qohelet's voice is that of a third way, not that of superficial affirmation as offered by preachers, nor the total negations of life and meaning provided by modern existentialists.

Here Gordis places Ecclesiastes in the category of criticism of religious thought and suggests that it is a literary expression of an 'I' who pushes against accepted religious boundaries. But he falls back in the face of negation. Though Qohelet discusses negative theology and the primacy of death as creator of existential boundaries, for Gordis he does not make this a bottom line to meaning itself. Gordis allows Qohelet to speak usefully to a mid-twentieth-century audience, but in such a way that traditional Christian frameworks are still endorsed. Ultimately, life, meaning and a recognizable deity are linked together with the bond of a purpose, a goal to which all life is moving. This interpretive stance allows Ecclesiastes to move into the field of 'otherness'. It produces a surplus of meaning which is not exhausted by being enclosed in traditional religious frames. But, at the same time, that otherness is then rejected, as the voice of Qohelet's self is shown to fit, none the less, into the sameness of traditional religion. Existentialism can be viewed as a bridge to a more advanced form of subjective philosophy, in the postmodern writings of Michel Foucault and Jacques Derrida.

Michel Foucault

Michel Foucault has developed further the philosophical exploration of boundary making and modelling. In a post-Enlightenment setting 'history' could become a tool for explaining coherences between past events, the extreme of which approach is to create pre-existent models of cause and effect into which actual events can be placed. Foucault offers a critique of such modes of action, 'that are challenged by the new history when it speaks of series, divisions, limits, differences of level, shifts, chronological specificities, particular forms of rehandling, possible types of relation.'[14] An exploration of past events does not bring about a sense of coherence and closure.

> Instead of finding reassurances in ... return and final confirmation, instead of completing the blessed circle that announces, after innumerable stratagems and as many nights, that all is saved, one is forced to advance beyond familiar territory, far from certainties to which one is accustomed, towards an as yet uncharted and unforeseeable conclusion.[15]

Foucault is led towards an argument against the existence of coherent bodies of discourse. It is always significant to ask of any statement, 'Who is speaking?', 'From what reading site?', 'What are the varied positions of the subject who speaks with regard to the objects of speech?'[16] Nor can a single statement be validly taken as the basis of objective discourse. 'We must not reduce the subject of the statement to the first person grammatical elements that are present within the sentence.'[17] Whereas George Steiner argued for the Word which lies behind all words, Foucault argues that no such Word exists.[18] There are only words, and words themselves shift content and value depending on who is using them, where and with regard to what. The nature of words is thus summed up as 'otherness'. Statements, including those concerning 'I', have coherence at the level of statements but have no necessary underlying coherence at grammatical, logical or psychological levels. All the statements of Qohelet belong together as statements by an individual voice, but they do not thereby have any necessary coherence, nor should any be sought, in logical or psychological aspects of individual mind or person.

Jacques Derrida

A further extension of this mode of treating words can be found in the work of Jacques Derrida. Whereas Foucault points out the variety of possibilities concerning words and discourse, Derrida stresses the inherent otherness at the heart of self-expression. Derrida argues for the priority of an interrogative stance to written words. Any apparently totally expressed and closed body of thought needs to be shaken so that it trembles and the extra meaning which is outside that closed expression can be found. It is this surplus of meaning, the alterity of writing, which alone reveals that which is. 'The historicity proper to philosophy is located and constituted in the transition, the dialogue between hyperbole and the finite structure, between that which exceeds the totality and the closed totality.'[19] This view leads Derrida to look for the 'difference', the division between what is articulated in text and that which constitutes it from outside. This is the foundation of meaning as expressed in structure. 'The attempt to write the history of the decision, division, difference runs the risk of construing the division as an event or a structure subsequent to the unity of an original presence, thereby confirming metaphysics in its fundamental operation.'[20] But, Derrida argues, it is the division which is prior to meaning-as-coherence.

The other is at the heart of this philosophical argument. It is not an object, but a subject. 'I could not possibly speak of the Other ... in the accusative. I can only, I *must* only speak to the other ... in the vocative.'[21] Here otherness is fundamentally a part of the identity of a self. It is through the negation of wholeness and the abandoning of sameness that a self comes nearer to meaning. Derrida addresses this alterity as negation of existence when he reflects that 'infinite alterity as death cannot be reconciled with infinite alterity as positivity and presence (God). Metaphysical transcendence cannot be at once transcendence towards the other as Death and transcendence towards the other as God. Unless God means Death.'[22] This thought can well be applied to Qohelet's own reflective voice. For human selves can think about life and eternity, says Qohelet in Ecclesiastes 3, but God as the provider of order offers death as the root of meaning.

Negative Theology

These explorations of contemporary thought feature meaning as the product of lack of a single coherent discourse and of the otherness of inscription. There is on offer here a theology which is negative in tone. It is possible to examine how Derrida's ideas have been picked up by theologians, especially how biblical commentators are beginning to use his paradigms as tools of biblical exegesis. K. Hart picks up Derrida's focus on negation. 'Death underwrites any text, any sign, any name. The proper name necessarily presupposes the bearer's death in order to function.'[23] Transferred to religious dialogue this leads away from a positive theology, which seeks to define what is, through identification in sameness, and towards a negative theology, which broods rather on the boundaries of meaning and on what is left out when sameness is the dominant encoder. 'As the negative theology longs for the God beyond Being, that is, who is beyond all philosophical determinations of Being, so the literary theorist searches for a literature and critical vocabulary that escape or thwart philosophical categories.'[24] The re-application of negative theory from philosophy to biblical commentary leads the commentator to pass beyond the position set up by Gordis, to accept as central to religious meaning that which is absurd and incoherent. It is through putting such marginal aspects in the centre of the gaze that a reader can come to a fuller interpretation of the 'Qoheletic self'.

M. Fox picks up the relevance of the concept of the absurd in the thought of Qohelet and in that of Albert Camus.[25] He does not wish to claim that these two writers are the 'same', but that there are echoes of a 'Qoheletic self' in the modern text. Fox supposes that this may be because Qohelet and Camus are responding to parallel social experiences, the one to social changes in Hellenistic Judaea and the other to changes in early twentieth-century Europe.[26] For Fox 'the affinity between Qohelet and Camus resides above all in their sensitivity to the absurd'.[27] Both writers desire to strip away illusion and to face the negativity of life experience. 'They are aligned also in their sense of the world's opaqueness, in their exaltation of the value of lucidity, and in the *zest* with which they invoke the power of unaided reason to undermine its own foundations – true instances of deconstruction long before the notion was invented.'[28] But having a vision of the 'absurd', seeing life as 'other', does not mean having no positive approach to that reality.

> Qohelet, like Camus, judges the world absurd and unfair by measuring it against a strict standard of values and rationality. This incongruity, more severe than any of the inconsistencies the commentators have focused on, dominates Qohelet's thought. This too should not be smoothed over in art or life ... because it is faithful to a disparity perceived in reality.[29]

By embracing the absurd as a source of meaning Qohelet 'seeks to recover meanings, values, and truths, to discern a Way of Life through the murky wasteland. So does Camus.'[30] Although Fox also, like Gordis, acknowledges that Qohelet is not an atheist, he has moved from viewing absurdity as an ultimate threat to meaning to arguing that it is that very absurdity which creates meaning. It is by examining the counter-rational that a reasonable understanding of existence can be formed. Otherness is a building block of selfhood. Fox defines the absurd as 'a disjunction between two phenomena that are thought to be linked by a bond of harmony ... Thus the absurd is irrational, an affront to reason.'[31] Fox continues by noting that absurdity is not a phenomenon but a relational concept, carried in the tension between reality and a frame of expectations.[32] Here, using Derrida's chosen vocabulary, the excess, the 'difference' which provides meaning, can be situated.

T. Beal also picks up on the positive value of disjunctive order.[33] He establishes the term 'cosmopolis' as a fundamental tool, indicating the fixed points of human experience, the *cosmos* of natural boundaries and the social frame of the *polis*.[34] But biblical literature also has recourse to the topic of chaos, a chaos which intervenes in the ordered cosmopolis – to form chaosmopolis.[35] In the Old Testament order can only be understood via chaos. 'The biblical God is both chaos monster and monster tamer.'[36] Beal argues that this mixture of (dis)order applies to Qohelet's last words in Ecclesiastes 12. 'Here in Qohelet's last words the crisis in wisdom's vision of a moral universe reaches critical mass in a vision of chaosmopolis – an undoing of creation, a re-intrusion of Chaos from God upon the divinely ordered cosmopolis. Chaosmopolis now.'[37]

Beal connects Qohelet's sense of the disjunction of order with Hamlet's view of existence as time out of joint, then notes how Derrida reads Hamlet. It is the very experience of the disjunctive that 'opens him to the possibility of justice – as relation to the other – that is infinitely beyond the law, and also beyond simple vengeance or restitution'.[38] Beal reapplies Derrida's comment on Hamlet to Qohelet's last words, which are then interpreted not simply as pointing to death as the other which takes away all meaning, but rather as providing a path to new meaning.

> They envision the end as *edge*, threshold – an ending/beginning, between uncreation and creation, chaosmogony and cosmogony ... on the edge of a chaotic desert, the edge of a wasteland, which is the place of a possible new relation to the other, a new creation, a new justice – excessive, beyond law and order, unnameable.[39]

Here Beal has passed fully into the thought patterns of a selfhood based on alterity. Meaning can still be found, but it is the meaning of the absurd, the disjunctive.

Holocaust Theology

A very particular example of negative theology is to be found in responses to the Holocaust events of mid-twentieth-century Europe. In *Strange Fire*, the editor T. Linafelt argues, the reader encounters a sustained reflection on how the Holocaust should affect modes of Bible reading.[40] Here, a modern atrocity is read alongside literature which is complex and disturbing; the aspect of strangeness, of otherness is key to both contexts. M. George reads Ecclesiastes in this hermeneutical mode. He points to the gap between the existence of a general order in creation and the possibility that human beings can live by such an order or claim that it adds up to predictable principles of justice.[41] Qohelet's voice speaks of the other, that is death, as the basis for self identity and personal values. George argues that this is precisely a suitable theology for a post-Holocaust age, 'a book that is, perhaps, "credible in the presence of the burning children"'.[42] The question to be raised is, can a focus for meaning-as-existence remain workable in a post-Holocaust age?[43] George likens Qohelet to the child in the Hans Christian Anderson tale of the Emperor's New Clothes. Having examined what traditional wisdom has to offer with regard to meaning, Qohelet is a lone 'I' who is prepared to speak the truth of experience. 'Having made his investigation, Qohelet boldly announces not only that he doesn't get it, but that there is nothing to get!'[44]

Negation climaxes in death. 'The only thing Qohelet knows for sure *is* death, and it is because of this certainty that death becomes the foundation for Qohelet's ontology and epistemology.'[45] George notes that Derrida also focuses on death as the foundation of philosophy. Social responsibility needs persons who act, but technological society erodes real individuality, stressing roles rather than persons. 'Derrida, however, argues that the construction of a unique person *is* possible in a technological civilisation because of the reality of death ... Death is a singular act, something that can only be experienced by oneself, and thus death forms the basis of a unique self.'[46] George sees a parallel here between the thought of Derrida and that of Qohelet, which is projected further by a comparison with Levinas, whose work 'suggests one way in which the reality of the Other can be understood in the creation of a unique self'.[47] Individuals only exist in relation to the other, because only then can a self know that it is such, distinguished as a self by the presence of the other.[48] Only by taking on that encounter with the other, as a positive event, can ethical relationships be created.

Thus Qohelet's self offers images for a post-Holocaust age. A self can only exist 'by constructing one's identity through the recognition, acceptance and taking upon oneself [of] not only the reality of one's own death, but also the reality of the deaths of all those who died in the Holocaust'.[49] Once again, as evidenced in different ways in the work of Beal and Fox set out above, a move has been made to pass through the negation of alterity and to find, through that engagement, a new perspective on what it means to be a self. In this engagement the 'I' who reflects in contemporary Europe encounters the others of both past and present thinkers who engage with death as the ultimate source of self-identity. For Beal this entails reading cosmic order through the lens of cosmic chaos, a view which takes the theme of difference to its extreme. Fox meanwhile stays within the model of absurdity, where the counter-rational becomes the source of reasonable meaning. Both these interpretations remain in touch with the original Qohelet's search for meaning, while re-expressing ancient text through new philosophical paradigms. George adds to this the contextualization of negative theology within the social and political realities of modern Europe.

Negative Theology and Women

It was suggested in the previous two chapters that the Western European concept of a self has been focused via maleness, over many centuries. That dominant self-identity can make an easy connection with Qohelet, the male intellectual. Just as, more generally, recent European thought has focused on alterity as a source of meaning, so, in particular, it has been possible to consider 'woman' as the male's 'other'. M. Grey is one example of a theologian whose work is opening up the field of feminist/womanist interpretation. Grey reminds readers that the woman as other brings a particular emphasis on 'flesh' as part of human identity.[50]

A key aspect of woman's identity is embodiment, as flesh that is often wounded by male violence and in need of healing. This leads into a wider emphasis on the theological value of the term 'embodiment'. It can become a metaphor for God, who is thus connected to world, being 'embodied' in it.[51] Embodiment thus becomes 'a metaphor for the activity and agency of God in the world'.[52] This image can be linked with Ecclesiastes where all treatment of God and order is boundaried by life *taḥat ha ššemešš*.

Grey notes how feminist writers have moved from body to the erotic aspect of human action. This aspect of human identity is to be included with divine embodied activity, since it is basically *good* energy. A further step, still, is to move into the 'bad' aspects of woman's sexuality. J. Kristeva, for example, has worked on female identity as expressed through that which is taboo, that which is 'abject', a concept which links human identity with what is other in terms of shame and dirt.[53] In male/female relations the woman may be regarded as dirty because of her sexual availability, and may be treated as dirt, as in the case of Korean women who were forced into acting as 'comforters' for Japanese soldiers in the twentieth century.[54] This casts a shadow over the theme of hospitality and nurture, an area often associated with women.

In an attempt to retrieve this theme as a positive value for woman's identity as 'other' than man, it can be noted that God is traditionally connected with welcome and food in Christian theology. A famous example of this imagery is the Rublev icon of the Trinity as the other who meets with Abraham at Mamre, in Genesis 18.[55] The themes of body, of sexuality, of hospitality at the table in a house can readily be applied to Ecclesiastes, since Qohelet's 'I' frequently reflects on the value of bodily pleasure and on the gain of procreation, while also urging his narratee to eat and drink. Furthermore, there is the link between these domestic topics and the role of *hōkmâ*. Wisdom is constantly the goal of Qohelet's search for meaning in existence. He pursues her, but does not find her easy to come by or, indeed, always a pleasant companion. In feminist thought Sophia is a key mode of access for women to a voice in social discourse. It is a concept valued by Old Testament books, and it is feminine, most especially in the form of Lady Wisdom.[56] Moreover the Solomonic guise of Qohelet aids the link between Ecclesiastes and Sophia, since Solomon is represented as specifically praying for her in the Wisdom of Solomon.[57]

But here the perspective of negative theology begins to impact on the reading of text. These themes do not easily offer a positive move from 'I' to 'other' as constitutive of the self, because in chapter 7 there is a metaphor about woman as snare and trap, which provides a major block. The Hebrew of this passage is difficult to untangle but most commentators agree that, whatever it means, it uses a thoroughly pessimistic approach to self-identity as promoted through woman as other.[58] C. Fontaine points out that the sages in biblical wisdom books are generally misogynistic, especially Ben Sira.[59] The form of misogynism in Qohelet cannot ultimately be displaced as part of the 'Qoheletic self'. Woman is marginal in value, a potential cause of shame and bitterness.[60]

Fontaine points out the Christian afterlife of the 'Qoheletic self' in the use of the passage in the construction of social relations in medieval Europe. 'With this philosophical and social matrix of female inferiority Qohelet's words on Woman, read with the customary negative slant, were scarcely perceived to be out of place among the teachings of the learned doctors of the Church.'[61] The climax comes with the *Malleus Maleficarum*, a text probably produced under the impact of social disruption in late medieval Europe, and one that sought an answer to these social evils, finding it in the demonization of women as witches who practised counter-order magic.

> The theological methods of these exemplars of the privileged, preserved male sex are clear enough; the eternally valid biblical text which at all times must be true ... is freely used to give meanings to the passage which ... were held in check to some degree by the contrary contours of Qohelet's own text. Now, the Preacher's words delineate a collective character for women which ... should leave men frightened indeed.[62]

But, in the modern world, where the marginal is at the heart of the self, what can be said about Ecclesiastes? Fontaine suggests that Qohelet's search for *hōkmâ* could be linked to the focus on Sophia as an expression of woman. Qohelet greatly values wisdom as essential to his self. He seeks her constantly, but finds her evasive or, when discovered, hard to accept.[63] In this context the other, necessary to selfhood, remains ambiguous and mysterious to the end. It remains truly in excess, outside. For the voice of Qohelet is a male voice, with a male view. But is this voice woman-hating on all counts? Apart from chapter 7 there are few direct references to woman, but E. Christiansen points out how many times the term womb (*beten*) is used.[64] There is, for example, the reference to human existence as coming empty from the womb and returning empty to the womb/grave. Then there is the example of a man and his one hundred sons. He has had great gain from the womb, but it brings him no *yitrôn*, for his sons abandon him at his death. Christiansen comes to regard Qohelet's womb imagery as part of his negative reversal of life and death, which provides death as positive source of meaning. 'The place of the womb, and the acknowledgement of its mystery, is chosen to convey one of Qohelet's most fundamental tenets: the inscrutability of the divine will.'[65] But the positive nature of womb/death imagery as the other of selfhood is linked with the pessimism about woman in chapter 7. Thus woman is the other of man's frustration and inability to complete himself. 'She is at once the recipient of lingual abuse and the cipher of the absurd.'[66]

It may be that identifying alterity with respect to gender in Ecclesiastes can only be carried out in terms of an absolute gap between self and other. There is practically no sense of sameness between Qohelet's male 'I' and women's voices. He seeks *hōkmâ* but finds her hard, since she is death to advantage through pleasure associated with bodily activity. In this case, reading for the other as a means of owning self means enunciating the female other in the teeth of the opposition from Qohelet's maleness. In a postmodern social discourse, with its discovery of the marginal, Qohelet functions as the other against which female principles of selfhood can know themselves. Christiansen notes the views of E. Reed who suggests that Qohelet's is an 'irregular discourse' against which feminist discourse can form its agenda, can come to know itself more clearly.[67] Here is a very particular form of negative theology in which the negative face of difference is inherent in the creation of self-identity.

Selfhood and Otherness

Throughout this chapter emphasis has been placed on otherness rather than sameness. This is in contrast to the identification of individual existence through sameness evidenced in the previous wave of European biblical exegesis. The rise of alterity as a key topic is linked with a suspicious attitude towards the historical-critical reading method. Historical reading methods claim that the Bible is a historical artefact whose meaning lies in an ancient society and that the proper attitude of readers to it is to search for the unadulterated 'truth' of its origins. This attitude involves a denial that the true meaning of a text has elements in it of the reader's own cultural and social context. Such a paradigm has been attacked by P. Davies in *In Search of Ancient Israel*, for instance.[68] Davies views the term 'Ancient Israel' as a scholarly construct which has not paid attention to the findings of archaeology as a check and balance on biblical narrative. K. Whitelam has added to this critique by describing the cultural use of the Christian Bible in Western Europe and the USA, highlighting the manner in which this religious inheritance has coloured ongoing political and economic relations between Israel, Palestine and the West.[69]

Postmodern readings, by distinction, acknowledge the role of the commentator in the creation of textual meaning. In the writing of Lyotard, for instance, there is a summary of three distinctive features of postmodern thought.[70] Under aesthetics it collapses the divide between high and low culture, and stresses the unsayable. In epistemology it tends to incredulity with regard to metanarratives. It brings in a political emphasis, with the suspicion that the desire for consensus, found in modernity, is phallocratic and universalizing, suppressive of heterogeneity. In these modes of thought the tendency is in each case towards plurality and not to privileging one interpretation above another in the name of truth. For truth, understood as norm or order, is itself a cultural artefact, in terms of its practical content and its link with power and authority. With regard to biblical texts truth is the meaning found by the reader, and these truths are used in European society, both modern and postmodern, to endorse, on the one hand, the status quo, and on the other, the current shifts in power balances.

Inherent in postmodernist thought is the concept of deconstruction. According to the Postmodern Bible Collective, 'deconstruction seeks out those points within a system where it disguises the fact of its incompleteness, its failure to cohere as a self-contained whole. By locating these points and applying a kind of leverage to them, one deconstructs the system.'[71] A development from deconstruction is the concern with the marginal, secondary, the repressed and the borderline. These are discovered by examining a totalizing account of an item or an event, and deconstructing this account. Thus, the marginal is identified as the other, which the account excludes but which is also necessary for its meaning. When it comes to statements as such, it is important to identify the speaker and the site of speech. Does this voice come from the centre or from the margins of a given social world? It has been stated in these last two chapters that Qohelet's textual voice, his autobiographical 'I', can be interpreted both from culturally central sites and from the margins. Whereas the search from the centre looks to the sameness of a modern selfhood with that of the ancient autobiographer, that which concerns itself with borders looks to the otherness already present in Qohelet's account of his experience of the social world of existence.

This brings the reader back to the topic of cultural exegesis. F. Mulhern, in offering a summary of the development of cultural interpretation in England since the start of the twentieth century, notes the shift from *kulturkritik* – the stance of a liberal elite who distance themselves from mass civilization and its values – to cultural studies.[72] The latter discipline has grown from the work of R. Hoggart and R. Williams, and, ultimately, finds matter for cultural discourse in the daily life of the whole of a society.[73] For Mulhern it is the first of these two movements which can be aligned with the search for a single metanarrative, a narrative worldview which in fact represented the interests of an elite. Thus, in English literature, for instance, it was appropriate to talk of a canon of texts, suitable for aesthetic pursuits. 'Kulturkritik spoke in the name of a rarified cluster of human values (culture) that survived in and against the prevailing generality of discourse (civilisation), culture was the true whole or universal, to be asserted against the false generality of modernity, with its riot of particular social interests.'[74]

By contrast,

> Cultural Studies has favoured a radical expansion of the field of relevant enquiry, and a strictly egalitarian ethic of attention within it … The justifying purpose of Cultural Studies has been to revoke the historic privileges of 'culture with a capital C' … and vindicate the active meanings and values of the subordinate majority.[75]

Art and literature as terms of classification and of value can now be used as titles for popular literature such as periodicals and for the visual images of cinema and video screen. That which was once the other, the excess left out of elite definitions of culture, is now a proper focus for analysis and intellectual critique. Since the marginalized majority have been placed at the centre of the social gaze, it may be asked what now is the excess which defines the structure? Or has the whole concept of structure, and thus of order leading to social value, vanished? Is the world of cultural studies technically meaningless? Or has the margin become the centre and the centre become the margin? Are the cultural canons of the past the other that gives meaning to the cultural self?

Just as in explorations of the 'Qoheletic self' commentators cannot decide which of his voices is central and which marginal, and cannot therefore be sure of the meaning of his key term *hebel*, so there is uncertainty about the movement of European culture. Mulhern fixes, in his summary, on the ever-shifting nature of culture. 'The excess has no fixed composition or tendency. It is a heterogeneous mass of possibilities old and new and never mutually translatable, possibilities no longer or not yet ... Culture is everything, in the sense that there is no social life outside formations of meaning, but it never adds up.'[76]

In this shifting pattern of cultural selves a further element has arisen which offers a new excess to meaning. So far it is the internal debates of European society which have provided meaning. But Europe is only one region within the world. Its cultural values have been exported through imperialism and colonialism, but are now challenged by the voices of social worlds from the margins of empire. Since the Christian Bible was exported along with other cultural signifiers, its role also comes under scrutiny here. In particular, further layers of the self may be added to the autobiographical 'I' of Qohelet, through the alterity of postcolonial biblical discourse.

Notes

1   This aspect of Qohelet's thought has been dealt with in the previous chapter, where Qohelet's activity as a subjective reporter was a matter of some concern to scholars who felt that he was speaking against, or outside of, normative social and religious boundaries.
2   A. Day, *Romanticism* (London, Routledge, 1996), p. 83.
3   Ibid., pp. 93–4.
4   Ibid., pp. 97–100.
5   Ibid., p. 101.
6   Ibid., p. 116.
7   Ibid., p. 121.
8   R. Gordis, *Koheleth: The Man and his World* (New York, Schocken, 1968), pp. 3–4.
9   Ibid., p. 113.
10   Ibid., p. 114.
11   Ibid., p. 115.
12   Ibid., p. 116.

13 Ibid., p. 118.
14 M. Foucault, *The Architecture of Knowledge* (London, Routledge, 1972), p. 10.
15 Ibid., pp. 38–9.
16 Ibid., pp. 50f.
17 Ibid., p. 93.
18 Steiner produces a metanarrative involving a transcendental value to words. This approach is reversed in a postmodern perspective which stresses instead the multiplicity of meaning involving words, as these are utilized in independent contexts.
19 J. Derrida, *Writing and Difference* (London, Routledge, 1978), p. 10.
20 Ibid., p. 40.
21 Ibid., p. 103.
22 Ibid., p. 115.
23 K. Hart, 'Reading the Text: Biblical Criticism and Literary Theory', in S. Prickett (ed.) *The Poetics of the Narrative* (Oxford, Blackwell, 1991), p. 308.
24 Ibid., p. 309.
25 M. Fox, *A Time to tear down and a Time to build up* (Grand Rapids, Mich., Eerdmans, 1999), p. 8.
26 Ibid., p. 9.
27 Ibid.
28 Ibid., p. 10.
29 Ibid.
30 Ibid., p. 11.
31 Ibid., p. 31.
32 Ibid.
33 This is to view order as produced not only by harmonious and continuous relationships between people and situations, but also by disharmonies and contrasts. It is thus possible to discourse on (dis)order.
34 T. Beal, 'C(ha)osmopolis: Qohelet's Last Words', in T. Linafelt and T. Beal (eds) *God in the Fray* (Minneapolis, Fortress, 1998), pp. 290–1.
35 Ibid., p. 291.
36 Ibid., p. 292.
37 Ibid., p. 303.
38 Ibid.
39 Ibid.
40 T. Linafelt, 'Introduction: Strange Fire Ancient and Modern', in T. Linafelt (ed.) *Strange Fire* (Sheffield, Sheffield Academic Press, 2000), p. 19.
41 M. George, 'Death as the Beginning of Life in Ecclesiastes', in Linafelt, *Strange Fire*, p. 281.
42 Ibid., p. 282.
43 Ibid., p. 283.
44 Ibid., p. 285.
45 Ibid., p. 288.
46 Ibid., pp. 290–1.
47 Ibid., p. 292.
48 Ibid.
49 Ibid., p. 293.
50 M. Grey, *Introducing Feminist Images of God* (Sheffield, Sheffield Academic Press, 2001).
51 Ibid., p. 76.
52 Ibid., p. 77.
53 Ibid., p. 79.
54 Ibid.
55 Ibid., p. 80.

56   The interlinking of Lady Wisdom as found in Proverbs 1–8 with the heavenly bride sought by Solomon in the Wisdom of Solomon has been radically explored in the recent work by C. Camp, *Wise, Strange and Holy* (Sheffield, Sheffield Academic Press, 2000).

57   Camp plays on the movement between a male wise Solomon and female wisdom. This can interestingly illuminate the figure of Solomon who is both royal and a sage.

58   This passage has had a long history of debate which has not reached consensus. Despite attempts to soften the misogyny of the text it does appear that the ancient writer uses a very negative image of woman here, even if 'only' symbolically. This view coheres with passages of Proverbs and Sirach which also use female metaphors for models of negativity. See C.-L. Seow, *Ecclesiastes* (New York, Doubleday, 1997), pp. 270–6.

59   C. Fontaine, '"Many Devices" (Qoheleth 7:23–8:1): Qoheleth, Misogyny and the Malleus Maleficarium', in A. Brenner and C. Fontaine (eds) *Wisdom and Psalms* (Sheffield, Sheffield Academic Press, 1998), pp. 138–9.

60   Ibid., pp. 152–3.

61   Ibid., p. 189.

62   Ibid., p. 164.

63   Ibid., pp. 167–8.

64   E. Christiansen, 'Qoheleth the "Old Boy" and Qoheleth the "New Man": Misogyny, the Womb and a Paradox in Ecclesiastes', in Brenner and Fontaine, *Wisdom and Psalms*, pp. 128–9.

65   Ibid., p. 130.

66   Ibid., p. 131.

67   Ibid., p. 134.

68   P. Davies, *In Search of Ancient Israel* (Sheffield, Sheffield Academic Press, 1992).

69   K. Whitelam, *The Invention of Ancient Israel* (London, Routledge, 1996).

70   F. Lyotard, *The Postmodern Condition*, trans. G. Bennington and B. Massumi (Manchester University Press, 1984).

71   Bible and Cultural Collective, *The Postmodern Bible* (New Haven, Conn., Yale University Press, 1995), p. 120.

72   F. Mulhern, *Culture/Metaculture* (London, Routledge, 2000).

73   See here the section on the growth of cultural studies in Chapter 2, p. 11.

74   Mulhern, *Culture/Metaculture*, p. 77.

75   Ibid., p. xix.

76   Ibid., p.174.

Chapter 10

Ecclesiastes and Religio-cultural Alterity

The last chapter stressed the importance of 'otherness' or 'alterity' as a key to deciphering the meaning of texts. In this context an 'I' is identified by that which it is not, even by that which stands in opposition to it. A particular kind of otherness is found in colonial and postcolonial cultural studies. Whereas postmodernist approaches to meaning seek the excess of signification left over when a fixed value is attached to words from within a European context, postcolonialism looks to the other meanings attached to words as cultural signs when these words are examined from a social setting which is non-European. European and non-European contexts are, however, linked within the common framework of imperialism. The concept of empire brings together those whose views represent the imperial authority and those who represent the people who are subjected to imperial authority. This is not a simple connection for, just as postmodernity is a complex term, composed of many varieties of meaning, so also postcolonialism is capable of different levels of content.

At the heart of questions of meaning lie the terms 'imperialism' and 'colonialism', two words that have often been used interchangeably.[1] They are linked into the process whereby one social group takes political and economic charge of territories which were originally autonomous; 'colonialism can be defined as the conquest and control of other people's land and goods'.[2] The eighteenth and nineteenth centuries saw the rise of a number of European empires in which British, French and German states especially took over parts of Africa and Asia.[3] The lands and peoples subordinated to foreign domination were culturally absorbed also, and their societies were defined and explained from the perspective of the dominant, originally foreign, culture. In the twentieth century these empires gradually collapsed as component social groups demanded independence. In the political process of the search for liberty the cultural norms of the imperial rulers were challenged and the viewpoint of margins of empire came to be asserted in the face of the view from the centre.

But the traces of colonial rule continue to exert cultural influence. 'We cannot dismiss the importance of either formal decolonisation, or the fact that unequal relations of colonial rule are reinscribed in the contemporary imbalances between "first" and "third" world nations', says A. Loomba. 'The new global order does not depend upon direct rule. However, it does allow the economic, cultural and ... political penetration of some countries by others.'[4]

The term colonialism thus continues to have relevance in literary studies, though its content shifts in the recent past. 'Postcolonial studies have shown that both the "metropolis" and the "colony" were deeply altered by the colonial process. *Both* of them are, accordingly, also restructured by decolonisation.'[5] Although the debates described here relate to modern empires and colonies it can be shown that similar power relations existed in antiquity.

In particular, the social setting for the original Qohelet is often said by scholars to be that of the Hellenistic Empire of the third century BCE.[6] If the author of the book of Ecclesiastes was operating in Hellenistic Palestine, then his perspective would be that of the colonized culture, and his work may be read as a work of postcolonialism, providing a study which offers a critique on the values of empire and its attitudes. The scene changes when this biblical book is taken into the canon of Hebrew Scriptures and then incorporated into the Christian Bible. It now becomes part of the culture of the European colonizers and forms part of the imperialist culture. But, since the Christian Bible passes from colonizer to colonized it can be resited. Read by the decolonized readers of Asia, Africa and Latin America from their own worlds of social discourse it once again functions as a resource for postcolonialism. Readers can investigate what meaning this text offers from the specific angle of an 'otherness' set over against a Eurocentric approach. The two layers involved here, the ancient and the modern postcolonialist interpretations of social discourse, can add further aspects of the 'Qoheletic self'.

Alterity

The last chapter picked up on the point that selfhood can be defined by that which is other, as well as by that which can be aligned with the self in a continuous sameness. Derrida, for instance, looked to the 'difference', the instability of the sign, which allows for a gap between words and their meanings.[7] The act of self-definition thus becomes a meaningful action only when this slippage is taken into account. If an 'I' defines its self, then this entails taking into self that which is outside 'myself'. Otherness or alterity here becomes critical to the interpretation of selfhood. When this concept is applied to postcolonial contexts it develops specific aspects. E. Said has argued that colonialism produces cultural norms which are binary – where the colonizer is rational, familiar, western and Us as against the colonized Them, which is irrational, strange and oriental.[8] 'This dialectic between self and other, derived in part from deconstruction, has been hugely influential in subsequent studies of colonial attitudes towards Africans, Native Americans, and other non-European people.'[9]

But, in his recent work *Culture and Imperialism* Said moves towards a more nuanced view of the connections between cultures. In a global context, which has moved beyond European territorial imperialism, European culture owes debts to its imperial past and land previously colonized has inherited traces of European cultural values. 'If at the outset we acknowledge the massively knotted and complex histories of special but nevertheless overlapping and interconnected experiences ... there is no particular intellectual reason for granting each and all of them an ideal and essentially separate status.'[10] The task is rather to preserve what is unique to each individual culture while also accepting that they exist within an overarching umbrella of human social experience.

Hybridity

In the centre of the complex and overlapping social discourses referred to by Said is an area of blurred identity boundaries. Loomba argues that 'post-colonial studies have been preoccupied with issues of hybridity, creolisation, *mestizaje*, in-betweenness, diasporas and liminality, with the mobility and the crossovers of ideas and identities generated by colonialism'.[11] Loomba notes one aspect of this crossover as it affects concepts of self and other. 'Even as imperial and racial ideologies insist on racial difference, they catalyse crossovers ... One of the most striking contradictions about colonialism is that it both needs to "utilise" its "others" and to fix them into perpetual "otherness".'[12] There is here a paradoxical view of selfhood in which an 'I' can only know its self by embracing otherness, but without abandoning the gap between self and other. The possibilities of sameness and alterity involved in this process lend themselves to the post-structuralist language of Derrida and Foucault.

H. Bhabha is one theorist who has taken up the concept of hybridity in a postmodern manner. He applies this concept, for example, to the task of translating words and ideas from the language of the colonizer to that of the colonized. The idea of a Christian revelation, enshrined in the Christian Scriptures, is deconstructed when situated in the context of Hindu and Buddhist cultural discourse, for there the term revelation has a pre-history shaped by those other religions. In the act of translation 'the word of divine authority is deeply flawed by the assertion of the indigenous sign, and in the very practice of domination the language of the master becomes hybrid – neither the one thing nor the other'.[13] The colonized subject cannot, then, be totally pinned down. It is a self that is other, that can be harnessed to another self in 'sameness', but slips past the boundary set by that self and produces meaning that utilizes the opposing self for its own meanings.

The interface of selves and others produces an alterity that has its own selfhood and is a hybrid, 'the otherness of the Self inscribed in the perverse palimpsest of colonial identity'.[14] There is here no stability. Identities shift, merging but still oppositional. 'It reveals the deep psychic uncertainty of the colonial relation itself: its split representations stage the division that cuts across the fragile skin – black and white – of individual and social authority.'[15] Neither colonialist self nor colonized other can stand on their own; it is that in-between hybridity which constitutes colonial otherness, what Bhabha describes as 'the white man's artifice inscribed on the black man's body'.[16] In this setting an 'I' reaches out to the other as a necessary component of selfhood. The other cannot therefore be an oppositional 'it' but is drawn into my-self at the same time as 'myself' is a term deconstructed by the 'difference' of the other.[17]

Whereas Bhabha employs the theories of Derrida as a linguistic tool to explore postcolonial identities, P. Hogan regards such theorizing as too abstract to be useful. He focuses instead on the narratives written both by colonizer and colonized and establishes his own version of hybridity.

> Postcolonisation literature is, in a sense, two literatures: one arising from the dominant or colonizer society, the other from the dominated or colonized society ... these literatures are united by a sort of dialectical tension ... but they also maintain a striking degree of thematic or structural congruence, often centring around the issue of identity.[18]

Hogan argues that a central facet of the relationship here is the region of contact between colonizer and colonized. In geographical terms certain regions have a high intensity of social contact between the two groups and this promotes cultural crossovers. These relations are 'often partially mediated by some third group, which is considered racially intermediate',[19] such as mulattos and mixed race groups. The interaction of groups produces, on the one hand, a loss of self-identity in the face of the culturally other, but, on the other hand, it leads to a reification of basic culture.[20] It is this cultural mix of the indigenous and the metropolitan which finds expression through literature. Through the literary medium the possibilities of mimeticism, of assimilation and of cultural independence can be explored. At one extreme is the syncretistic self, which assimilates cultural influences to an indigenous base. At the other is an alienated self 'estranged from both traditions ... the paralysing conviction that one has no identity, no real cultural home, and that no synthesis is possible'.[21]

Postcolonial Biblical Studies

Despite methodological disagreements both Bhabha and Hogan are agreed on the existence of an area of cultural interchange in which cultural and social identities are both threatened and reconstructed. Important for both writers is the pairing of sameness (syncretism) with otherness (alienation), as key terms for the investigation of social identity. Meaning is found 'in-between' the two outer boundaries of syncretism and alienation. Postcolonial biblical studies can be situated within this concept of the in-between. The biblical texts belong to the 'I' of the European imperialist culture, 'along with gunboats, opium, slaves and treaties, the Christian Bible became the defining symbol of

European expansion'.[22] but they are now owned as a source of relevant cultural meaning by the 'I' of the colonized. Yet it became an other that 'has been transmitted, received, appropriated and even subverted by third world people'. Sugiratharajah argues that a key factor in this shift is the setting up of the British and Foreign Bible Society.[23] The aim of this society was to make biblical books available in every culture and language. 'The Bible was promoted as the only text among all the sacred writings of the world which could be made readable "for men of every colour and in every country".'[24] But this was part of colonialist cultural norms, involving the displacement of local cultures.[25]

Otherness, as a response of the colonized to the 'I' of colonial biblical interpretation, took the forms of resistance and of assimilation.[26] The Bible, a tool of the colonizer's selfhood, could be turned around against the colonizer. A Native North American, William Apess, was able to use Old Testament narrative to authenticate his own culture. 'In invoking the lost tribes of Israel, and identifying Native Americans as the genuine heirs of the biblical tribes, Apess's intention was to affirm a common pedigree for all humanity ... [which] meant that every native North American was just as much a human person as the invading white.'[27] K. N. Banerjea's intertextual reading of biblical narratives and Vedic texts offers an example of assimilation.[28] He took, for instance, the theme of sacrifice to show a common link between the Bible and the Vedas. Thus he intended to show that Christianity was not a foreign religion but a fulfilment of Indian religious tradition.[29]

Kwok Pui-Lan's book *Discovering the Bible in the Non-biblical World* brings together in the authorial self these two aspects of the cultural impact of colonization – syncretism and alienation. As an Asian woman theologian she was trained in the interpretive methods of the colonizing culture. But she is also aware 'that contemporary mental and intellectual space is controlled by the cultural hegemony of the West, the white gaze and the unceasing self-representation of the male'.[30] In this context the task of the Christian Asian reader is to dialogue with the other in terms of Asian religions and Asian society. The reader's gaze must extend beyond that which is the same to the radically other, while still offering an authentic source for examining identity and social values. 'Our goal is not to generalize and distill abstract principles from the Bible in order to apply them prescriptively in other situations, but rather to respect the particularity of the stories ... and to learn from them religious insights for dealing with the common issues that face all human societies.'[31] The goal here is to encourage the development of a self-identity which is not self-centred but whose nature is 'to destabilize all imperialistic claims of truth for the liberation of all'.[32] Liberation here means a freedom from the truth claims of the colonial culture and also from any unexamined utilization of the cultural values of any given society. The topic of liberation is also examined by R. Sugiratharajah: 'liberation hermeneutics is postmodern in its desire to take the Other – the poor, women, indigenous and all the marginalised peoples – seriously. In doing so, it rightly overrides the Enlightenment concern with the non-believer, and focuses on the non-person'.[33]

Communal Bible study engages readers who share a common world of social discourse in seeking their communal self within the biblical texts. 'The appeal of the Bible is that it not only contains liberative memories of an oppressed people but it also provokes participation.'[34] These views, though expressed in different words are not dissimilar to the views of Kwok Pui-Lan. They urge the need for a global context for Bible reading where all readings have an equal value since all cultures have equal weight. E. Tamez is one theologian who has produced a reading of Ecclesiastes within this broad cultural perspective of a postcolonial search for identity. Her emphasis is on Qohelet as a man living in a colonized province and the opportunity this offers a modern reader for resiting Ecclesiastes in contemporary postcolonialist experiences.

When the Horizons Close

Tamez begins her study with the current reality of social/cultural despair which, she argues, is a result of a capitalist economic system, whose strategy is to create a culture of despair.[35] Tamez views the current global climate of despair as one with that of Ecclesiastes whose cultural setting in the Ptolemaic Hellenistic Empire was a similar mix of international commerce and human beings controlled by economic and social forces beyond local control. 'The narrator experiences reality as a great emptiness, masked by the change and agitation around him; he is anguished by his inability to envision a liberating future.'[36] Yet Qohelet's self-identity is as an 'I' who insists on a Utopian future, breaking free from despair to assert the rewards of happy social relationships in the present moment.

Qohelet discusses power politics, the roles of kings and leaders, but sees no hope for true justice and freedom there. 'Perhaps in its context, this is what his people have experienced in the changes of Empire and the empty hopes of his contemporaries for a better life – from Sennacherib to Nebuchadnezzar, from Nebuchadnezzar to Alexander the Great, and then to the Ptolemies and the Seleucids, and later the Romans.'[37] Tamez notes how Qohelet stresses the lack of newness. But this is at odds with the real world of the Hellenistic empire of his day. 'Qoheleth challenges the newness of the dominant foreign system, perhaps because its impact does not lead to human fulfillment.'[38] Yet Qohelet is not totally sympathetic to his indigenous Jewish culture either. 'It has been suggested that ... the author belongs to the Palestinian aristocracy in Jerusalem. More specifically, he would be a sage who imparts his wisdom in the circles of young Jewish aristocrats, warning them against the apparent newness of the Hellenistic system and culture.'[39]

Yet Qohelet does offer a personal voice of positive, if limited, utopian aims. He proposes a logic that follows the heart and the eyes, that is the subject's consciousness and sight.[40] Not knowing the times intended by the deity leads to frustration that is cut away by reframing the times as beyond his own control, so acknowledging his 'I' to be one governed by limitation, the human condition.[41] The future is opaque and the past alienating[42] so only the present offers meaning. But the person as subject is not centred on rational argument so much as on social discourse, around the household table. 'The utopia of everyday enjoyment is a viable, humanizing way of repudiating the present [of ceaseless toil] but at the same time living it by a contrary logic.'[43]

Tamez' interpretation of the Qoheletic self is one that stands in its indigenous culture, experiencing that culture as helpless in the face of foreign domination and so alienated. But some of the ancient writer's specifically Jewish traditions are continued since Qohelet's personal voice is not one of assimilation to foreign culture. The propaganda of new economic and social forms, the growth of syncretistic religious and philosophical beliefs, do not offer the hope of real solutions for a pain free existence. Instead they are regarded as a form of entrapment. The only worthwhile act is to turn back to a subjective 'I', which both owns what makes imperialism tick and traces a connection with past native tradition. This personal voice at the same time creates a critique of imperialism. It accepts the empires as realities but is not personally subsumed to their otherness.

Tamez then reads across from colonialist past to present culture. The Qoheletic self is an 'I' with which a reader's self can easily empathize, in the mode of sameness. Here the 'otherness' of a text presented as part of colonial culture is retrieved as useful for the oppressed society. 'Sameness' means one with the underdog society and produces a perspective which must be read as 'other' by the imperial culture. Tamez wishes to make the postcolonial version of meaning accessible to more readers, however, and does this by defining the reader of the modern period more generally, as one who experiences alienation and struggles with the otherness of contemporary cultural norms. 'Obviously the reading of Qoheleth presented here has been done in the context of our present reality, with the globalisation of the free market. But there is an extraordinary similarity between those Hellenistic times and our own.'[44]

For Tamez there is no need to interpret the text specially for the modern day. To understand the colonized context of the Qoheletic self is to be part of that 'I'. Both colonizer and colonized experience the otherness of global imperialism, especially in its economic form, and find themselves as others and aliens in such a cultural context. Tamez can now read Qohelet from a European viewpoint, as a postmodern relativist in his focus on present existence, and can raise about the ancient text questions asked concerning modern European cultural theory. 'Is embracing the present sufficient for human fulfillment in our world today? Doesn't it lead to the trap of postmodern sentiment?' She allows that these queries are valid but argues that, in spite of the issues it raises, for example, its lack of praxis, we cannot deny the importance of discussing Qoheleth's proposal in depth.[45] Thus

Tamez bridges the difference between European and postcolonial worlds by focusing on the common otherness (alienation) of all world societies from the cultural meaning offered them by some forms of globalist activity.

Diasporic Postcolonial Experience

In Tamez' approach Qohelet can be interpreted as a wanderer between worlds. In the current period these worlds are those defined by modern forms of imperialism, but the model engages also with the ancient, original Qohelet. Not fully 'Jewish' and not fully 'Greek' he crosses and re-crosses the religio-cultural boundaries of these two identities. This is a common experience for modern postcolonialists. The migrant who has no localized status, as R. Bromley points out, 'confronts the "localised" with those very ontological anxieties – of temporariness, of transience, of instability, of contingency and the arbitrary'.[46] The 'I' of such a figure is hyphenated, represented in modern times by, for instance, American–Asian identity. In Qohelet's case the equivalent is Greek–Palestinian. Bromley claims that in diasporic literature

> figures look in from the outside while looking out from the inside ... They are figures with hyphenated identities, living hybrid realities which pose problems for classification and control, as well as raising questions about notions of essential difference ... The narratives are involved in a process of endless locating and undermining: belonging is always problematic, a never-ending dialogue of same with other.[47]

Interpreting Beyond Borders

F. Segovia uses these diasporic models of discourse as his inspiration in editing a volume of essays on diasporic biblical studies. 'In the light of the diasporic phenomena involved in ... the increasing presence of the non-Western Christians in the West, Diasporic Studies can also be brought to bear on every aspect of Christian Studies.'[48] In a later chapter from the same volume Segovia explores his own self-stance as a diasporic reader of texts. He notes the early stage of development of biblical diasporic studies. 'It is only with the advent of cultural studies, as the construct of the informed and universal reader yields to that of the real reader, that scientific reading and textual silence begin to be examined and evaluated ... as critical options rather than givens.'[49] In the new context empiricism, objectivity and hierarchism give way to a conscious exploration of the texts and their readers 'as aesthetic, strategic and political constructs'.[50] This shift of emphasis provides 'the elan of diaspora hermeneutics, with its combined search for the otherness of the text and engagement with such otherness'.[51] Segovia further interprets this by a technique of 'reading across' in which 'the imperative attitude before texts, readings and readers is not critical silence but critical dialogue'.[52]

The editors of *Return to Babel* also focus on the need to engage critically with texts and readers, noting the importance of reading biblical texts from a variety of global perspectives. This is in line with Segovia's basic stance of dialogic encounter with readers and texts. Babel often stands for a limitation of human strength in which the babble of tongues is a punishment, but an argument can be made for a reading of Genesis 11 in which the destruction of an imperialist tower and the scattering of people represents 'the signal event in the restoration of a desirable diversity, of a positive return to indigenous tongues and thus to the multiplicity of nativist experiences'.[53] In the essays that follow 'each writer begins by foregrounding those aspects of his or her particular context that have the potential to provide a vantage point for fresh interpretations'.[54] These cultural settings in Latin America, Africa and Asia are then linked with specific elements of the biblical text. The biblical material under scrutiny thus 'migrates' across three cultures, crossing boundaries of social identity.

Ecclesiastes 3: 1–16 is such a text, diasporically interpreted by Tamez, Lumbala and Song.[55] The original text is Qohelet's account of human time and can be read either optimistically (there *is* a time for all things) or negatively (all things are determined by a pre-existent order of events and cannot be creatively re-timed by human beings).[56] Tamez views the poem as offering hope. She locates the text in Nicaraguan society where a woman cannot afford to send all five of her children to school, contrary to her subjective values. Can such a woman find hope of 'good times'?[57] Tamez believes that Qohelet has a confident utopianism that there is a time order which offers real life in the midst of slavish toil.[58] This hope can be set against the hope of better things offered by the present capitalist imperialism. The secular values of capitalism have not provided a way forward for Nicaraguans.[59] In this context Qohelet is to be read not as pessimistic but as other. He offers an alternative self-identity focused on Christian religious values in which faith in God's timing frees an 'I' from the paralysing effect of *hebel*. Thus Tamez views the personal voice of Qohelet as a way towards true self-identity and a liberation from the oppressive otherness of an imperialism which poses as being one with the reading subject. Only by a true choice of cultural otherness can cultural values be upheld.

As Ecclesiastes 3: 1–16 migrates to Africa a change of reader produces a change of meaning. Lumbala locates Qohelet with African Bantu beliefs which emphasize the link between present reality and an unseen world beyond human life. Happiness involves harmony between these two universes.[60] In this setting time has many layers and human time overlaps with heavenly time and mythical time.[61] Like Bantu religion Qohelet seeks for the means of human happiness. Qohelet's 'I' may view time pessimistically but Bantu readers hear in the poem its rhythm and its refrain. 'The rhythm carries us to the heart of the universe's rhythm, which for us constitutes an essential element in the harmonisation of existence.'[62] What counts is the event not the time measure itself; so the events of life should be long and fully explored as each comes into being. Only by reading Ecclesiastes against the grain of its pessimism can Bantu readers find meaning for their native culture and its religious values.

Once again the text migrates – to Asia. This time the readerly selves focused on are the *burakumim*, or outcasts, in Japanese society. The long-term effects of belonging to a caste of persons rejected in their own culture is engraved on the bodies of contemporary members.[63] They are hopeless, for they cannot change history. When such selves read Ecclesiastes they can align with the 'I' of the ancient autobiographer. They, too, can share his sense that society is morally in ruins and that human beings are enslaved to humiliating toil. But this Qohelet is a rich man who stands helpless and negative before moral anarchy, even though condemning it. The Japanese reader who has crossed into the ancient writer's worldview, and sees with the same eyes, can now change that vision around to otherness. 'What he must have also said in utter helplessness can be heard as a call to action on the part of those who have suffered from a world that is hostile to them.'[64] There is a time for *all* things, so now there is a time for the *burakumim* to break their age-old silence in the face of oppression and to cry out against their treatment. Thus '*kairos* has broken out of the historical time of Japan'.[65]

Thus one text can produce three individual readings as it crosses cultural boundaries. Diasporic interpretation entails the rating of all three readings as equally valuable in the development of a Qoheletic self. Taken together they offer variations on a 'same' selfhood; treated as individuals the readings offer three 'other' selves. They are each both same and other with regard to the biblical text since all three readings depend on the same root, a book within the Christian Bible, while each finding a different message from reading this same book. Plurality of readings, in a global marketplace of interpretation, ensures that Qohelet's 'I' has many stalls offering different produce and the buyer may shop at them all.

Native and Indigenous Readings

The above exploration of readings of Ecclesiastes leads to a focus on 'native' take up of 'foreign' texts. This returns the study to the themes of resistance and assimilation. As the colonized become conscious of their identity and separate themselves from the colonizer's ownership of their cultural identity they come to seek their own expressions of identity. As E. Boehmer states, 'the typical nationalist quest for self truth ... was marked by a struggle to give shape to an everyday ... reality in resistance to images ... transmitted by colonial literature'.[66] Yet this is not a straightforward break in selfhood between same and other, involving a rejection of the colonizer's 'same' as in reality alien. 'To be true to oneself in borrowed robes: this was the core dilemma of the colonial nationalist.'[67] Boehmer argues that the search for independence itself had to be carried out in language, literary traditions, institutions and political ideologies which in part derived from European templates.[68] The original nationalist writers created an imaginary homeland for themselves, ironically moving nearer to the cosmopolitan metropolis as they sought political independence.[69]

In the current time, following independence, a new stage of postcolonial writing has arisen. Independence as such has not brought economic and social stability or growth to many postcolonial states. The neo-colonialism of the capitalist world continues to shape their economies and political systems. Boehmer argues that a new search for meaning takes decolonized thinkers back to colonial traditions as well as indigenous ones. Modern colonial texts can be viewed as hyphenated works, straddling several worlds, as postcolonial authors examine their own social world as selves alienated from its confusion, thus participating 'in the time-worn processes through which those in the West scrutinise the Other the better to understand themselves'.[70]

These events can be aligned with the development of biblical studies. There is a move to own these texts from the western traditions but to understand them as religious resources for cultural meanings inscribed in the bodies of decolonized subjects. One example of the creation of local meaning taken from the Christian Bible is that of Seree Lorgunpai who provides a commentary on Ecclesiastes via the lens of Thai Buddhism. In western biblical scholarship missionary translators put a low value on Ecclesiastes, a book that none the less offers a mode for self-identity to Thai Buddhism.[71] Lorungpai attempts to reclaim the book as a means of dialogue for Christians with the other selves of Thai Buddhists. He notes that the Qoheletic self is often taken as alien and other by European commentators, who see it as an isolated and marginal perspective within the Old Testament. Conversely the book of Ecclesiastes speaks well to Thais.

Qohelet focuses on the *hebel* nature of human experience. In translation this concept becomes *anitjung* which means unreliable and is a key term in Buddhism. 'Buddhists are taught to think that everything in this world is *anitjung*. If Ecclesiastes was separated from the Christian Bible and handed to Thai Buddhists to read, they might consider it to be a Buddhist book.'[72] The book resonates with the Buddha who sought enlightenment through a knowledge of the suffering of everyday human living. Life is viewed as empty, imperfect, full of conflict.[73] The original Qoheletic self can be linked with this attitude to human affairs and also to the Buddha's stress on the illusion of desire. Qohelet argues that seeking pleasure and putting stress on life's advantages is a dead end philosophy and leads to pain. Death is the real boundary of desire. From there the two traditions diverge.

The Buddha teaches the importance of human efforts to re-orientate mind and spirit towards that which is eternal via proper conduct. Qohelet in the end leaves all to God and focuses on the here and now as the only gain which humans possess. Yet in both traditions the limits of temporality form a distinctively Qoheletic self. 'Both of them were seeking for the truth, responding to similar circumstances and pursuing similar paths' and areas of common ground could be used to facilitate mutual understanding between Thai Christians and Thai Buddhists.[74] So here there is a plan for the enrichment of a specifically regional culture via indigenous sources, some of which were originally alien and imperial, but which can be reclaimed for native purposes in a truly non-imperialist culture.

Qohelet's Postcolonial Selves

In this section on postcolonial biblical interpretation three versions of reading Ecclesiastes have been explored. In Tamez' commentary Qohelet was viewed as a counter balance to the oppressive imperialism of global capitalism, a reading intended for Latin America but available also for any region of the modern world since all are subject to one common economic network. In the plurality of responses to Ecclesiastes 3 the focus was firmly on the individuality of regional biblical criticism and in the case of Thai culture the biblical text was gathered into a setting fixed by a previously established regional religious tradition. The variety of these readerly perspectives indicates a central aspect of postcolonial interpretation, namely the departure from the Enlightenment view that there can only be one authorized meaning to textual passages. Wherever the reader stands is where the text is read from and every siting produces an individual reading, as argued by Foucault. The uniting force here is that of alterity. It is the very difference which links the readings together. Qohelet's 'I' moves from context to context, a migrant, hyphenated self, crossing over between same and other.

It is this unity and yet separation between colonized and colonizer which raises questions about the nature of postcolonial writing. How far have the decolonized moved from European influence? Loomba notes that 'Arif Dirlik calls "postcolonialism" a "child of postmodernism" which is born not out of new perspectives on history and culture but because of the increased visibility of academic intellectuals of Third World origin'.[75] These intellectuals, it is suggested, owe a great deal to First World patterns of thought. They are caught in a form of mimeticism in which there is no truly other manner of thought, but rather the once colonized cultures still look to the old imperial societies for the means of creating their self-identity, even if only by opposition to what they see therein.

Loomba argues for the need to think about the local and the marginalized and their relations to larger structures in another manner. So far the narratives of the colonized and the oppressed revise the meaning of colonialism and modernity, but they do not transcend the thought patterns of the past. 'We need to move away from global narratives not because they necessarily *always* swallow up complexity, but because they historically have done so.'[76] What is needed is an approach to stories of the self which would avoid placing Europe at the centre of the scene. 'If postcolonial studies is to survive in any meaningful way, it needs to absorb itself far more deeply with the contemporary world, and with the local circumstances within which colonial institutions and ideas are being moulded into the disparate cultural and socio-economic processes which define our contemporary "globality".'[77]

Boehmer stresses the impact of migrancy in funding postcolonial attitudes: 'from national bonding to international wandering, from rootedness to peregrination'.[78] In the 1990s the postcolonial writer tended to have a self-identity which had a Third World focus but in other ways was part of the metropolis of western culture.[79] Here otherness and sameness interweave so that literary styles hybridized on the colonial outskirts now become more intensely hybridized by being returned to the post-imperial western city.[80] The difficulty is still that of the seeming impossibility of separating the postcolonial from the imperial. And yet there remains a haunting otherness which is in search of its own world of social discourse. It may be that the underlying similarity between postmodern culture in Europe and postcolonial society in decolonized regions is a shared uncertainty about self-identity. 'Both discourses are clearly products of a time notable for the growing unsteadiness of Enlightenment thinking and the institutions which have fostered it ... Both are also clearly spin-offs of ... the disintegration of Western culture and political authority in its imperial form.'[81]

There are ironic echoes here of a Qoheletic view of human affairs. The continuing pull of a collapsing world order can resonate with the argument that there is nothing new *taḥat ha ššemešš*. At the same time this gravitational force offers only *hebel* as an explanation of human existence. It does not liberate the subject to find gain or advantage in living. The move towards local individuality, however, like Qohelet's stress on the immediate here and now of the social world, creates, potentially, a space within which individual selves, persons and social groups can respond freely with their portion in life. They can exercise some degree of alterity with regard to the wider global systems. As with the original Qohelet's message, this may be read hopefully or pessimistically. Tamez, Lumbala and Lorungpai choose to read with some hope, taking the biblical text as a resource for localization.

Notes

1 A. Loomba, *Colonialism/Postcolonialism* (London, Routledge, 1998), p. 1.
2 Ibid., p. 2.
3 Loomba shares a common view of the extent of colonialization, that by the 1930s colonies and ex-colonies accounted for 84.6 per cent of the world surface (p. xiii).
4 Ibid., p. 7.
5 Ibid., p. 19.
6 This is to accept the majority opinion that the text dates from the third century BCE.
7 Loomba, *Colonialism/Postcolonialism*, p. 36.
8 Ibid., p. 47.

9   Ibid.
10 E. Said, *Culture and Imperialism* (London, Vintage, 1993), p. 36.
11 Loomba, *Colonialism/Postcolonialism*, p. 173.
12 Ibid.
13 H. Bhabha, *the location of culture* (London, Routledge, 1994), p. 33.
14 Ibid., p. 44.
15 Ibid.
16 Ibid., p. 45.
17 Ibid., pp. 51–2.
18 P. Hogan, *Colonialism and Cultural Identity* (Albany, State University of New York Press, 2000), p. 3.
19 Ibid., p. 5.
20 Ibid., p. 6.
21 Ibid., p. 17.
22 R. Sugiratharajah, *The Bible and the Third World* (Cambridge, Cambridge University Press, 2001), p. 1.
23 Ibid., pp. 52f.
24 Ibid., p. 59.
25 Ibid., p. 65.
26 Ibid., p. 74.
27 Ibid., p. 90.
28 Ibid., pp. 90f.
29 Ibid., p. 94.
30 L.-P. Kwok, *Discovering the Bible in the Non-biblical World* (Maryknolln NY, Orbis, 1995), p. 26.
31 Ibid., p. 23.
32 Ibid., p. 24.
33 Sugiratharajah, *Bible and Third World*, p. 241.
34 Ibid., p. 219.
35 E. Tamez, *When the Horizons Close* (Maryknoll, NY, Orbis, 1999), p. 1.
36 Ibid., p. 2.
37 Ibid., p. 8.
38 Ibid., p. 14.
39 Ibid., p. 15.
40 Ibid., p. 25.
41 Ibid., p. 19.
42 Ibid., p. 24.
43 Ibid., p. 25.
44 Ibid., p. 143.
45 Ibid.
46 R. Bromley, *Narratives for a New Belonging* (Edinburgh, Edinburgh University Press, 2000), p. 13.
47 Ibid., p. 5.
48 F. Segovia, *Interpreting Beyond Borders* (Sheffield, Sheffield Academic Press, 2000), p. 23.
49 Ibid., p. 64.
50 Ibid., p. 65.
51 Ibid.
52 Ibid., p. 66.
53 J. Levison, 'Introduction', in J. Levison and P. Pope-Levison (eds) *Return to Babel* (Louisville, Ky., Westminster John Knox, 1999), p. 2.
54 Ibid., p. 3.
55 E. Tamez, 'Ecclesiastes 3:1–16', in Levison and Pope-Levison, *Return to Babel*, pp. 75–92.

56 This comment touches once again on the fundamental question of the intention of the ancient writer as to whether any visible order in the world of human affairs is a sign of hope for human advantage or not.

57 Tamez, 'Ecclesiastes 3:1–16', p. 76.

58 Ibid., p. 77.

59 Ibid.

60 F. Lumbala, 'Ecclesiastes 3:1–16', in Levison and Pope-Levison, *Return to Babel*, p. 81.

61 Ibid., p. 82.

62 Ibid., p. 84.

63 C.-S. Song, 'Ecclesiastes 3:1–16', in Levison and Pope-Levison, *Return to Babel*, pp. 87–8.

64 Ibid., p. 89.

65 Ibid., p. 92.

66 E. Boehmer, *Colonial and Postcolonial Literature* (Oxford, Oxford University Press, 1995), p. 109.

67 Ibid., p. 115.

68 Ibid.

69 Ibid., p. 123.

70 Ibid., p. 239.

71 S. Lorungpai, 'The Book of Ecclesiastes and Thai Buddhism, in R. Sugiratharajah (ed.) *Voices from the Margin* (London, SPCK, 1995), p. 339.

72 Ibid., p. 342.

73 Ibid., p. 343.

74 Ibid., p. 347.

75 Loomba, *Colonialism/Postcolonialism*, p. 247.

76 Ibid., p. 249.

77 Ibid., p. 257.

78 Boehmer, *Colonial and Postcolonial Literature*, p. 232.

79 Ibid., p. 233.

80 Ibid., p. 234.

81 Ibid., p. 244.

SEQUEL

Chapter 11

The Interpretation of Selves

This entire study has entailed a play on the interpretation of self-identity. It has raised questions about the content of the first person address 'I' and how this relates to 'you' and to 's/he', persons who can themselves be 'I'. A critical line of interpretation in this context is the interaction between self as the same and self as other. In particular the focus has been the autobiographical self of Qohelet, with its mutually dissenting voices of hope and pessimism. These voices have been explored internally, through the text of Ecclesiastes, and externally, through some cultural afterlives of that text.

Qoheletic Selves

It was noted in the Preamble that the biblical character Qohelet is shaped by the narrative framework provided in Ecclesiastes. Thus Qohelet is royal and powerful. Linked with Solomon, a great wise king, the voice of Qohelet then speaks as that of a wisdom teacher and sage, advising the young through a monologue of personal reflection. This Qohelet can be placed alongside the figure of Montaigne in his autobiographical *Essais*. The personal voice of the autobiographer here turns less to an ordered and coherent account of the external details of life events than to a kaleidoscope of scenes and feelings, which offer the 'flavour' of one human being's experience of human affairs and the values for living which can be extracted therefrom.

In literary terms this is the voice of a narrator whose account of affairs is both reliable and unreliable. It is the thoughts of the inner self which are displayed and these have a foundation in truth. What a person thinks, especially on serious matters of life fortunes, is what a person thinks. But there are two voices here – *hebel* and no *yitrôn*, and eat, drink and enjoy family life. These two voices may be harmonized in various ways or one may be stressed above the other, but both have to be accounted for. The narrative voice as a whole is both reliable and unreliable in its commentary on life and meaning.

Stressing the role of the narrative voice as a tool for expressing selfhood in autobiographical material leads to a Qoheletic self wholly created by language. The observer only knows something of the biblical Qohelet because Ecclesiastes is a book of 'his words'. In speaking out Qohelet speaks himself into existence. The self thus created is open to critique by readers. The

Qoheletic self may be viewed as a 'tragic hero', pushing out the boundaries of human understanding,[1] or may be interpreted as a symbol of human frustration and emptiness because the pursuit of knowledge is itself *hebel*. Von Balthasar's comment can stand here: 'What remains in the end is *hebel* the "great wind"; not *ruach* the divine breath that blows where it wills.'[2]

Wise sayings that present a valid tool for interpreting human affairs or an inevitable flawed view of the value of social discourse, drawing only on finite and temporal understanding – these are two strands of the Qoheletic self which continue to shape the responses of readers as Ecclesiastes moves into the domain of received text. Through the application of reader response perspectives the Qoheletic self gains new layers of meaning contributed by the variety of human responses to the text. But these responses are not the product of individuals in social isolation. Just as the original 'I' of Qohelet was expressed within and shaped by social context, so also the 'other selves' of Qohelet are culturally patterned.

In this process readers become centres of conscious attention and thus 'I's who approach the ancient autobiographer as a conversation partner, both 'you' and 'he'. Readerly selves sit together with Qohelet in sameness – or stand apart in otherness. European academics can view Qohelet as a fellow wise man. But such a Qoheletic self may be other to postcolonial readers. Yet otherness can shift ground. Postmodern European thought, such as that of Derrida, addresses the 'excess' of meaning produced when any coherent view is expressed in language. Reading Qohelet through this approach means seeking out that otherness as a significant element of selfhood. Postcolonial views, which are in excess of an imperialist account, are the other that vitally contribute to a fuller collection of Qoheletic selves.

Interpreting the Self

An essential part of this study has been an exploration of the shape of auto-biography. Modern autobiographical literature can be defined as an account of a life, given through the eyes of the one who has experienced that life. As D. Bjorklund states, 'they are much more than straightforward attempts at personal histories; they are an amalgam of cultural ideas, scruples, art, imagination, rhetoric and self-presentation'.[3] Bjorklund wants, in particular, to address autobiographies as products of culture and as social acts.[4] This is in keeping with the approach to Qohelet as self offered in this book. The text is addressed to a reader, the young man, and to readers, the *Qahal*, and then taken up by cultural interpretations across time. Bjorklund's comment that 'autobiographies are, therefore, a good resource for investigating changing ideas about the self. They are historical records that have been steadily produced and preserved over a lengthy time period', fits with the present perspective. This involves not only Qohelet as a self, but also the 'Qoheletic self' across the modern period.

It is possible to use how people talk about the self as an indicator of how the world of social discourse sorts itself out. The micro-world, which is the key to reading and managing the full historical universe of social experience, can be shaped through first person speech and reflection. Bjorklund argues that 'the ways in which individuals construe their world and their experiences are not simply arbitrary but are influenced by their cultural and historical vantage points'.[5] Thus, whereas one reader experiences Qohelet as king and sage, a source of stability and wisdom from the centre of the social stage, another reader views Qohelet as a 'decentred self' whose wisdom moves from centre stage to periphery, and a third can describe this character as 'migrant and hyphenated'. The autobiographical text simply provides a skeleton of selfhood which can be fleshed out in many social profiles and which produces differing cultural products.

Whatever possibilities the original autobiographer offers with regard to self-identity, these are added to by the process of social interaction involved in the act of reading/hearing a text read. 'The self ... arises not only out of the interaction process with specific others but also by using ideas available for constructing a viewpoint of the self. Selves are culturally as well as socially constructed.'[6] Developing Bjorklund's argument here, it can be postulated that individual examples of interpreting the personal voice of Qohelet are not only products of social discourse but themselves exemplify key features in the culture in which that reading takes place. The term 'Qoheletic self' thus links both original author and later interpreters in a cultural construct which is socially constructed, but also socially deconstructed.

The First Person and Scripture

G. Salyer raises the issue of how to treat Qohelet within such an autobiographical context. He argues that Qohelet's key tendency is a move towards 'truth', viewed as a valid approach to life and the world of social affairs.[7] This is a major issue and invites response of some significance, so it draws readers fully into the text. 'In a book such as Ecclesiastes, where the protagonist speaks almost exclusively from personal experience, the necessity of public validation is immediately given prominence.'[8] This is represented in the text by the epilogist, 'Qoheleth symbolises private knowledge while the Epilogist serves as an indice for public knowledge.'[9] In this cultural model the 'Qoheletic self' is a social tool by which a never-ending testing of the personal voice against that of the assembly takes place.[10]

Such a tension between public and private voices presents a wider issue with regard to reading biblical text. From the seventeenth century onwards the historical style of exegesis subordinated the private voice to that of a publicly accepted meaning. But this binding together of historical meaning, single voice and faith profession has been eroded more recently. 'Beginning in the late 1960s there developed a return to earlier Renaissance models of intellectual enquiry, such as those advocated by Montaigne and Erasmus ... they accent the rightful place of skepticism, and in particular, the concrete, transitory and practical aspects of human experience.'[11]

This move places less emphasis on the original historical culture of the text and more on the text as migrating through generations of readers. The text can even be viewed as going through social isolation as it moves from culture to culture, and as in need of recurrent resocialization. 'Reading becomes a "remedy" by which distanciation is rescued from cultural estrangement ... Ultimately, reading is the act of making the text's otherness one's own.'[12] Salyer's point can be taken to indicate that the Qoheletic self is a textual self, hyphenated with particular cultural settings. The potential for such a constantly renewed selfhood is the 'surplus' of meaning present in the text, left over from the definition of Qohelet within his original historical context in Hellenistic Judaism.

In Ecclesiastes this distancing which can give space for meaning is created already in the text by the contrast between order, expressed in poems of time and space, and *hebel*. The tension between these two perspectives 'defamiliarises the reader's understanding of the world, giving the reader the necessary hermeneutic he or she will need to understand the narrator's radical worldview'.[13] Like Bjorklund, Salyer here suggests that first person discourse has a particular social function.

> The reading contract that is initiated by the use of 'I' signals to the reader to begin a process of characterisation, humanisation, subjectivisation, and embodiment that essentially limits the credentials of the narrator. On the other hand, the very act of embodiment has abundant powers of suasion that act to build the credibility of the narrator.[14]

It is between these two poles that the autobiographical voice moves. The reader takes the part of Qohelet, the critic of society and its religious traditions. But s/he also takes the part of the rhetorical response of the assembly to that critical voice, found in Ecclesiastes 12.[15]

Bjorklund points to the fictive element in autobiography, Salyer to the excess of meaning created by the balancing of distancion of text with the meaning provided for it by the figure of a reader. In both instances the stress falls on the open-endedness of the autobiographer's character. Qohelet's 'I' is a speech act which itself is an act of (self) imagination. When this piece of imagination is taken to be part of a canonical collection of texts it also acts as 'biblical imagination'. The afterlives of the text, its meanings as provided by a succession of readers, are drawn into the act of biblical imagination. Qohelet's 'I' speaks itself into existence 'as if' the voice of a traditional wise man and ruler. Further readings of this 'asness' are also voices which speak 'as if' they were Qohelet. The voices of the reading assembly become acts of biblical imagination in their turn.

Notes

1   A discussion of the possible role of Qohelet as a tragic hero can be found in Chapter 4, p. 49.
2   H. Von Balthasar, *The Glory of the Lord* (Edinburgh, T. and T. Clark, 1991), vol. VI, p. 142.
3   D. Bjorklund, *Interpreting the Self* (Chicago, University of Chicago Press, 1998), p. x.
4   Ibid.
5   Ibid., pp. 2–3.
6   Ibid., p. 7.
7   G. Salyer, *Vain Rhetoric* (Sheffield, Sheffield Academic Press, 2001), p. 14.
8   Ibid.
9   Ibid., p. 17.
10   Ibid.
11   Ibid., p. 34.
12   Ibid., p. 45.
13   Ibid., p. 99.
14   Ibid., p. 125.
15   Ibid., ch. 4.

Chapter 12

The Art of Biblical Imagination

It is time to return to the beginning of this study, to move from a summary of some narrative and cultural aspects of reading autobiography to the methods and issues of biblical interpretation. The middle section of this book was written as a 'narrative' – a story about an ancient autobiographer and the migrations of that personal voice across some aspects of modern culture. The intention which fuelled this narrative was to contribute to contemporary readers' understanding of the book of Ecclesiastes. But this was not a move towards one single explanation of meaning, it stressed instead the plurality and variety of meanings, which offer choice to the 'reader as purchaser'. Now this process leads back to the overarching questions concerning biblical criticism and the place of 'biblical imagination'.

Maps and Myths

A useful point of reference in this matter of biblical interpretation through use of the imagination is the recent work by R. Walsh, *Mapping Myths of Biblical Interpretation*. It is difficult to define the term myth, but Walsh offers three lines of thought here, in what he calls the popular, romantic and sociological modes. Each involves the construction of symbolic universes within which to situate selfhood and its link with human affairs, thus offering 'maps of meaning'. Walsh argues that humans need to create ordered patterns of reality in order to provide maps for life; but this can be stultifying. 'Myth, like gods, religion, and definition itself, imposes needful, if Protean, order upon the chaos of experience.'[1] In order to do so it 'uses the other to structure and empower. The three definitional tendencies simply reflect different attitudes to the mythic other.'[2] The other may be someone else's popular account, usually viewed as false, or it may be imagination as owned by a Romantic aesthetic, as opposed to the popular viewpoint or the pluralist others of a sociological mode in which myths are the products of cultural perspectives.[3] Commonly all three definitions of myth relate to the outsider, thus creating boundaries of definition by contrast.[4] Myth 'is the epistemological other – either abhorred, tolerated or desired ... a limit-setting exercise, epistemological and/or sociological'.[5]

When the concept of myth is applied to the Christian Bible, Walsh notes a reluctance by biblical scholars to own the part played by this way of reading text. 'For most of the history of biblical scholarship, myth has been the necessary but unwanted other.'[6] Not that scholars could argue away the role of myth but there was a tendency to use the word as a label for what was not accepted. At the same time, the Christian myth has been an essential part of European identity, and has been utilized to define cultural self-identity in the region, holding at bay the non-European other. Biblical scholarship, including the 'scientific' mode of historical criticism, has had a role in that creation of cultural selfhood.

In a postmodern setting the emphasis falls on plurality. Walsh suggests that new settings need new meanings and, as part of this, proposes to move 'myth' from noun to verb. 'To myth', Walsh argues, is what is done in biblical criticism all the time; it produces meanings that are plural and diverse. The context for this view includes the work of Roland Barthes. For Barthes, myth is a matter of cultural constructs.[7] In the creation of these social models the ordinary image gains new layers of meaning. 'For Barthes, myth presents value as if it were fact.'[8] The significance of this work of myth is that it provides 'maps of social order'. Walsh suggests that

> to myth is not necessarily to create a myth ... but to live within and use an available myth to form the chaos of human experience ... Behind myth stands a power which we may conceive as the gods, as simply the relentless flow of experience ... or as death ... To myth is not merely to order, but also to situate oneself with respect to this power.[9]

Barthes criticized the act of mything, using contemporary images in French imperialist culture, since the end result was to convince the viewer that truth resided in a single social reality. Walsh acknowledges the possibility of putting readers into boxes by the act of reading biblical material through myth, but argues that this is not inevitable. His focus here is 'border' rather than 'box'. This is in line with Todorov's descriptions of fantasy as related to border-crossing. The reader hesitates on the border between history and that which is beyond, and it is that moment of pause which constitutes the genre of fantasy. With regard to interpretation of text this can be redefined as a hesitation between one line of explanation and another. 'If there is no Archimedian point, no non-mythic place, from which we might innocently critique a, ours or another's myth, we have left the myth of the one true interpretation behind for the myth of inevitably diverse interpretations.'[10]

In relation to the unpacking of the concept of the self it is not a matter, then, of assuring the reader of the stability of sameness but of encouraging a sense of the instability and variety of selfhood. It is not a question of asking how we may interpret the world, rather 'postmodern fiction asks which world am I in and which self is relating to it'.[11] In an era of postcolonialization the Christian biblical myth is only one culture, one 'social fiction' among others.

Awareness of our belief in fictions also commends a tolerance and generosity toward the myth of others. Such might limit, if not prevent, the tribal violence of mythic certainty which recurrently mars human history. After all the other is necessary to us. Without the other we have no possibilities of avoiding mythic certainty and boredom.[12]

And so it is reasonable to read the Qoheletic self as one mythic map offered by biblical studies. It holds together both same and the other, and offers both order and its disordering. It asserts order only to critique it, but then returns to an assertion of the importance of order in daily life.

Autobiography as Map/Myth

In autobiography the 'I' who speaks can be related to matters both of mapping and 'mything'. It has two strands, the mapping and mything of that personal voice and the mapping and mything of the social world in which such a voice is contextualized. These two moves are not ultimately separate, but interweave in the move from personal subject to social discourse. The mything and mapping of a self produces a profile of human existence. Qohelet focuses on death as providing a tool for these activities. It is not birth and life that ground human existence but, paradoxically, their opposite, death and cessation of being.

In Ecclesiastes 3 the autobiographer can conceive of life going on without limit, but all that can really be proved, in terms of human boundaries, are the correct moments of time for human events. Thus death exerts its mapping and mything authority; time, like all human experience, can only be fairly represented by limit and finitude. The reversed role of life and death can then be read back to all human evaluations of experience. What human beings 'ought' to be doing is the reverse of what they do. The search for gain is foundational, but which map shows the way to it? Human beings map a path through wealth, through commerce, through public building on a vast scale, through owning more, through many sons. All these are illusions; they map the human quest deceitfully. The myth they employ is not a profile of humanity which succeeds in the quest for gain from existence. Only by reversing the mapping and mything based on ever expanding material wealth can a better map be discovered. This mything of selfhood tends always towards otherness. It is by avoiding the 'same' and by embracing the unfamiliar just as such, that human selves come to true understanding.

Qohelet's map and mything is a mirror which reflects not an image of sameness but pictures of difference. This flows into cultural usage of texts. L. Dupre notes that 'culture does far more than equip a society with the norms and values needed for coping with the material conditions of its existence. It holds out a spiritual surplus that urges humans beyond the satisfaction of immediate needs.'[13] This comment could be read as ironic with regard to

Qohelet because his personal voice returns to the ordinary events of life, but finds in them that spiritual surplus. By using the vocabulary of trade and finance Qohelet creates a broad world map to serve his mything. 'Through the symbolic meanings we attach to it, human existence escapes the drudgery of the ordinary.'[14]

The cultural context of human life thus becomes the place where spiritual meaning emerges. Spiritual meaning in the Qoheletic self cannot be separated from the map of what is visible *taḥat ha ššemeš̌*. Insofar as an invented social world can compare with the actual social world experienced by a reader, this perspective from under the sun aligns the readerly self with the man of business and public affairs. It is this parallelism which provides a new point from which to read the map of human affairs, both part of daily life and set aside from daily toil. Theo de Boer raises the question of how far fiction can be an instrument of investigation in meaning, and suggests that

> it is only when we place what has actually happened against the background of what could have happened that we gain insight into history ... It is not the reproduction of the facts but the distance in the imagination and the mental representation of how things might have been otherwise that creates its insight.[15]

Applying this viewpoint to Ecclesiastes involves a bringing together of the real business man and the 'as if' person of public affairs to which Qohelet's personal voice gives shape. The imaginary man of affairs allows the reader the distance necessary for looking at the real business setting with different eyes.

The aim of mapping and mything is to meet the demands of identity seeking. Qohelet himself is a useful resource in this context since his autobiographical self includes both the subject as an individual identity and the social world within which that individual operates. In the modern world of readers 'the idea of an established world order and of a tradition based upon that order has lost its authority. The intrinsic teleology of nature has given way to an extrinsic one determined by the modern subject.'[16] But readers still seek to map, and so to myth, human identity, even if that identity is viewed as a shifting reality, as dialogic, caught up in moving relationships.[17] Postcolonial theory, in particular, uses space to order identity, with concepts such as displacement, placelessness and exile as central components.[18] Pursuing this approach leads to putting nomadism forward as the foundation of identity. Qoheletic selves are viewed, in this context, as changing, migrating across cultures, regions and times.

The 'original' Qohelet was a nomad insofar as he passed across events, places and through the time of his own life span. His voice 'migrates' between hope and uncertainty. Here biblical imagination takes a particular form – that of autobiography, personal voice, future reality, cultural input. There is a stable core to this identity, rooted in social discourse and the repeating patterns of nature, but it is also volatile, deconstructing the sense of divine beneficence towards human beings. For some readers, Jewish and Christian, the scandal of the text is its focus on human attempts to grasp the world; where is putting the deity first in this perspective? Is God not the power which constantly thwarts such hedonism? Yet it is also true that human beings do not in fact see the glory of God in what goes on *taḥat ha ššemešš*. Ecclesiastes, and Qohelet, speak to this readerly condition. Even Von Balthasar, who places this text on the negative balance in his biblical aesthetics, agrees with the validity of some of its insights.[19] Qohelet is a transcendentalist who can stand apart from physical events and critique self-understanding of inner-worldly concepts.[20] Moreover, Qohelet's final words, focusing towards death 'with a great becalming of the movements and the sounds of life, is surely the climax of the Book of Qoheleth and one of the summits of the whole Bible'.[21]

So what are the links between autobiography and biblical imagination? P. Fiddes notes that 'Koheleth and his colleagues have clearly identified some features of the world which present a problem to be answered: the world appears elusive in its complexity, and yet also staled by habit.'[22] This identifies the term 'autobiographical voice' as linked with the concept of problem. This link is elucidated through the use of complexity and polarity in the thought of the book, and is further associated with mystery. This mystery surrounds the endeavour of human beings to search for reasons and meaning for the way their lives progress. Literary imagination, according to Fiddes, gives characters a pattern for finding themselves, in what would otherwise be a meaningless set of events.[23] 'The imagination thus reaches out towards mystery, towards a reality that is our final concern but which eludes empirical investigation and bursts rational concepts.'[24] Fiddes argues for a connection between the free play of imagination in the arts and its role in theology. Just as the nature of story shapes the imagination of the hearer,[25] so 'the theologian, too, is always dealing ... with the interaction of primary forms of faith (metaphor, symbol, story) and systematic statement'.[26] This involves dialogue between boundaries or limits and the free play of imagination. In religious contexts this dialogue is between the limits of the tradition and the current personal voice which engages with that tradition. Qohelet is clearly an example of such religious dialogue, illustrating the fact that this dialogue is not only part of the modern world, 'since biblical writers are themselves in creative tension with the religious traditions of the communities to which they belong'.[27]

In the book of Ecclesiastes the literary genre of autobiography provides a setting for an example of such creative tension at work. There is no sense in the book that the ancient writer is 'godless', the deity is still the ultimate metaphysical centre of world power. But the order and stability thus provided are in tension with the personal voice of an 'I' who cannot find in this religious teaching any ease, any easy resolution of life's vagaries. Instead the 'I' who speaks produces polarities in dialogue. The ultimate pair of such opposites is that of *'ôlām/taḥat ha ššemešš*, with death as the bridging force between these time and spatial borders. Implicit here is the boundary between freedom and limits. And that boundary is the heart of mystery, which itself is related to uncertainty, a clouded vision of reality. 'A man has a thought in his mind, but there is an element of unpredictability about how that will emerge as a spoken word. Or, a man may plan how he will walk, but something may trip him up.'[28] Fiddes here demarcates the mystery surrounding human affairs in language which resonates with Qohelet's personal voice. Qoheletic selves are centred on this boundary, constantly revisiting the interchange of freedom and limitation which human beings have in their responses to their worlds, imagining and re-imagining what it is to be a self.

Notes

1   R. Walsh, *Mapping Myths of Biblical Interpretation* (Sheffield, Sheffield Academic Press, 2001), p. 14.
2   Ibid., p. 11.
3   Ibid., p. 30.
4   Ibid., p. 51.
5   Ibid.
6   Ibid., p. 129.
7   See here the parallel comments on the thought of Barthes made in Chapter 2.
8   Walsh, *Mapping Myths*, p. 141.
9   Ibid., p. 140.
10   Ibid., p. 145.
11   Ibid., p. 148.
12   Ibid., p. 163.
13   L. Dupre, 'Cultural Variety and Metaphysical Unity', in M. Bal (ed.) *The Practice of Cultural Analysis* (Stanford, Stanford University Press, 1999), p. 256.
14   Ibid.
15   T. De Boer, 'Desire, Distance and Insight', in Bal, *Practice of Cultural Analysis*, pp. 281–2.
16   Dupre, *Cultural Variety*, pp. 264–5.
17   I. Hoving, 'Three Local Cases of Cross-Atlantic Reading: A Discussion on Space and Identity', in Bal, *Practice of Cultural Analysis*, p. 203.
18   Ibid., p. 204.
19   Von Balthasar's series of volumes under the title *The Glory of the Lord* are works of systematic theology whose methodology is said by the author to be that of 'aesthetics', understanding *aisthesis* as indicating 'beholding' of divine glory, revealing itself in the Christian Scriptures.
20   H. Von Balthasar, *The Glory of the Lord* (Edinburgh, T. and T. Clark, 1991), vol. VI, p. 138.
21   Ibid., p. 142.
22   P. Fiddes, *Freedom and Limit* (Macon, Ga., Mercer University Press, 1999), pp. 44–5.
23   Ibid., p. 8.
24   Ibid., p. 11.
25   Ibid., p. 25.
26   Ibid., p. 39.
27   Ibid.
28   Ibid., p. 56.

Bibliography

Alter, R. (1981) *The Art of Biblical Narrative*, London, Basic Books.

Austen, J. (1975) *How to do Things with Words*, Oxford, Oxford University Press.

Avis, P. (1999) *God and the Creative Imagination*, London, Routledge.

Bakhtin, M. (1998) *The Dialogic Imagination*, trans. M. Holquist, Austen, University of Texas Press.

Bal, M. (1997) *Narratology*, Toronto, University of Toronto Press.

Bal, M. (ed.) (1999) *The Practice of Cultural Analysis*, Stanford, Calif., Stanford University Press.

Barker, F. (1984) *The T P Body: Essays on Subjection*, London, Methuen.

Barthes, R. (1972) *Mythologies*, New York, Hill and Wang.

Beal, T. (1998) 'C(ha)osmopolis: Qohelet's Last Words', in T. Linafelt and T. Beal (eds) *God in the Fray*, Minneapolis, Fortress.

Bewer, J. (1962) *The Literature of the Old Testament*, rev. E. Kraeling, New York, Columbia University Press.

Bhabha, H. (1994) *the location of culture*, London, Routledge.

Bible and Cultural Collective (1995) *The Postmodern Bible*, New Haven, Conn., Yale University Press.

Bjorklund, D. (1998) *Interpreting the Self*, Chicago, University of Chicago Press.

Boehmer, E. (1995) *Colonial and Postcolonial Literature*, Oxford, Oxford University Press.

Booth, W. (1983) *The Rhetoric of Fiction*, Harmondsworth, Penguin.

Brenner, A. and Fontaine, C. (eds) (1998) *Wisdom and Psalms*, Sheffield, Sheffield Academic Press.

Bromley, R. (2000) *Narratives for a New Belonging: Diasporic Cultural Fictions*, Edinburgh, Edinburgh University Press.

Brown, W. (1996) *Character in Crisis*, Grand Rapids, Mich., Eerdmans.

Brown, W. (2000) *Ecclesiastes*, Louisville, Ky., Westminster John Knox.

Brueggemann, W. (1993) *Texts Under Negotiation: The Bible and Postmodern Imagination*, Minneapolis, Fortress.

Bruss, E. (1976) *Autobiographical Acts*, Baltimore, Md., Johns Hopkins University Press.

Buss, M. (1999) *Biblical Form Criticism in its Context*, Sheffield, Sheffield Academic Press.

Camp, C. (2000) *Wise, Strange and Holy: The Strange Woman and the Making of the Bible*, Sheffield, Sheffield Academic Press.

Christiansen, E. (1998) *A Time to Tell: Narrative Strategy in Ecclesiastes*, Sheffield, Sheffield Academic Press.

Clines, D. (1995) *Interested Parties: The Ideology of Writers and Readers*, Sheffield, Sheffield University Press.

Clines, D. (1997) *The Bible and the Modern World*, Sheffield, Sheffield Academic Press.

Cohan, S. and Shires, L. (1988) *Telling Stories*, London, Routledge.

Crenshaw, J. (1988) *Ecclesiastes*, London, SCM Press.

Culpepper, A. (1983) *The Anatomy of the Fourth Gospel*, Minneapolis, Fortress.

Day, A. (1996) *Romanticism*, London, Routledge.

Davies, P. (1992) *In Search of Ancient Israel*, Sheffield, Sheffield Academic Press.

Davies, P. (1998) *Scribes and Schools*, Louisville, Ky., Westminster John Knox.

De Lubac, H. (1998) *Medieval Exegesis*, trans. M. Sebanc, vol. I, *The Four Senses of Scripture*, Edinburgh, T. and T. Clark.

Derrida, J. (1978) *Writing and Difference*, trans. A. Bass, London, Routledge.

Dyck, J. (2000) 'A Map of Ideology for Biblical Critics', in M. Daniel Carroll (ed.) *Rethinking Contexts, Rereading Texts*, Sheffield, Sheffield Academic Press.

Eagleton, T. (2000) *The Idea of Culture*, Oxford, Blackwell.

Easthope, A. (1991) *Literary into Cultural Studies*, London, Routledge.

Exum, C. (1992) *Tragedy and Biblical Narrative*, Cambridge, Cambridge University Press.

Exum, C. and Moore, S. (eds) (1998) *Biblical Studies: Cultural Studies*, Sheffield, Sheffield Academic Press.

Fewell, D. (ed.) (1992) *Reading Between Texts: Intertextuality and the Hebrew Bible*, Louisville, Ky., Westminster John Knox.

Fiddes, P. (1999) *Freedom and Limit*, Macon, Ga., Mercer University Press.

Fokkelman, J. (1999) *Reading Biblical Narrative*, Louisville, Ky., Westminster John Knox.

Foucault, M. (1972) *The Architecture of Knowledge*, trans. A. Sheridan Smith, London, Routledge.

Fox, M. (1999) *A Time to tear down and a Time to build up*, Grand Rapids, Mich., Eerdmans.

Genette, G. (1983) *Narrative Discourse*, New York, Cornell University Press.

Gordis, R. (1968) *Koheleth: The man and his World*, New York, Schocken.

Grey, M. (2001) *Introducing Feminist Images of God*, Sheffield, Sheffield Academic Press.

Gunn, D. and Fewell, D. (1993) *Narrative in the Hebrew Bible*, Oxford, Oxford University Press.

Hamilton, P. (1996) *Historicism*, London, Routledge.

Hart, K. (1991) 'Reading the Text: Biblical Criticism and Literary Theory', in Prickett, S. (ed.) *The Poetics of the Narrative*, Oxford, Blackwell, p. 308.

Hawkes, D. (1996) *Ideology*, London, Routledge.

Hayes, J. (1979) *An Introduction to Old Testament Study*, London, SCM Press.

Hogan, P. (2000) *Colonialism and Cultural Identity*, Albany, State University of New York.

Huwiler, E. (1999) 'Ecclesiastes', in R. Murphy and E. Huwiler, *Proverbs, Ecclesiastes and the Song of Songs*, Carlisle, Paternoster.

Iser, W. (1980) *The Act of Reading*, Baltimore, Md., Johns Hopkins University Press.

Jameson, F. (1996) *The Political Unconscious: Narrative as a Socially Symbolic Act*, London, Routledge.

Jay, P. (1984) *Being in the Text*, Ithaca, NY, Cornell University Press.

Johnson, T. (1998) 'Imagining the World Scripture Imagines', in J. Jones and J. Buckley (eds) *Theology and Scriptural Imagination*, Oxford, Blackwell.

Kitzberger, I. (ed.) (1999) *The Personal Voice in Biblical Interpretation*, London, Routledge.

Kwok, P.-L. (1995) *Discovering the Bible in the Non-biblical World*, Maryknoll, NY, Orbis.

Levison, J. and Pope-Levison, P. (eds) (1999) *Return to Babel: Global Perspectives on the Bible*, Louisville, Ky., Westminster John Knox.

Linafelt, T. (2000) *Strange Fire: Reading the Bible after the Holocaust*, Sheffield, Sheffield Academic Press.

Longman, T. (1998) *The Book of Ecclesiastes*, Grand Rapids, Mich., Eerdmans.

Loomba, A. (1998) *Colonialism/Postcolonialism*, London, Routledge.

Lyotard, F. (1984) *The Postmodern Condition*, trans. G. Bennington and B. Massumi, Manchester University Press.

Marcus, L. (1994) *Auto/Biographical Discourses*, Manchester University Press.

Milner, A. (1996) *Literature, Culture and Society*, London, University College Press.

Montaigne, M. (1958) *Essais*, trans. J. Cohen, Harmondsworth, Penguin.

Mulhern, F. (2000) *Culture/Metaculture*, London, Routledge.

Ogden, G. (1987) *Qoheleth*, Sheffield, Sheffield Academic Press.

Olney, J. (ed.) (1980) *Autobiography: Essays Theoretical and Critical*, Princeton, NJ, Princeton University Press.

Perdue, L. (1994) *Wisdom and Creation: The Theology of Wisdom Literature*, Nashville, Tenn., Abingdon.

Perry, T. (1993) *Dialogues without Kohelet*, University Park, Pa., Penn State University Press.

Pippin, T. (1999) *Apocalyptic Bodies*, London, Routledge.

Prickett, S. (ed.) (1991) *The Poetics of the Narrative*, Oxford, Blackwell.

Prickett, S. (1996) *Origins of Narrative*, Cambridge, Cambridge University Press.

Ricoeur, P. (1984) *Time and Narrative*, trans. K. McLaughlin and D. Pellauer, 3 vols, Chicago, University of Chicago Press.

Ricoeur, P. (1992) *Oneself as Another*, trans. K. Blamey, Chicago, University of Chicago Press.

Riley, D. (2000) *The Words of Selves*, Stanford, Calif., Stanford University Press.

Rimmon-Kenan, S. (1999) *Narrative Fiction*, London, Routledge.

Said, E. (1993) *Culture and Imperialism*, London, Vintage.

Salyer, G. (2001) *Vain Rhetoric: Private Insight and Public Debate in Ecclesiastes*, Sheffield, Sheffield Academic Press.

Sauter, G. and Barton, J. (eds) (2000) *Revelation and Story*, Aldershot, Ashgate.

Segovia, F. (2000a) *Decolonizing Biblical Studies: A View from the Margins*, Maryknoll, NY, Orbis.

Segovia, F. (ed.) (2000b) *Interpreting Beyond Borders*, Sheffield, Sheffield Academic Press.

Seow, C.-L. (1997) *Ecclesiastes*, New York, Doubleday.

Smith, S. (1993) *Subjectivity, Identity and the Body*, Bloomington, Indiana University Press.

Solomon, A. (1993) *Blake's Job*, London, Palambron.

Spengemann, W. (1980) *The Forms of Autobiography*, New Haven, Conn., Yale University Press.

Steiner, G. (1989) *Real Presences*, London, Faber and Faber.

Steiner, G. (2001) *Grammars of Creativity*, London, Faber and Faber.

Sternberg, M. (1985) *The Poetics of Biblical Narrative*, Bloomington, Indiana University Press.

Suelzer, A. and Kselman, J. (1990) 'Modern Old Testament Criticism', in R. Brown, J. Fitzmyer and R. Murphy (eds) *The New Jerome Biblical Commentary*, London, Chapman.

Sugiratharajah, R. (ed.) (1995) *Voices from the Margin*, London, SPCK.

Sugiratharajah, R. (2001) *The Bible and the Third World*, Cambridge, Cambridge University Press.

Tamez, E. (1999) *When the Horizons Close*, Maryknoll, NY, Orbis.

Todorov, T. (1981) *Introduction to Poetics*, trans. R. Howard, Minneapolis, University of Minnesota Press.

Tompkins, J. (ed.) (1980) *Reader-Response Criticism*, Baltimore, Md., Johns Hopkins University Press.

Toolan, M. (1988) *Narrative: A Critical Linguistic Introduction*, London, Routledge.

Von Balthasar, H. (1991) *The Glory of the Lord*, vol. VI, *Theology: The Old Covenant*, Edinburgh, T. and T. Clark.

Walhout, C. (1999) 'Narrative Hermeneutics', in R. Lundin, C, Walhout and A. Thiselton, *The Promise of Hermeneutics*, Carlisle, Paternoster.

Walsh, R. (2001) *Mapping Myths of Biblical Interpretation*, Sheffield, Sheffield Academic Press.

Walton, H. and Hass, A. (eds) (2000) *Self/Same/Other*, Sheffield, Sheffield Academic Press.

West, G. (1999) *The Academy of the Poor*, Sheffield, Sheffield Academic Press.

Whedbee, W. (1998) *The Bible and the Comic Vision*, Cambridge, Cambridge University Press.

White, H. (1991) *Narration and Discourse in the Book of Genesis*, Cambridge, Cambridge University Press.

Whitelam, K. (1996) *The Invention of Ancient Israel*, London, Routledge.

Whitlock, G. (2000) *The Intimate Empire: Reading Women's Autobiography*, London, Cassell.

Zimmerman, F. (1973) *The Inner World of Qohelet*, New York, KTAV.

Index